7/12

$26.95
338.19 THU
Thurow, Roger
The last hunger season

THE LAST
HUNGER
SEASON

ROGER THUROW

A YEAR IN AN AFRICAN FARM COMMUNITY ON THE BRINK OF CHANGE

THE LAST HUNGER SEASON

THE CHICAGO COUNCIL
ON GLOBAL AFFAIRS

PUBLICAFFAIRS
New York

338.19
THU

PUBLICAFFAIRS books are available at special discounts for bulk purchases
in the U.S. by corporations, institutions, and other organizations. For more
information, please contact the Special Markets Department at the
Perseus Books Group, 2300 Chestnut Street, Suite 200, Philadelphia, PA 19103,
call (800) 810-4145, ext. 5000, or e-mail special.markets@perseusbooks.com.

Editorial production by Lori Hobkirk the Book Factory.
Design by Cynthia Young at Sagecraft.
Maps created by Chas Chamberlin.

The Library of Congress has cataloged the printed edition as follows:
Thurow, Roger.
The last hunger season : a year in an African farm community
on the brink of change / Roger Thurow.—1st ed.
p. cm.
Includes bibliographical references and index.
ISBN 978-1-61039-067-5 (hardcover); 978-1-61039-068-2 (e-book)
1. Farms, Small-Kenya.   2. Subsistence farming-Kenya.
3. Food supply-Kenya.   4. Hunger-Kenya.   5. Agricultural development
projects-Kenya.   6. Kenya-Rural conditions.   I. Title.
HD1476.K43T485 2012
338.196762-dc23
2012003785

First Edition

10 9 8 7 6 5 4 3 2 1

For Anne
And for the smallholder farmers of Africa

CONTENTS

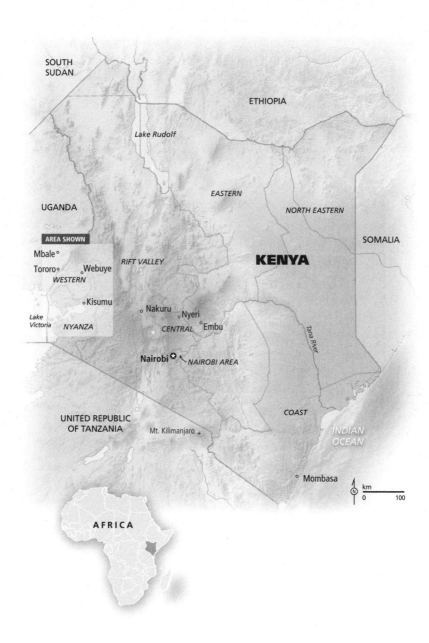

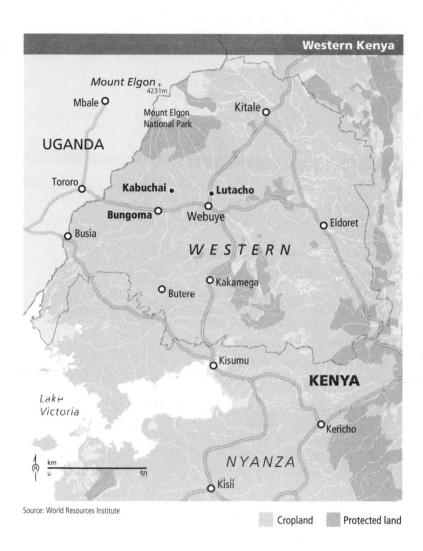

PROLOGUE

I wasn't in western Kenya long before I met my first Wanjala.

He was Francis Mamati, a smallholder farmer, unfailingly gracious, who smiled relentlessly as he lugged chairs and tables from the dark sitting room of his little house to the expansive shade of an avocado tree. With a slight breeze stirring, Francis began telling the story of his life as a farmer. He mentioned that he was born in 1957. We were the same age. I asked the date of his birth.

"I don't know a day," Francis said, "but I think it must be May or June."

"Why's that?"

"Because my mother gave me a third name: Wanjala," he said. "*Wanjala* is our word for hunger, for the time of year when we run low on food. The hunger season. And that is usually May and June."

Francis Wanjala Mamati. "You can call me Hunger," he said.

In western Kenya, the Luhya people like to name their children for the time of year in which they are born. Sitawa, for instance, is a girl born during the time of flying termites. Wamalwa is a boy who arrived during the brewing season. Nasimiyu is a girl delivered during the hot, dry months. Particularly popular are boys' names that match the rhythms of the growing season: Wafula (rains), Wanyonyi (weeding), Wekesa (harvest).

The most common name of all, it seems, is Wanjala. There are an awful lot of people called Hunger. That is because the hunger season can be the longest, stretching from the time the food from the previous harvest in August and September runs out to the time when the new crops begin to come in. It is a time when food prices soar with the shortages, and parents scramble for whatever income they can find and scrounge whatever assets they can sell to afford daily nourishment. Household food rations are cut and meals eliminated. Three meals become two, then one, and then, on some days, none. Work in the fields slows, children drop out of school, the littlest battle for survival. May and June are the high season for hunger in western Kenya, but for some families the *wanjala* can begin in April or even in January.

After Francis, I would meet many more Wanjalas, and Nanjalas, the female version of the name. Teachers, preachers, taxi drivers, shopkeepers, aid workers, farmers. Especially farmers.

HUNGRY FARMERS. That is perhaps the most confounding, troubling phrase on a confounding, troubled continent. "Hungry farmers" should be an oxymoron. How can farmers, who rise every morning to grow food, be hungry? But in my frequent travels to Africa's hunger zones as a reporter for the *Wall Street Journal*, I knew that phrase to be one of the continent's saddest truisms: her smallholder farmers, the people who grew their own food, were also her hungriest people.

It was this discordant fact that brought me to the hardscrabble homesteads of western Kenya, a paradoxical region of breathtaking beauty and overwhelming misery. The area that stretches from Lake Victoria north to the slopes of Mount Elgon on the border with Uganda is one of Kenya's breadbaskets, especially for the production of corn, which is known across much of Africa as maize. But it is also the region that leads the country in malnutrition and poverty. Collectively it may boast the nation's highest agriculture output per acre, yet individually millions of smallholder farmers struggle to grow enough to feed their families throughout the year. Few families escape the annual *wanjala*.

Hungry farmers are the legacy of the "criminal negligence" of agricultural development foretold by Norman Borlaug, the father of the Green Revolution, for which he won the Nobel Peace Prize in 1970. "We will be guilty of criminal negligence, without extenuation, if we permit future famines," Borlaug warned back then. And that is indeed what came to pass. After Borlaug's new breeding system produced a wheat strain that conquered famine in India, Pakistan, and other places in Asia in the 1960s and '70s, and after the Malthusian worry that the world would run out of food was diffused by the transformation of formerly hungry countries into new food powers, a long era of abundant and cheap food dawned, and the world turned away from agricultural development. The movement to spread new farming advances to hungry countries derailed before it could reach Africa. Aid to farmers and investment in rural areas in Africa by both the international community and the continent's governments declined precipitously, shrinking to negligible levels through the 1980s and '90s and into the twenty-first century. The private sector, particularly the agriculture industry, likewise largely ignored the smallholder farmers tending less than five acres of land, deeming them too poor and remote for its attention. Neglecting the well-being of the largest segment of the population on the world's poorest continent defied logic. Yet this was the pre-vailing development philosophy in the United States and other rich precincts of the world: our farmers, who are heavily supported by our governments, are producing vast stockpiles of food cheaper than farmers anywhere else. Better the poor countries buy their food from us than produce it themselves. And if they are hungry—if famine were to flare from drought, turmoil, or evil politics—we'll feed them with our food aid.

And so it went for decades, even as the world's population grew and strains mounted on the global food chain—until the worldwide food crisis of 2007 and 2008. Shrinking stockpiles of some major grains sent prices skyrocketing, triggering food shortages and riots in dozens of countries. The ranks of the chronically hungry on the planet soared past one billion. The era of cheap, abundant food was over. Once again, the prospect loomed of a *wanjala* for all mankind.

I FIRST MET ANDREW YOUN in the middle of a Chicago snow-storm at the end of 2009. He was just back from western Kenya, where the hot, dry season reigned, but he insisted on keeping our appointment, even as blizzard conditions escalated. We ordered warm drinks in the café area of a bookstore.

Andrew eagerly told me about the farmers he had encountered when he arrived in western Kenya a few years earlier. He was a budding social entrepreneur, then working on his MBA at North-western University's Kellogg School of Management. He didn't know much about farming, but he did know that what he was see-ing on the rural homesteads didn't add up. With all of the agricul-tural advances in the world, he wondered, how was it that the farmers he met couldn't feed their families for the entire year? The rain was plentiful; the soils, though overworked and depleted, were laden with potential. Yet the *wanjala* persisted.

It was there, during the hunger season, that Andrew had his epiphany. For the first time in his life, he had come face-to-face with hunger. He watched one farmer's adolescent daughter stretch a thin mixture of maize porridge for the family's only meal of the day. It was an image he couldn't shake from his mind. He founded a social enterprise organization to reverse the neglect of the smallholder farmers by providing access to the seeds and soil nutrients and planting advice that never made it deep into the rural areas. The "social" aspect was to banish the hunger season; the "enterprise" part was to do it as an efficient business. He called his operation One Acre Fund.

"The existence of a hungry farmer is completely crazy. It's mind-boggling. A hunger season shouldn't exist," Andrew said on that cold Chicago day, as the wind howled and the snow drifted beyond the bookstore's windows. "Our mission as an organization is to make sure it never, ever happens."

In that bleak winter setting, far from Africa, I recognized this passion, for it was also mine. I repeated to Andrew what an aid worker for the World Food Program (WFP) had told me during the Ethiopian famine of 2003: "Looking into the eyes of someone dying of hunger becomes a disease of the soul. You see that nobody should have to die of hunger." It was that profound connection that led me to write the book *Enough: Why the World's Poorest Starve in an Age of Plenty* with my *Wall Street Journal* colleague Scott Kilman. And it was what subsequently led me to leave the *Journal* to continue to pursue the story that had come to seem more important to me than any other, and one I felt unable to stop covering regardless what else was dominating news headlines that day or that year: Why were people still dying of hunger at the beginning of the twenty-first century when the world was producing—and wasting—more food than ever before? For me and my own diseased soul, *Enough* hadn't been enough. From my new post as senior fellow at the Chicago Council on Global Affairs, I set out in search of smallholder farmers I could follow for a year to both chronicle the impact on people's lives of the "criminal negligence" Dr. Borlaug had warned of, and to illustrate these farmers' potential to grow enough to escape the hunger season and benefit the global food chain.

Andrew told me that One Acre was then working with nearly twenty thousand farmers who were doubling and tripling their maize yields. He was optimistic they had the *wanjala* on the run. "I really believe," he said, "that agriculture is the fundamental humanitarian challenge of our time."

The urgency of attacking that challenge was palpable. We both believed that smallholder farmers, who were the majority of the population in most African countries, would be central to any success. In the wake of the 2007–2008 food crisis, agriculture economists and development theorists had begun clamoring that the world needed to nearly double food production by 2050 to keep up with a growing global population and the growing prosperity of that population. Estimates placed another 2.5 billion people on earth in that time, which would be the equivalent of feeding another two Chinas or two Indias. In addition, there were already one billion people in the world who were chronically hungry. Adding to the challenge, this doubling would need to happen on roughly the same amount of arable land and with less water than was being used in the existing agricultural breadbaskets. All the while, a growing demand for biofuels that was channeling more and more food, corn especially, into gas tanks instead of stomachs, and extreme climate patterns that were wreaking havoc on harvests from the Russian steppe to the Texas panhandle, would be adding to the unprecedented strains on the global food chain.

Where would the needed doubling come from? Likely not from the present breadbaskets of the United States, Canada, Europe, and Australia, where the great jumps in yields over the past decades have been narrowing. Nor can we confidently count on repeat performances of the large gains in productivity in green revolution stars such as India, China, and Brazil, where future growth depends on continued costly investments in infrastructure and research. In fact, under some scenarios, water scarcity in India and China could cut wheat and rice production by 30 to 50 percent by 2050, even as demand for these crops in those countries was expected to rise by the same amount over the same period.

From where, then, will come the quantum leaps in production?

Only from Africa, food's final frontier. Because it is so far behind the rest of the world agriculturally, Africa now has the potential to record the biggest jump in food production of any region by applying technologies and infrastructure and financial incentives that are common most everywhere else. Africa, where the hybrid seeds that revolutionized American agriculture in the 1930s are only now beginning to spread, is the one continent where yields of maize, wheat, rice, beans, and an array of local crops, have yet to have their growth spurts, and lag as much as 90 percent behind the yields of farmers elsewhere. With only 4 percent of its farmland irrigated, Africa has water resources that are underutilized. With one-third to one-half of its harvests routinely going to waste, Africa could give an immediate boost to the world's food supplies with improved storage facilities and more efficient markets.

With all this potential, Africa's long-neglected smallholder farmers, who produce the majority of the continent's food, have thus become indispensable for our future. It will be impossible to multiply global food production without creating the conditions for them to grow and bring to market as much as they possibly can—to at least feed themselves, their communities, and their countries—and to not only stop being a drain on the world's food supply, but to add to it. They need to be at the vanguard of a new agriculture economy for the twenty-first century, an economy where all farmers are encouraged to grow as much nutritionally beneficial food as possible and then be rewarded through the global market for doing so. The farmers who have been fed by the world's food aid are now needed to help feed the world. We continue to neglect Africa's smallholder farmers at our own peril.

Andrew Youn embraced all this. He invited me to come to western Kenya and meet the farmers.

INCREDIBLY, much of rural Africa is the same today as it was in the 1930s when a classic tale was told about farming in Kenya.

"I had a farm in Africa, at the foot of the Ngong Hills," begins Karen Blixen's endearing and enduring memoir, *Out of Africa*. Her farm, a coffee plantation in the central Kenyan highlands, was in many ways typical of white landholdings during the colonial period in Africa. It was a sprawling six thousand acres, full of various crops, and wildlife, too. But even more typical were the farms of her African neighbors, who worked on her farm and tilled their own small plots called *shambas* in a corner of her land. She wrote,

> Whenever you walk amidst the Kikuyu *shambas*, the first thing that will catch your eye is the hind part of a little old woman raking in her soil, like a picture of an ostrich which buries her head in the sand. Each Kikuyu family had a number of small round peaked huts and store-huts; the space between the huts was a lively place, the earth hard as concrete; here the maize was ground and the goats milked, and children and chickens were running.

That stooped farmer raking in her soil, children and chickens running over concrete-hard dirt between her tiny mud house and the flimsy small round storage huts with peaked thatched roofs— that's Leonida Wanyama and Rasoa Wasike and Zipporah Biketi, and it is Francis Wanjala Mamati. You will meet them all in the pages of this book. One Acre Fund farmers, they have been working their *shambas* at the foot of the Lugulu Hills in western Kenya in much the same manner as Karen Blixen described three-quarters of a century ago. The political landscape of Kenya has changed greatly since the time of *Out of Africa*; the country gained its independence in 1963. But life on the *shambas* is still very similar. Kenya's, and Africa's, smallholder farmers toil in a time warp, living and working essentially as they did in the 1930s.

If anything, the rhythm of the seasons has grown harsher, and the harvest yields more miserly over the years. The romantic ideal of African farmers—rural villagers in touch with nature, tending bucolic fields—has hardened into a horror scene of malnourished children, backbreaking manual work, and profound hopelessness. No one should dare mistake the romantic for the reality, for rural Africa is a nightmarish landscape of neglect. There is, in the main, no electricity or running water. Health care is distant and meager. Sanitation is rudimentary. Roads are wretched. Growing food is the driving preoccupation; buying additional food consumes almost every spare shilling. And still the farmers don't have enough to eat. The *wanjala* abides.

THIS IS THE STORY of a year in the life of African farmers, in particular four farmers in western Kenya—Leonida, Rasoa, Zipporah, and Francis—on the brink of change.

As their year began, international efforts to finally reverse the neglect of agricultural development couldn't have been more important—or more threatened. In the first days of 2011, staple food prices were soaring to record highs around the globe. In another part of Africa, north of the Sahara, the outrage ignited when a food vendor in Tunisia lit himself on fire was spreading. Unrest partly fueled by the escalating cost of food and deepening poverty was roiling North Africa and the Middle East, toppling governments. A drought was creeping across East Africa, including Kenya, threatening millions with famine. In Kenya itself, commodity prices and the value of the country's currency, the shilling, were beginning a turbulent ride (the shilling/U.S. dollar rate jerked from 80 to more than 100 and back to 80 again). In rich world capitals, the building debt crisis was eroding promises to invest more in agricultural development. In Washington, DC, President Barack Obama and his administration were readying for battle with Congressional budget cutters to save his Feed the Future initiative, which sought to assert American leadership in the push to end hunger through agricultural development, particularly among smallholder farmers.

And on the *shambas* of western Kenya, the farmers were stirring with the fervent hope that this would be their last hunger season.

CHAPTER 1

SIMIYU

(The Dry Season)

A song began to form near the front of the Kenya Assemblies of God church, and the hundred or so farmers filling the simple, wooden benches rose to join in the praise. Leonida Wanyama, wiping her brow, straightened slowly. Even though the day was still young, she was exhausted. The forty-two-year-old mother of seven had been up long before the sun, toiling since 4 a.m.

By the light of a kerosene lantern, Leonida had milked her two cows and dispatched several liters to the morning market. Then she gathered charcoal and wood for the breakfast fire and prepared a meager serving of tea and maize porridge for her family. As dawn arrived, Leonida grabbed her *jembe*, a crude, short-handled hoe, and hacked at a patch of stubborn soil on her small farm plot, breaking ground for the coming planting season. She paused frequently, arching her back, catching her breath, summoning more energy. She knew this feeling—was another bout of bone-wearying malaria coming on?

It was the second Friday of the New Year. This was the hottest, driest season in the Lugulu Hills of western Kenya. The day had dawned cloudy, and during the early morning hours when Leonida began her work it had been relatively cool—but by the time the farmers of the Lutacho community began their journey to the church it was sunny and scorching. Even Mount Elgon, one of Africa's loveliest peaks, seemed sweaty and weary as it shimmied in the distance, hulking over the Kenya-Uganda border.

Leonida left her field and washed the dust off her hands and feet with water from the nearby stream that she and her daughters had collected in plastic barrels the night before. Retreating to her small, two-room house, she changed out of her ragged skirt and blouse and slipped into her church clothes—a smart blue dress. She tied a white kerchief on her head and rummaged through a worn dresser for the broken remnants of a vehicle's rearview mirror; through the cracks and chips, she checked her appearance. After working barefoot in the field, she now stepped into a pair of brown shoes, her toes threatening to poke through the worn leather. Then she set off down the dirt path beyond her *shamba*, walking five minutes to the church.

It was a rare house of worship as poor as its parishioners. The walls were made of sticks and mud, the floor a hard-packed mixture of dirt and cow dung. Silver sheets of corrugated metal formed the roof. Beams of sunlight and a little breeze squeezed through a couple of small windows carved imprecisely into the walls and through the two rough, wooden doors that hung slightly askew on wobbly hinges at the back and on the right side of the church. At the front, a framed homily hanging on the wall behind the simple altar proclaimed, "To this day, I have had help from God and so I stand here testifying to both great and small."

The farmers, more than two-thirds of them women, with calloused hands and feet as tough as leather, were coming to testify to small harvests in the past that left their families hungry, and to express their expectations for great harvests this year. This was the first One Acre Fund training session of the new growing season, and it was designed to be a kind of pep rally, devoted to whipping up enthusiasm for the possibilities that lay ahead. The anticipation of salvation filling the church had shifted from the ecclesiastical to the agricultural. The wobbly, wooden pulpit, which normally stood front and center and anchored sermons of fire and brimstone, had been moved to a corner. In its place were the elements of manual farming—hoes, buckets, small bags of seed, and fertilizer.

The song that began with a lone tremor picked up momentum, and the Lutacho farmers formed a mighty *a cappella* chorus. Leonida, standing before the second pew, perked up as the voices soared. On Sundays, she led the church choir, belting out songs of worship: "Alleluia, all the praise and honor to Christ." This morning, she fervently joined in a new hymn of hope.

> *We are strong farmers*
> *We are One Acre Fund*
> *One Acre Fund*
> *One Acre Fund*

A wave of rich African voices—sopranos, tenors, baritones—unaccustomed to singing together but now naturally harmonizing like a well-rehearsed choir rolled through the church.

> *We help our neighbors*
> *We are One Acre Fund*
> *We work to increase our harvests*
> *We are One Acre Fund*

One Acre Fund
One Acre Fund
We work to end poverty
We are One Acre Fund
Mapambano (struggling)
Mapambano (struggling)
Bado Mapambano (still struggling)
We are One Acre Fund

As the voices softened after a fourth chorus, a cell phone crackled with a ring tone from the holiday just past. "Jingle Bells." Laughter filled the church. An embarrassed farmer rifled through her pockets, seized the phone, and silenced the ringing.

"Happy New Year," said One Acre field officer Kennedy Wafula, joining in the laughter. He was a thin, cherubic man named for an American president and a long-ago rainy season. Kennedy was still smiling broadly, shaking his head at the comical interruption, as he taped a large, white paper to a tattered blackboard on the front wall of the church. The paper asked, "What Does the Song Talk About?"

"The song describes our core values," Kennedy explained, referring to the One Acre jingle, and not "Jingle Bells." "We are strong farmers; we are willing to work hard to see good results in our fields. We work together, we help our neighbors; we are stronger together than we are by ourselves. We work to increase our harvests. We work to end poverty by working together for many seasons to come."

Kennedy was performing an age-old agriculture service, that of a rural advisor traveling the back roads to bring the latest technology and practical knowledge to the farmers. Such wandering wise men, known as "extension agents" in agriculture parlance, had been essential in spreading the agricultural revolutions in every part of the world: North America, Europe, Asia, Australia, Latin America. Everywhere except Africa. In most African countries during the past three decades, the sighting of an extension agent had been about as rare as spotting a black rhino. Government budgets didn't have enough money to fund them; international development agencies, in their negligence of agriculture, believed that Africa, alone among the continents of the world, could do without them. As a result, Africa's extension services deteriorated to a woeful state, and new knowledge seldom reached the smallholders' fields.

And so it was that the Lutacho farmers who gathered in the Kenya Assemblies of God church adroitly wielded the latest in twenty-first-century cell phone technology—in fact, they had skipped technological generations, never having used landline telephones—but didn't have access to farming technology, such as hybrid seeds, developed at the beginning of the twentieth century. The cell phone purveyors, among the most aggressive entrepreneurs on the continent, had pushed their products far into the African bush so that most every farm family had at least one tiny phone, which could do all sorts of magical things, such as transfer money and monitor commodity prices in addition to calling relatives in far off places. But agriculture companies, with only a few exceptions, had never viewed those very same farmers as worthwhile customers for their seeds or fertilizers or farming advice. Too poor, they reckoned. Too insignificant. So while the Lutacho farmers clutched their cell phones, changing ring tones with the seasons, they remained subsistence farmers unable to feed their families.

Kennedy and his fellow field officers at One Acre were out to rectify that incomprehensible imbalance. Though an American with a business school degree founded One Acre, more than three hundred Kenyans who intimately knew the rhythms of the local growing season and commanded the trust of the local farmers were doing the critical fieldwork. One Acre armed them with a lively script of extension advice and provided sturdy bicycles to travel over the rutted dirt roads.

A smallholder farmer himself, Kennedy had pedaled his bike nearly two kilometers from his house to the Lutacho church that morning and left it leaning against the wall near the front door. Churches were a favorite One Acre gathering place, for they offered seats and refuge from the sun. Inside the Assemblies of God church, Kennedy captured the farmers' attention by preaching what he called the "Obama method." It was a simple sequence of planting techniques known to most every farmer and backyard gardener in the United States and other rich areas of the world. But the methods were still alien concepts to the smallholder farmers of western Kenya and most of Africa, farmers who sought—and almost always failed—to feed their families and eke out a living from a couple of acres of land. Kennedy hoped to capitalize on the American president's popularity in Kenya by hitching the set of farming instructions to the Obama aura. Barack Obama's father had grown up tending goats on a small farm just a few hours' drive south of the Lugulu Hills, and his relatives still worked the land there. President Obama's election was greatly celebrated in Kenya, where he was highly revered; and three years later, many people still wore his image and name on shirts and dresses and caps. His smiling face beamed from the mud-brick walls of many rural houses where One Acre members also proudly displayed the organization's calendar.

That One Acre calendar even had pride of place on the front wall of the Assemblies of God church. It hung beside a poster depicting Jesus on ascending stairs. "CHRIST, OUR ONLY WAY TO HEAVEN," the poster proclaimed in large letters, and then added, "Jesus said . . . I am the Way, the Truth and the Life; no one comes to the Father except through me."

The One Acre planting method, Kennedy told the farmers, is the way to better harvests and the alleviation of hunger. He taped another poster to the altar wall. It asked,

Why do we space our seeds when planting?

- To avoid competition on fertilizer and sunlight.
- To know the number of plants in your farm.
- To get high yields.
- To give easy time for weeding.

As he paced the front of the church, punctuating his advice with the Swahili words *sawa, sawa*—"OK, OK"—Kennedy plunged into the heart of his sermon on the basics of planting maize, which has long been the staple crop for the smallholder farmers of Kenya but rarely a cash crop. Wiping beads of sweat from his forehead, he told his congregation that each group of farmers would need to fashion a planting string. He unraveled a length of twine, seventy-five centimeters long. "Seventy-five," he said. "That is the distance between rows. *Sawa sawa*?"

"Seventy-five," the farmers repeated.

Kennedy then held aloft a thicker spool of twine, wound around a tree stick. He slowly unrolled it, and every twenty-five centimeters he tied a strip of plastic torn from a bag. "Twenty-five. This is the distance between plants. How far?"

"Twenty-five," came the reply.

"You dig a hole every twenty-five centimeters and put in one seed. *Sawa sawa*. Only one seed, so there is no competition between many seeds for the fertilizer and water and sun."

Kennedy led the farmers outside, through the side door, to practice the measuring and the preparation of their land. It demanded discipline and patience—a great departure from the traditional planting method of grabbing a fistful of seed and scattering it willy-nilly over the soil, as if throwing dice or tossing feed to chickens. That carefree method often left multiple seeds in a hole. The farmers thought that increased their odds of at least one seed germinating and one plant surviving. In reality, it crowded the sprouts as they pushed through the soil and stretched toward the sun. The frequent result: stunted maize stalks with under-formed cobs and harvests far below potential.

The farmers gathered around a sample plot in the churchyard. The sun was bearing down from a clear, blue sky. Kennedy tied the planting string to two sticks anchored at opposite ends of the plot. Leonida grabbed a *jembe* and led the demonstration as Kennedy narrated. "Turn the soil, remove the weeds," he instructed. "Break up the big chunks of soil, make it as fine as possible. Bend over, dig hard."

Leonida, bending deeply at the waist in her blue dress, hacked robustly at the soil for a minute or so, moving along the planting string, digging a hole at every plastic marker. Other farmers followed her, completing the planting process: one put a tiny scoop of fertilizer in the hole, the next covered it with a layer of dirt, then one dropped a single seed, and finally one filled in the hole. More farmers stepped forward to take their turns. Leonida handed off the *jembe*.

ONE ACRE FARMERS worked together in groups of eight to twelve, friends and neighbors coming together to form their own little farming cooperatives. They gave their groups inspirational names like Hope or Faith or Mercy or Grace or Happiness or Success. Leonida's group of eight women and one man was called *Amua*. The name conveyed hope and faith but also determination and ambition. *Amua*, in Swahili, meant "decide."

"What have you decided?" Leonida was often asked by fellow farmers.

"We have decided," she would proudly reply, "to move from misery to Canaan."

Canaan was the Old Testament land of milk and honey, a place of abundance, the land of deliverance. Before they'd banded together, the members of *Amua* had each watched other farmers in their region double or triple the size of their maize harvests. Those farmers, with maize that grew tall and robust, were advancing to Canaan, progressing beyond being merely subsistence farmers. What were they doing, Leonida had wondered, that I'm not?

Leonida, one of Lutacho's village elders, sought more information. Agnes Wekhwela, a nearly toothless farmer thirty years her senior, told Leonida about a new organization that she had joined the previous year: how it delivered seeds and fertilizer on time and in abundance, how it followed up with planting and tending and harvest advice, how that was all provided on a credit of about forty-five hundred shillings (about US $50) per half acre of maize, how it all led to harvests more bountiful than she had ever seen. It was called One Acre Fund.

Joining such a group, taking on debt for the first time in their lives, putting their trust in seeds and methods and technologies foreign to their long-practiced agricultural traditions, would be a leap of blind faith. Leonida and her neighbors sought assurance and inspiration in the Scriptures. They found it in Exodus 3:17: "And I have promised to bring you up out of your misery in Egypt into the land of the Canaanites . . . a land flowing with milk and honey."

Misery? Leonida and her neighbors certainly knew misery. The very area where they lived was called Malaria. There was a stream nearby, a great blessing in that it provided water for drinking and cooking and washing only a few minutes' walk away. But it was also a dreaded curse, for with the slow-moving water came a thicket of mosquitoes. And with the mosquitoes came malaria, an energy-sapping affliction of fever, chills, and headaches that could be deadly for children and debilitating for adults.

The malaria, though, wasn't the greatest misery in Leonida's neighborhood. The big one was hunger. Struggling with depleted soils, tired seeds, and fickle rains, the farmers of Lutacho and their families lived with a chronic, gnawing emptiness in their bellies. It was at its worst during the annual hunger season. As the *wanjala* dragged on, the littlest children were the earliest casualties. In this area of rural western Kenya, one of seven children died before reaching their fifth birthdays, most of them from hunger and malnutrition or related diseases. Of those who survived, half were stunted physically and mentally. Leonida worried that her youngest child, four-year-old Dorcas, was tinier and quieter and sicker more often than she should be. For the women farmers of western Kenya and all of Africa, that was the deepest misery of all: being a mother unable to stop a hungry child from crying, and then watching that child retreat into the shrinking shell of malnutrition.

Misery, yes, Leonida and the farmers of Lutacho knew it all too well. This new organization, this One Acre Fund, offered promise. But also peril. Should the farmers trust the new seeds, the new practices? How would they handle the new credit? The farmers fought the same qualms that rattle any farmer in the world who is trying something new: What if it doesn't work?

It was yet another risk for farmers who already bore 100 percent of the risk of their operations; not only were they solely dependent on rains, but they also had no crop insurance or price surety or government support like farmers in the United States and many other rich parts of the world enjoyed if their crops or the market failed.

But if little Dorcas and their other children were to ever have a chance to grow up healthy and smart, did they really have another choice? If they were ever to break the cycle of the annual hunger season, they had to try something different.

Amua. They decided. Leonida joined One Acre in 2010, and through the year she watched in astonishment as her maize grew tall and strong. At harvest time, her maize was more bountiful than ever before. It was a first step in her exodus from misery. She knew it would be a journey requiring repeated years of plentiful harvests, but this was a start. She recruited other neighbors to join. As a village elder, she wanted everyone to see such improvement, to join in the exodus.

Now, as 2011 began, she eagerly helped Kennedy spread the word about the One Acre way.

BACK INSIDE THE CHURCH, Kennedy taped a third paper to the wall:

Importance of Land Preparation:

- To kill and remove the weeds from the field.
- To allow the plants to penetrate the soil easily.

What Kind of Land Should You Use for Planting?

- Flat, free of rocks and trees, and not swampy.

Kennedy asked for volunteers, and eleven farmers eagerly joined Leonida at the front of the church. Six of the farmers, including Leonida, squatted in a row. They represented new maize sprouts. The other six farmers stood behind them. They were weeds. Kennedy instructed the standing farmers to press down on the shoulders of the squatters. He then ordered the squatters to stand. They tried and tried, but they couldn't straighten up. It was a hilarious scene, earnestness turning to slapstick, and the church again shook with laughter. Kennedy, stifling a laugh himself, explained the serious message: This is what weeds will do; they will hold down the maize plants. Be diligent about killing the weeds, he implored. Give the maize a chance to grow.

The farmers returned to their benches, sprouts and weeds still giggling together. Kennedy requested two more volunteers, "strong, fit farmers, a man and a woman." Two of the younger farmers jumped forward. Kennedy gave the woman a single stick and told her to try and break it. With a quick flex of her arms, she snapped it easily. The man was given a thick bundle of sticks bound together. Kennedy told him to try and break it. He flexed his muscles and heaved his chest and failed. He tried to break the bundle over his knees and failed. He huffed and puffed, growing angrier at every attempt as laughter increased, but the sticks didn't break.

"If you work in your fields alone, like one stick, the work will break you easily," Kennedy explained, throwing an arm over the shoulder of the frustrated man. "But if you come together and work in a group, like the bundle of sticks, you will be strong and you will be hard to break from the labor. *Sawa, sawa.*"

Next, Leonida appeared again, carrying a bucket of water to the altar. As the farmers moved to the edge of their benches, curious about what was to come, Kennedy told them it was important to understand the principle of receiving the seeds and fertilizer on credit—forty-five-hundred shillings for those planting a half acre of maize, eighty-eight-hundred shillings for one acre—and the importance of paying it back. It was a practice at the core of One Acre's method: Nothing comes free.

Another woman farmer emptied the bucket of water into a second bucket and handed the full bucket to Leonida. "This is a gift," Kennedy said. "With a gift, you can do with it what you want. But once you use it, it is over." To symbolize using the gift, Leonida walked to the door and tossed the water into the churchyard. She returned with an empty bucket.

"The gift won't make you work hard," Kennedy said. "But if you get a loan, you must take care. *Sawa, sawa*. You will work hard to repay it."

Leonida's demonstration partner produced another bucket of water. Leonida grabbed a green plastic cup and began pouring the water from that bucket into the empty one, cup by cup. That was the repayment system. When the water had moved from one bucket to the other, the second farmer moved the water back, cup by cup. Leonida and her partner did this several times, moving the water from bucket to bucket.

"It is a continuous process," Kennedy explained. "Just like this water circulates from bucket to bucket, so will our money. *Sawa, sawa*. One Acre will supply the seeds and fertilizer and advice; you pay us back bit by bit. Then we have money to supply the inputs next year, and you pay us back. This means that One Acre will continue to provide inputs and services. We will stay here with you; we will stay in business. If it is a gift, we give it to you one time, and we are gone. A gift ends, but a loan continues, it circulates year after year. *Sawa, sawa*."

The demonstrations complete, Kennedy handed slips of paper to the farmers and asked them to write down their farming goals and then share them with others. Leonida retrieved a pen from a black bag boldly emblazoned with the slogan, "Your vote, your future"; it was from a community voter registration drive she had organized the previous year when Kenya's new constitution was up for popular ratification. She quickly and decisively wrote her goals, which remained the same from her first One Acre meeting: "Educate my children. Have enough food for my family. Have enough food to help others in need, be a person who helps others. Buy a dairy cow to earn more money."

She swapped goals with another farmer, who had written, "To have a good house, enough food, more income, send children to school." From the conversations in the church, it seemed that two goals appeared on every piece of paper: Feed my family, educate my children.

Kennedy asked the gathering, "How can you reach these goals?"

"Work hard," the farmers answered in unison.

"Say it again," Kennedy implored.

"Work hard!"

THE WORDS—"feed my family, educate my children"—resonating around the mud-and-sticks church, one of the humblest settings on earth, echoed words uttered almost exactly two years earlier, on January 20, 2009, at perhaps the most powerful location on earth, the steps of the U.S. Capitol in Washington, DC. In his Inauguration Day address, President Obama said, "To the people of poor nations, we pledge to work alongside you to make your farms flourish and let clean waters flow, to nourish starved bodies, and feed hungry minds."

Food and education. These were the same priorities, the same dreams the Lutacho farmers scribbled on their scraps of paper. From its first minutes in office, the Obama administration had made ending hunger through agricultural development a top foreign policy priority and an essential element of America's deployment of "soft power." Before 2009 ended, those thirty words on Inauguration Day had become the presidential initiative called Feed the Future, an effort to create the conditions for the world's poor smallholder farmers—farmers precisely like those gathered in the Assemblies of God church as well as other One Acre members—to be as productive as possible, to feed themselves and their communities, and to hopefully have surpluses to boost their incomes, which could mean better education for their children.

In April 2010, the United States was the lead founding donor of the Global Agriculture and Food Security Program, known by its unfortunate acronym, GAFSP (which, when spoken, sounds like gaffes or gasp). It was a new, international financing facility administered by the World Bank to reverse the neglect of farming over the previous three decades by supporting agricultural development projects drawn up and prioritized by the poorest nations. The founding donors, including Canada, Spain, South Korea, and the Bill & Melinda Gates Foundation, pledged an initial injection of $880 million into the fund.

Bill Gates, the cofounder of Microsoft and the cofounder with his wife of the world's largest private philanthropy, said on the launch day that the intention was to "put smallholder farmers, especially women, front and center." Investing in smallholder farmers, he added, "is an incredibly effective way to combat hunger and extreme poverty. History has proved it many times."

U.S. treasury secretary Timothy Geithner, looking out of place talking about farming, proclaimed, "A world where more than one billion people suffer from hunger is not a strong or stable world. A world where more than two billion people in rural areas struggle to secure a livelihood is not a balanced one."

And U.S. secretary of agriculture Tom Vilsack offered the reminder that "just one lifetime ago the United States was a country of subsistence farmers." He maintained, "There are no better innovators than those who farm the land."

This new agenda to improve smallholder farming had been moving quickly, as the Obama administration envisioned leading the greatest assault on hunger through agricultural development since the Green Revolution a half-century earlier. American researchers, philanthropists, and politicians powered that movement, which eliminated famine in many parts of the developing world. By the fall of 2010, a new Bureau for Food Security was up and running in the U.S. Agency for International Development (USAID) to coordinate this new agricultural development push. The bureau was to be the cornerstone on which a new USAID would be constructed after years of being neutered by previous administrations, a revitalized agency that would put agriculture growth at the center of development efforts. President Obama asked Congress for $3.5 billion over three years to fund the ambitious agenda.

But as Leonida and her One Acre neighbors gathered in the Assemblies of God church at the beginning of 2011, a new Congress was gathering in Washington, DC. At their swearing in, member after member—particularly those from the Republican Party and its new Tea Party wing—swore that they would corral government spending and slash the federal budget. One of the prime targets was foreign aid. Florida Republican congresswoman Ileana Ros-Lehtinen, the new chair of the House Foreign Affairs Committee, said, "There is much fat in these budgets." Some in Congress even called for killing off USAID altogether.

The new appropriations committees in the Senate and House of Representatives were quick to begin carving into Obama's agricultural development requests; indeed they embarked on a paradoxical pursuit for "fat" in programs to reduce hunger. Soon, GAFSP was gasping for money, and Feed the Future was in danger of an unceremonious early death, just as Leonida and her neighbors were preparing their soil to come to life again.

The stakes were high: would the administration be able to truly provide the leadership necessary to drive an agricultural renaissance in the developing world for the benefit of farmers such as

Leonida, and for the entire global food chain and world stability? Would members of Congress and parliaments across the rich world hear the aspirations of the farmers in the Assemblies of God church in an area called Malaria and realize that there was really nothing "foreign" about any aid that would help them achieve their goals? What the farmers wanted was universal: food and education.

THE SUN WAS APPROACHING its noontime peak as the One Acre training session ended and the farmers of Lutacho trudged back to their *shambas*. As the temperature rose, the pace in the village slowed. Farmers retreated from the fields to the shade of trees or to their little houses. Leonida plopped into a wooden chair at her living room table. She ran her right palm over her face, wiping away the sweat.

A sturdy, graceful woman, Leonida had a full, expressive face that could shift quickly from joy to concern. Mostly, it conveyed weariness and worry. After years of barefoot farming, what did she have?

Her homestead was two acres in total, most of it cropland with several mud-and-stick structures clustered in one corner. Her house, though small, was the largest of the buildings, a rectangle of about 450 square feet. Like the church, the house had a sheet metal roof and a dirt-and-dung floor. There were two rooms. The living room was populated with four wooden couches, six wooden chairs, two tables, and one cabinet. The couches had no upholstery or padding; they were covered only with a blanket or a sheet. The chairs were unadorned. The tabletops were draped with tattered cloth in red-and-white paisley patterns. Two small windows introduced slivers of light when the blue wooden shutters were open. Off the living room was a small bedroom where Leonida, her husband, Peter, and their youngest child, Dorcas, slept.

The living room walls were decorated with assorted calendars from various years—2009 from a cow management program, 2010 from a flour company, 2010 and 2011 from the One Acre Fund. Election posters from past campaigns joined the eclectic mix on the walls, as did a gallery of family photos from earlier days, better times. Beside the door hung a faded photo in a blue-and-white wooden frame. It was from their wedding day in 1986; Leonida was eighteen then, Peter thirty-eight. Leonida smiled beneath a bushy Afro. Peter looked dapper and cocky in a beret.

Peter had bought this patch of land near other family members, and they eventually settled here to farm. The house they built with mud and sticks was meant to be temporary, until a more solid brick house could be constructed. But still it stood. All their dreams from back then had given way to the daily grind of subsistence farming and raising a growing family, which now numbered seven children and two grandchildren. A large clock—"high quality quartz," a script on the face proclaimed—hung forlornly on one of the living room walls. It, too, was set rather majestically in a blue-and-white frame, along with a plastic red rose, but no one looked to it for guidance anymore. The clock hands had stopped at high noon on some long-ago forgotten day when the battery died and progress on the *shamba* came to a standstill.

An even smaller mud-and-sticks house, standing unevenly behind a hedge of bushes, was where the eldest son, Francis, twenty-four, stayed when he was in the area. The "kitchen" was in a separate small hut; the two middle daughters, thirteen-year-old Jackline and ten-year-old Sarah, slept there in a ramshackle bed beside the cooking pit. A round, thatched hut was used to store grass and fodder for the cows, and it was also the sleeping quarters for two orphaned nephews, Lukas and Peter, who began living with Leonida after their fathers died in a car accident. It's also where the second-oldest son, Gideon, fifteen, stayed when he was home from high school. Between the structures, the cows grazed, and a half-dozen chickens pecked away at the hard ground.

The *shamba* was without electricity and running water. Meals were cooked over a fire; the children studied by the light of kerosene lamps, which emitted a sickly smell and wavering light. Water was gathered from the Malaria stream a short walk away; rainwater was harvested by two gutters loosely attached to the metal roof of the main house, which funneled the runoff into plastic barrels. A mud-and-sticks outhouse perched precariously over a pit latrine at the back of a small grove of banana trees.

Sitting on a chair in the living room, her arms resting on the table in front of her, Leonida pondered the first steps of her exodus from misery to Canaan. The harvest several months earlier, in August, had been her best ever. Her half-acre planted with the One Acre method had yielded ten ninety-kilogram bags of maize, which was triple her usual production. She had rented the plot from a neighboring farmer who couldn't do the work himself. Much of her own *shamba* had been planted with sugarcane, which took eighteen months to mature for harvest. Still, she had a few open patches where she had hedged her One Acre bet, in case these new methods didn't work. On those patches, adding up to another half acre, she planted maize as she always had, randomly scattering seed she had saved from the previous harvest, forgoing fertilizer, haphazardly pulling the weeds. The results on those patches were also as they had always been: a paltry total of three bags. The total harvest, thirteen bags, filled the bedroom, which also served as the storeroom. Leonida felt wealthy beyond imagination.

And yet, five months after the harvest, only one bag of maize remained. It, too, sat on a chair in the living room in a dark, cooler corner a couple of feet off the ground to give it some protection from

weevils that could easily chew through the plastic mesh. The farmers called the most evil weevils "Osamas," after Osama bin Laden.
They were especially destructive.

A few days earlier, Leonida had made a momentous decision—
her first big decision since joining One Acre and a decision made
possible only by her increased harvest. She decided to sell all ten
bags of maize from her One Acre production for twelve hundred
shillings per bag (about US $13). She then spent those twelve thou-
sand shillings on an initial payment for Gideon's third year in high
school, fees that were due when classes began in January. The family
had already consumed two bags of maize since the harvest. As the
year began, their food supplies were running close to empty. Their
wanjala would be starting soon.

Leonida's two goals as a farmer, as she listed in church, were to
educate her children, to feed her family. There was no *and* between
those two goals. In the first year of her exodus, even with her
increased harvest, her dream remained an either/or proposition.
Either food *or* education. In past years, she hadn't grown enough to
do either. But at least now, with her better harvest, Leonida had a
choice for the first time. She could either keep her maize in storage
to feed the family for the year, or she could enter the market for the
first time as a maize seller to raise money for school fees.

It was a heavy decision. Leonida weighed the options with her
husband, who said he would support whatever choice she made.
Leonida lost sleep, tossing and turning in her bed, just several feet
from the stored maize bags. She feared that the consequences of selling would be felt by the family every day of the year as they struggled for food. She focused on the practical reasons for selling now.
They lacked proper storage facilities. How long could the bags be
kept in their bedroom before the maize would begin to spoil with
mold and deadly aflatoxins? How long could she fend off the

Osamas? Besides, she reckoned, they were used to dealing with food shortages and hunger. They would just have to endure for one more year.

Mainly, Leonida strongly believed education was the surest route out of poverty, for her individual children and for her family as a whole. An educated person with a good job beyond the farm wouldn't have to depend on rain and sun and outwitting the weevils to make it through the year. There would be a salary that could be shared with those back home. That would be Leonida's social security in old age. She often told her children, "Education is the most important thing in this century. You must concentrate on your studies."

The children knew their mother's story well. She had not had the chance to go to high school; her father died when she was very young, and she had to drop out of school in the seventh grade to save money on school expenses and help her mother with the farm work. She had wanted to be a police lady, she told her children, to help maintain law and order. But for that, she needed a high school diploma.

She wanted better for her children. In Kenya, primary school education was essentially free; parents were expected to cover costs for tests and for supplies such as pencils and paper and uniforms. But high schools charged tuition; the better the school, the higher the fees. Leonida hoped to enroll her children in the best high schools possible, and that would likely mean sending them away to a boarding school where they could live and indeed concentrate on their studies. Such schools would be costly—basic tuition fees of more than two hundred dollars a year were a huge sum for subsistence farmers. Leonida and all the farmers knew that education in the government day schools, though much cheaper, was notoriously uneven. Many of the teachers weren't well educated themselves;

even those who were often lacked motivation when their salaries weren't paid on time, which was a frequent problem. School supplies were short, and classrooms were overcrowded. Books and desks were shared. Discipline was lax. And, most worrisome for Leonida, there were too many temptations in the hours outside of the classroom, too many opportunities to get into trouble while walking back and forth to school.

She had learned much of this from the experiences of her older children. Francis, her eldest, hadn't performed well in school and now was unemployed, wandering about looking for construction work. Her two oldest daughters, twenty-two-year-old Hellen and twenty-year-old Melsa, had both gotten pregnant in school and dropped out. Melsa was now working on a sugarcane plantation in the southern part of Kenya and Hellen was continuing her education in the capital city of Nairobi, cared for by one of Leonida's brothers who lived there. Leonida had two grandchildren but no children with high school diplomas.

She was determined that her next oldest, Gideon, would graduate from a top-notch school. She had high hopes for him. He was an excellent student, a quiet, earnest boy. He had liked to read from the time he was little. Leonida often found him sitting with the Bible, which was one of the few books in the house. He had performed well in primary school and on the national tests, which brought invitations from some of the better high schools in the area. Leonida knew that these boarding schools also struggled for funding, but she believed in their reputation for setting higher academic standards, giving more individual attention to the students and maintaining better discipline. Leonida calculated that the higher tuition was a necessary sacrifice, for a good high school education could lead to college maybe, but certainly to a better job in a city somewhere and money to support her in old age.

Gideon chose the best-performing school among those which recruited him, the Milo Friends Boys High School in the town of Webuye. He told his mother the distance from home was two hundred—by which he meant not kilometers but shillings, the cost of hiring a bicycle driver to take him on the thirty-kilometer ride. That's how distance was routinely measured in rural western Kenya, not by the length of the journey but by the cost. The basic fee for tuition and boarding at Milo High was twenty-three thousand shillings (about US $255) a year. For Gideon's first year, Leonida came up with the money by selling a big shade tree on her *shamba* to people who came and cut it down for lumber and making charcoal. The second year, she sold some tree saplings that had been provided by One Acre and by government arborists for the farmers to nurture. But that covered only part of the fees, and Gideon had been sent home from school at various times of the year to bring more money. Each time, his education was interrupted, and his grades suffered; he wasn't doing as well as he could.

As he entered his third year, which began in early January, Gideon owed the school nine thousand shillings in unpaid fees from the previous term, plus the twenty-three thousand for the new tuition. Leonida wanted to make a sizeable first payment to show the school that she was serious about Gideon continuing his education. She didn't have other assets that could fetch a sizeable sum; if she sold the cows, the family would be without daily income from the milk. And for Gideon to drop out now would be a bitter defeat for her. *Amua*, again. Leonida decided to sell the maize.

She was about to receive an education herself in the crazy economics of African commodities markets. At the time she sold her maize, the price was still near the seasonal low that followed the harvest, when the market was flush with food. She received about twenty-six shillings per *goro-goro*, the standard two-kilogram measure for maize in the local markets. It wasn't a very good price, but it was the going market rate. She had hoped that the price would have risen some by January, more than four months after the harvest, but it hadn't; the post-harvest surplus was still plentiful in western Kenya, keeping the price low.

When the contents of the lone remaining bag of maize ran out—that would happen in less than a month, Leonida calculated—she would need to purchase maize on the market. Food reserves stored in other households would also be dwindling, as would the regional and national supplies, increasing demand in the markets. So with each passing week, the maize price would creep higher, ascending until the next harvest, now about eight months away. By then, according to the price escalations of recent years, maize might be two-and-a-half times more expensive than in January.

Africa's smallholder farmers generally operated opposite of the old stock market principle of "buy low, sell high." Many of them sell low and buy high. Forced to cover debts or pay school fees, like Leonida they sell in the months right after the harvest when local and national food stocks are highest and, therefore, the prices are lowest. Or, with lousy storage facilities, they sell to at least get something from their maize before the Osamas or the molds get to it. Then later they enter the market as buyers when maize is scarcer and the prices are higher. They end up being net buyers of the very products they grow. It was perverse economics, and one of the powerful forces trapping smallholder farmers in their poverty. Leonida needed the money in January; she couldn't wait to sell at higher prices.

The year had begun with Kenyan newspapers trumpeting stories of maize price craziness. The world price of maize was soaring to record highs, but Kenya's farmers weren't benefitting since local prices were depressed by post-harvest surpluses. In addition, a grand African paradox was beginning to form in Kenya: food shortages and surpluses side by side, simultaneous feast and famine. Drought was spreading in the northern and eastern reaches of Kenya, threatening herders and their livestock. The government declared a food shortage in the country and said it would be necessary to import food, either by purchasing from neighboring countries or inviting food aid, to feed the growing ranks of the hungry. Estimates were that anywhere between two and five million Kenyans would need food assistance in the coming months. At the same time, farmers in the breadbasket regions of western Kenya and the Rift Valley were complaining about the low prices they were receiving for their maize.

"Can the government tell us what food shortage they are talking about?" an incredulous North Rift parliamentarian was quoted as saying in the Kenyan newspaper, *Daily Nation*. "Most farmers have maize, but there is no market."

Politicians and the press were hectoring the government to buy local maize to feed fellow Kenyans rather than relying on food aid from abroad. After a few weeks of clamor, the government directed immediate purchase of food from the surplus regions to distribute in the drought areas and to replenish the country's strategic grain reserves. And the government offered to pay a premium price for the maize, but even that didn't help the smallholder farmers. The government and its contract purchasers often didn't pay until one or two months after taking possession of a farmer's maize. So they mainly did business with larger commercial farmers or traders who could wait to get their money. For smallholders, if they sold, it was because they needed the money immediately.

Like Leonida. She contacted a local buyer who came to her *shamba* riding a bicycle. In a couple of trips, he had carried away all the maize.

THE MEALTIME SCRIMPING had already begun. Leonida was reducing the daily portions of maize to stretch the remaining bag. For many Kenyan families, particularly in the western region, a day without maize in some form is considered a day without food. But Leonida had no choice than to begin relying on the sweet potatoes, cassava, bananas, and vegetables such as cowpeas and kale that she also grew on small plots around her house. The first step was to cut back on maize porridge for breakfast.

She described a typical day's menu:

Breakfast: black tea, no milk.

Lunch: sweet potatoes or boiled bananas or *githeri*, a beans and maize mix.

Dinner: small portions of *ugali*, a favorite staple of maize meal, and maybe some vegetables like *sukuma wiki*, the local kale.

Anticipating a squeeze on their maize, Leonida had resisted the temptation to celebrate the bigger harvest with a Christmas feast. She told her family her head was buzzing with school fee worries. The children had hoped for a meal with chicken, rice, bread, and juice, all things they normally didn't eat because of the expense. But their mother didn't want to sell any maize to purchase this other food. So all they got for Christmas dinner was boiled bananas.

Even though chickens scampered around the *shamba*, they weren't for eating. They were the family's emergency fund; in case of medical care or another sudden expense, the chickens would be sold to raise money. Eating a chicken was an extravagance, like a beach vacation, or a foolhardy act, like smoking a one-thousand-shilling bill.

In fact, eating meat of any sort was a true rarity. And, for Leonida, a painful irony. The family name, Wanyama, meant "meat," such as the meat consumed at festival time. It provided a line of gallows humor: "The Meat family has no meat," Leonida would tell her children with a sarcastic chuckle.

The sale of the maize for Gideon's school fees didn't buy Leonida much of a respite from money pressures. A few days after the One Acre training session, Dorcas and the two orphan nephews returned home from school in mid-morning. Leonida was puzzled; it wasn't lunchtime yet. She met the children outside the house and asked what had happened at school. Dorcas, who was just beginning kindergarten, spoke softly. She told her mother they had been sent home to collect school fees. Leonida raised her hands in supplication, as if to say, what can I do?

Leonida had wanted Dorcas and the boys to be day borders in the government primary school, so they could stay for lunch and spare them the two-kilometer walk home and then back to school. There would be a modest fee, but she had hoped the school wouldn't press for an initial payment for a couple of months.

Leonida wrapped her arms around Dorcas and pulled her close in a hug. Then she fished around in her bag and pulled out a crumpled one-hundred-shilling note. Leonida wrapped the bill in a gold-colored cloth and tied the ends into a knot. She handed the precious little bundle to Dorcas, who tucked it firmly into the pocket of her school uniform, a blue dress with yellow trim.

It seemed like a pathetically small amount; one hundred shillings was little more than one U.S. dollar. But Leonida hoped the school principal would see it as a good-faith gesture by a parent who was struggling. It was a deposit on good intentions.

Dorcas would return to school in the afternoon. But now she was tired; she put her head on a table in the sitting room and closed her eyes. Her mother had given her the middle name of Nasimiyu, since she was born during the season of drought, a time of stress. Even in kindergarten, her name was fitting.

LEONIDA KNEW she would have to continue to come up with money to meet the relentless demands for school payments. She could earn fifty shillings a day by helping other farmers in their fields. And there was the milk money from her cows. Together the cows produced between five and eight liters a day, depending on how much grass and fodder she was able to scrounge up for them, a difficult task in the dry season. Leonida would keep some of the milk for her children and sell the rest for thirty shillings per liter.

She was also a village elder, watching over the people of Malaria, settling disputes among neighbors, advising the local chief on community matters. It was an unusual position of authority for a woman, particularly in rural Kenya. But Leonida, who had wanted to become a police lady, commanded her neighbors' respect. They came to her to adjudicate community issues, like petty theft and arguments between neighbors and within families. She organized a neighborhood watch and talked tough to idle boys and men, telling them to make themselves useful in the community. It wasn't a paid position, but sometimes people gave her something for her assistance.

Shortly after Dorcas came home from school, a thin man silently walked into the sitting room, bowing his head as he came through the open door. He sat on a couch without saying a word, simply making a reverential clasp of his hands. When Leonida had finished speaking with Dorcas, she looked at her visitor. He stood up and gave her a wrinkled, brown envelope. She peeked inside and nodded. The man turned to leave as silently as he had come, clasping his hands a second time, never speaking a word. She thanked him and put the envelope on the table. "I will bring it up with the chief," she said.

Moments later, Leonida's husband, Peter, entered the house, slowly, painfully. He had been unable to do any heavy labor since being seriously injured in a traffic accident ten years earlier. He had been a *matatu* driver in the western Kenya town of Kakamega; *matatus* being the ubiquitous passenger vans that swarm throughout the country, rushing Kenyans where they need to go. One night, a truck swerved into Peter's path, and a few days later he woke up in a hospital, wondering how he got there. He remembered nothing. A severe chest injury—"I must have hit the steering wheel," he speculated—left him disabled with chronic breathing problems.

Peter couldn't work in the field with the *jembe*, so he conducted the family's milk trade. After Leonida finished milking the cows at 4 a.m., she set a liter or two aside for the children and poured the surplus milk into bottles and lined them up in a box Peter could carry on the back of his bicycle—the family's only mechanical means of transport. Peter would also buy additional liters of milk from neighbors and add that to his cargo. Then, while the morning sky was still dark, he pedaled the bike to the town of Webuye, an urban area where fewer people had their own cows and demand for milk was greater. The sixteen-kilometer journey was a swift downhill sail, a perilous slalom run between potholes; on the arduous return trip, Peter would often dismount and push the bike up the hill.

Now he had returned from the daily milk run; exhausted, he gingerly sat down beside Leonida at the living room table. He had 120 shillings from four liters of milk. Leonida tucked it under the tablecloth. They agreed they would save as much money as they could for the school fees and to begin making repayments on the One Acre credit for the coming year. Repaying the loan wasn't a priority in January; in fact, One Acre encouraged the farmers to pay it off bit by bit, aiming to be finished by harvest time. But Leonida wanted to set an example in her group, so all the members would be diligent in making repayments. After all, she had led the repayment demonstration at the training session, moving water from one bucket to another.

Peter said the One Acre credit had been a good investment; from 4,500 shillings in seed, fertilizer, and planting advice they had reaped 12,000 shillings worth of maize. He told Leonida that her decision to join One Acre was the best choice she ever made, other than marrying him. He squeezed her arm and laughed. "Ten bags of maize on a half acre! I didn't think that was possible," he said. Perhaps, he suggested, they should get a credit to plant one acre this year. "Imagine if one day we can plant two acres," he told his wife. "We will do very well."

Leonida agreed. She had already been thinking of doubling her bet on the One Acre method, stepping up to an acre of maize, increasing the pace of their exodus from misery to Canaan. "We will keep moving forward," she told her husband. Now she squeezed his arm. "We will succeed."

A WOMAN WITH A BIG SMILE looked over their shoulders. She was posing with her three sons in a photo on the One Acre calendar. Leonida admired that picture because the people looked so carefree, so at ease with life, apparently unburdened by school fees and any looming *wanjala*. The calendar woman was Rasoa Wasike, a One Acre farmer on the other side of the Lugulu Hills, in the village of Kabuchai. She also was determined to succeed in rising above subsistence farming. And she too had made a crucial choice, full of promise and peril, in the first days of the year.

Rasoa looked much younger than her thirty years; indeed, her face didn't convey the worry that so haunted Leonida. Often, people who had seen Rasoa's calendar picture insisted that she couldn't be the mother of those three boys; she must be their sister. Whenever Rasoa heard this, she doubled over in laughter, her incandescent smile brighter than ever.

Her appearance was indeed striking in the harsh, rural setting. Squatting beside the cooking fire in the tiny kitchen hut behind her mud-and-sticks house, Rasoa seemed impervious to the smoke billowing all around, stinging the eyes, choking the throat. In that dark, smoky setting, her smile with brilliantly white teeth was all that you could see, like the grin of the Cheshire cat that remained alone while the body and face magically disappeared. If she had been born in Nairobi, Rasoa might have been spotted by a talent agency, and her smile would be lighting up magazine ads and billboards across the city. Instead, she was like millions of Kenyan women born in the rural areas, working the soil by hand to feed her family. The only place she was a cover girl was on the One Acre calendar. She was a leader of her One Acre group, called Kabuchai Women Self-Help. Whenever she spoke the name, she stressed the word *women*. For women, she often said, did most of the hard work on the *shambas*, and women, by improving their agriculture production, would lead their families and their communities out of poverty.

Like Leonida, Rasoa was spearheading an exodus to a place where there would be no hunger. One woman eagerly joining her column as the New Year began was Zipporah Biketi. Zipporah was determined to live up to her name, which is recorded early in the Bible, in the second chapter of Exodus. Zipporah was the wife of Moses.

The twenty-nine-year-old Zipporah Biketi had formed a new branch of the Kabuchai Women Self-Help group; she was desperate to turn her *shamba* into her own land of milk and honey. Zipporah lived with her husband and four young children in a tiny hut with a thatched roof that leaked into the bedroom. Money and food were perpetually scarce. The two youngest children—a two-year-old son and four-year-old daughter—appeared trapped in the season of their birth. The boy's belly was swollen, a common sign of malnutrition, and he was plagued with a persistent cough. His name was David Wanjala. David Hunger. The girl was thin as a twig. Her name was Tabitha Nanjala. Tabitha Hunger.

"When you, as a parent, see your child not eating enough to be satisfied, you are hurt, but you are not in a position to control the situation," Zipporah said during her first One Acre training meeting at the Kabuchai Baptist Church Elgon View. She was soft-spoken, with a reluctant, nervous smile, a stark contrast to Rasoa's confident, booming smile. Through One Acre, Zipporah hoped to assert control over her *shamba*. She would be devoting the entire acre to the One Acre way of maize growing. For her and her family—especially for the two children of *wanjala*—it was a matter of survival. Zipporah herself was a Nekesa, born in the time of harvest, but her latest efforts mocked her name. Her previous harvest had been a disaster, yielding less than two bags of maize. Now, that was long gone; in January, they were already deep into their hunger season.

It was a shared ambition in Kabuchai Women Self-Help to conquer the *wanjala* by transforming the family farm into a family business, through increased yields and diversification. For Rasoa, 2011 had dawned full of opportunity.

Rasoa, like Leonida, had harvested ten bags of maize on a half-acre in her first year with One Acre. It was more than double her previous best harvest. She rejoiced that for once she might have enough maize to stretch through the year, sustaining her husband, herself, and their three boys: Timothy Wafula (Rain), eleven; Arnest Wanyonyi (Weeding), nine; and David Wekesa (Harvest), six. None of her children had been born during the *wanjala*. Now, she hoped, her bountiful harvest would eliminate that season altogether.

In the post-harvest months she was storing her maize in a corner of their bedroom. By the beginning of the year, they had consumed one-and-a-half bags of maize, alternating maize meals with bananas, cassava, and vegetables. At that rate, Rasoa calculated, the remaining bags would last them until the next August harvest.

But in the second week of January, she received a tantalizing offer. A neighbor was desperate to sell a calf in order to raise money for high school fees. She was selling the calf for 8,500 shillings, which Rasoa thought to be a very good price. Rasoa checked the maize price in her village of Kabuchai. It was 1,200 shillings per bag, the same price Leonida received. For eight-and-a-half bags, that would be 10,200 shillings.

Rasoa and her husband, Cyrus, huddled in their house and pondered the decision. Their house, too, was a mud-and-sticks shack that was meant to be temporary but still remained twelve years after their marriage. They had built a crude kiln in a corner of the *shamba* and begun to make bricks from clay. But it was slow going; a permanent house remained a distant dream.

Now, though, with a bumper maize harvest, they could begin working on another dream—diversifying their farming to help provide an education for their children. Sitting on the unadorned wooden chairs in their house, they were surrounded with inspiration. It was written on the walls. Literally, with chalk. "With God Everything is Possible," Rasoa had scrawled on one wall of her living room. And other exhortations as well: "Lord is Good All the Time" and "Nothing but Prayer."

These words served as art—words instead of pictures or paintings or decorative wallpaper. "Welcome Visitors Feel at Home," proclaimed the far wall of her living room, a greeting that was seen immediately by all those who entered the house. A framed homily hung near the door, proclaiming Proverbs 24:3–4. "By wisdom a house is built and through understanding it is established. Through knowledge its rooms are filled with rare and beautiful treasures."

Today's rare and beautiful treasure, realized from the knowledge of better planting methods, was the eight-and-a-half bags of maize that remained from their harvest. Those bags gave Rasoa and Cyrus a rare choice in life. They could either keep the maize and eat it throughout the year, or they could sell it and buy the cow. Rasoa pointed out that the cow would last longer than the maize. It would be an investment for the future and help them realize their goal of good education for their boys. Rasoa was a high school dropout; her parents couldn't afford the fees, and she needed to work on their *shamba*. Cyrus had a high school education and was working as an agent at the local M-Pesa shop in the Kabuchai village. M-Pesa (M is for mobile; *pesa* is Swahili for money) was the method Kenyans used to facilitate cash transactions with their cell phones. Cyrus, working behind a counter wrapped in chicken wire, accepted the clients' money and credited it to their phone accounts. That job provided a base salary of fifteen hundred shillings a month, which could increase depending on the volume of business at his shop. Without his high school diploma, he wouldn't have the job.

Rasoa and Cyrus wanted each of their boys to have a high school education and the chance for a future beyond subsistence farming. Like most farmers, they didn't have a formal savings account in a bank. There was no such thing as a 529 education savings plan, no 401(k) saving strategies. But Rasoa and Cyrus were now thinking of a 401(Cow) plan. The calf would grow like an investment account. In two years, when their oldest son would be entering high school, the calf would be bigger, a full-grown dairy cow, and it would sell for twice the price. That would go a long way toward covering a year of tuition. In the meantime, as the calf matured, it would begin to produce milk. That would be the accumulating interest. The cow would be both a longer-term investment and a true liquid asset.

There were also more immediate, practical reasons for selling. Rasoa and Cyrus wondered whether they would be able to preserve their maize until the next harvest; like farmers and entrepreneurs all over the world, they sought to eliminate risk. There was the threat of spoilage from the humid climate and pests, but there would also be pressure to share with relatives and neighbors who didn't have enough to eat, a cultural custom that often left everyone hungry. A cow would be a hedge against these downsides.

So they decided to sell the maize. And by the third week of January, a young black-and-white calf of the premium milk-producing breed stood in the middle of their *shamba*, picking at the grass. It was tethered to a rope anchored to a wooden stake hammered deep into the ground. Rasoa named the calf "One Acre" so it would remind the family of the benefits that had come from using better inputs, following up-to-date farming advice, and reaping a harvest that gave them choices.

Her *shamba* was becoming more diversified. Her tiny house was bordered by a patch of sugarcane and a garden of vegetables on one side, a small grove of banana plants and passion fruit trees and Napier grass on another, and a half-acre of dark soil where the maize would be planted on a third side. In front was the scrawny yard where One Acre grazed.

The family already owned one mature cow, which was chomping on the Napier grass. With enough nourishment, that cow was producing five liters of milk in the morning and another two or three in the afternoon. Rasoa would keep some for her boys, and sell the rest. A second cow, though, added another mouth to the *shamba*; One Acre needed to be fed throughout the year, along with the three boys. With the dry season bearing down, the grass in Rasoa's yard had already been chewed to a nub by the older cow. And now there would be added stress on the Napier grass.

In January, the market price of maize was still low. Rasoa was comfortable with the family's daily menu: tea with milk for breakfast, boiled bananas and cassava for lunch, a good serving of *ugali* and vegetables for dinner. "The boys feel happy," she assured Cyrus. "They have a healthy diet."

Rasoa was counting on the milk money, plus the money she had left over from the maize sale after buying the calf, to supply the cash to purchase maize on the market for the next couple of months and keep her boys well fed. And Cyrus's salary, which went to purchase other necessities like sugar and vegetables and kerosene, provided a bit of a cushion. But Rasoa, like Leonida, knew that higher maize prices loomed as the year moved forward. She didn't show it behind her big smile, but she was as worried as Leonida.

They had both pushed all their chips on education, betting that somehow they could cheat the hunger season.

Chapter 2

MASAMBU

(Preparing the Land)

After weeks of slow-motion work in the baking heat, life on the *shambas* shifted into a higher gear at the end of February. The daytime temperatures remained high, in the nineties, but there was much to be accomplished in the fields. The long rains would be coming soon, and when they did, the soil needed to be ready for planting.

Teams of oxen and their handlers roamed the dirt roads, listening for a shout from a farmer to come and work her land. The bulls did the heavy labor, dragging plows that churned through the concrete-hard dirt. Stout men walked behind the single-blade contraptions, tightly grabbing the wooden handles, fighting to stay on a reasonably straight path. Often the plow would pop up above a resistant patch of dirt and veer off to the side. The plowman, holding on desperately, would swing wildly behind the plow, battling mightily to return the blade to the furrow. Up at the head of the team, another man walked with a eucalyptus switch, prodding the oxen with sharp flicks to keep them moving straight ahead. The turns at the end of the rows provided constant adventure and comedy, with the plow skidding on its side and the men scrambling to catch up as the animals jerked to head in the opposite direction.

Nowhere was a tractor to be seen.

The hardened fields often required two or three sessions with the oxen; the more frequent the plowing, the finer the soil for the planting. Farmers who didn't have enough money to hire the oxen would be forced to do the work with their *jembes*, a lengthy and backbreaking exercise. The *jembes*, with their short handles, required the farmers to bend deeply while attacking the soil. They seemed to be terribly awkward tools, in desperate need of longer handles to allow the farmers to remain upright. But these hoes were especially tailored to the women who, as was the custom of subsistence farming, did most of the work in the fields. Often they dug at the soil with babies on their backs; the deep bending position with the back horizontal to the ground was the most practical for mother and child.

Leonida needed the oxen to turn her soil three times. She would be planting her maize on a half-acre where sugarcane had once grown. For eighteen months, as the cane matured, the soil remained largely undisturbed. So it was especially hard at the end of the dry season. Three plowing sessions would be barely enough, but at five hundred shillings each time—money saved from the daily milk deliveries—Leonida couldn't afford a fourth or fifth. So in the early mornings and late afternoons, in the cooler stretches of the day, she would head to the field with her *jembe* and attack the large clumps of dirt. Her back was killing her, but she knew the seeds and fertilizer would soon be arriving from One Acre and that they would work best if they were placed in a soft bed of soil. She thought of her exodus to the land of milk and honey and kept digging.

IN BUNGOMA, the main city in western Kenya about an hour's drive from Leonida's *shamba*, activity was also accelerating in warehouse 10 at the National Cereals and Produce Board. The sun was just coming up on a late February morning, peeking over the grain silos that were the tallest structures in Bungoma. At their base was a row of cavernous, concrete warehouses. In the warehouse at the end of the row, rented by One Acre Fund, Andrew Youn began to scale a mountain of seed bags.

He stepped awkwardly from bag to bag, as though he were ascending wobbly stairs. The earthy smell of burlap merged with the dank odor of sweat. Thousands of dust specks twinkled in the rays of sun that streamed through the open warehouse doors. When he reached the summit, Andrew looked down on a conga line of strong-backed men carrying twenty-five- and fifty-kilogram bags on their shoulders. The workers wore an array of rags to protect themselves from the dust—one decided to wear a dress—as they snaked their way through a labyrinth of towering columns of farming ingredients to the fresh air of the loading dock where a fleet of trucks waited.

The One Acre founder looked terribly out of place amid the grunting warehouse labor. He was a skinny, bespectacled, bridge-playing, thirty-two-year-old details geek from Minnesota, the earnest son of Korean immigrants, a Yalie with a Northwestern MBA who would likely stagger under the weight of a big fertilizer bag. But Andrew did his heavy lifting with numbers, calculating his task ahead as nimbly as the burly Kenyan warehouse workers completed their task at hand. Andrew really was in his element. From his lofty perch, he filmed the scene with a small video camera cradled in his right palm. Below the camera was a broad smile. For in each bag of seed or fertilizer he saw a prospering farmer.

"One of my favorite days of the year," he declared to no one in particular.

This was an Input Distribution Day on the One Acre Fund calendar. It was a day when farmers would receive their seed and fertilizer in advance of the rains and the planting season. It was a day of great anticipation. Singing and dancing and prayers of thanksgiving would greet the arrival of the trucks.

For Andrew, it was a day of great fun that provided a measure of how much the organization had grown. But it was also a day of sober assessment of how much more work needed to be done. He descended the mountain of seed sacks and joined Andrew Wanyonyi, One Acre's purchasing manager who was standing on a stack of empty burlap bags near the warehouse door. He, too, was a slender, bespectacled, numbers man, a Kenyan who had worked with One Acre almost from the beginning when they didn't even need a warehouse to service the first couple hundred farmers. Now he carried a clipboard heavy with computer printouts, which recorded the needs of every farmer.

"How are we doing?" Andrew Youn asked.

"It's really hard to imagine what we've become," answered Andrew Wanyonyi (named for the time when weeds were pulled). "I look at what's going on in this warehouse and say, 'Wow!'"

Wanyonyi knew his boss wanted hard numbers to back up the exclamations. Flipping through the printouts, he came to the warehouse totals: This year, he reported, they would be moving 201 metric tons of maize seed and 2,010 tons of fertilizer to their farmers in Kenya who were ready to plant a total of 20,100 acres. It would all fill about four hundred ten-ton trucks.

"That is pretty ridiculous," Andrew Youn said gleefully in his own burst of astonishment. Ridiculous was a favorite word of his. "In our first year, we couldn't even fill one pickup truck. And this year, four hundred? In five years I hope we'll laugh at how small this operation today was."

Actually, he had a little chuckle now, a melancholy little chuckle, as he put this operation into perspective. "Every time I think about the need, it's amazing how big it is. Four hundred trucks seem like a lot, but each truck is just an eye drop in the ocean of need. A meaningful eye drop, but we need so many more."

As the warehouse emptied of stock, it filled with a great sense of urgency, for this would be a pivotal year for One Acre as well as for the farmers. It was a year that would test the organization's ambitious growth projections. On that February morning, One Acre was working with about fifty thousand farmers in western Kenya and Rwanda after only five years of operation. Andrew was eyeing expansion to Burundi and Ghana and points beyond, perhaps even to Asia; he plotted an annual doubling of the number of farmers served. It was a tremendously rapid rate of growth for a humanitarian organization—a "nongovernmental organization," or NGO, in the parlance of the development world. But for Andrew it was hardly satisfying; in the corporate realm, where he had worked for a couple of years as a consultant to Fortune 500 companies, such ambition was expected. His mid-range goal was to be serving 1.5 million smallholder farm families by 2020. His long-term goal was mindboggling.

"Today we're satisfying a fraction of 1 percent of the market," Andrew told his colleagues who had gathered around him on the warehouse loading dock. "The total potential market is over one hundred million farm families in the world. We think fifty million at least in sub-Saharan Africa. We have our work cut out for us."

Andrew and his One Acre cohorts knew their warehouse work was in stark contrast to what was happening in warehouses in other parts of Kenya. The newspapers had recently been filled with stories describing the escalating relief effort to feed Kenyans who had been left hungry by the spreading drought. The United Nations' World Food Program (WFP) was distributing maize and rice and beans, most of it coming in from foreign countries, to feed about 1.6 million Kenyans; predictions were that the number of hungry would soar to more than five million in coming months. Thus, in warehouses in the eastern and northern parts of the country, it was bags of food aid that were being loaded into trucks also making their way to hungry farmers.

Andrew shook his head and frowned when he contemplated the contrast. He appreciated the need for emergency food aid to keep people from starving. But, he wondered, "How much more efficient is one bag of seed than one bag of food? Each bag of seed produces ten bags of food." Indeed, in One Acre's experience, one five-kilogram bag of hybrid maize seed produced an average of ten ninety-kilogram bags of maize. "The idea of bringing in food aid to feed farmers, whose profession is to grow food, is totally absurd, feeding them, creating dependence, rather than empowering people to grow food themselves and feed themselves." There was a rare flash of frustration in his voice. "That's terribly uncreative. The human race is much more creative. We can do better than that."

This determination—"We can do better than that"—placed Andrew and One Acre at the vanguard of a new wave of social entrepreneurs who were upending the development doctrine and practices of the past generation. Talk of poor African farmers succeeding, of growing enough to feed themselves and others, of managing an agricultural enterprise that would improve their standard of living, would have been preposterous a decade or two earlier when those same poor African farmers were being ignored by the development community. At institutions like the World Bank, proposing an agricultural development project was a surefire way to be booted down the career ladder. Hungry smallholder farmers were seen as the problem; they must get out of farming to end their poverty.

Now here was Andrew Youn in a warehouse filled not with food aid but with farming aids, sounding like a revolutionary with his talk of catering to the needs—the business needs!—of the world's poorest and hungriest. He dared called them "customers." He refused to see them as welfare recipients and wanted One Acre's approach to stand in contrast to NGOs that came to Africa and freely handed out food and supplies for a couple of years and then left. "The minute you feed one person, another one hundred are lined up with their hands outstretched," he told his colleagues. "You realize that handouts won't solve a thing, unless you're ready to feed millions of people every year, forever. The only way to make a real difference is to somehow empower the poor to solve their own problems."

Andrew and One Acre were determined to go beyond the old Band-Aid approach of charity relief and emergency aid and pursue new business-based methods of long-term, sustainable agricultural development. He had the audacity to believe that Africa's farmers should see farming as a business, as a way to make a living, rather than merely farming to live.

In the past, very few enterprises had been willing to take on Africa's smallholder farmers as clients. That was why the higher-yielding hybrid seed that had boosted yields in the United States seventy years earlier was so minimally used across Africa, why fertilizer use—even just a thimbleful per plant, as the continent's agronomists prescribed for smallholders—was so rare, why the farming methods were so ancient. Agriculture suppliers simply dropped off seed and fertilizer and tools at supply stores in the big cities. If the remote smallholder farmers needed any of that, the suppliers reckoned, they would come into town and get it.

Andrew didn't understand that philosophy. From business school, he knew there were plenty of case studies that emphasized distribution. He had zeroed in on Coca-Cola's strategy to put a bottle within arms' reach of every person on the planet. Indeed, Coca-Cola had pushed its products out to the remotest points of the African bush. He had also studied the ubiquity of cell phones in rural areas and the customer service tailored to those needs. Similarly, Andrew believed it was possible to inundate every corner of Africa with farm services. "Our secret business ingredient," he often told the One Acre staff, "is distribution."

In passion and ambition, he was the agriculture version of Paul Farmer, the American physician and anthropologist who for twenty years had been challenging the way the world was dealing with health inequalities, be it HIV/AIDS and tuberculosis treatments or horrible hospital infrastructure. Farmer cofounded Partners in Health and went to work in some of the most difficult places on earth, such as Haiti and Rwanda. Andrew greatly admired Farmer. He liked how Farmer lived with the poor to understand their problems, liked how he tirelessly pushed for greater innovation, liked how he asked questions too daring for most set-in-their-ways development organizations. Andrew particularly liked the question, "How can the world do this better?"

IN 2005, ANDREW YOUN had set out for Africa, seeking to help physicians and social workers increase their treatment capacity to serve more AIDS patients. In South Africa's teeming townships, crammed with the very poorest of that widely skewed society, he found that patients desired economic empowerment along with health care so they and their families could eventually thrive on their own. He also began hearing about the woeful conditions of rural Africa, which sparked his curiosity to explore other parts of the continent. Andrew had a few weeks to spare before returning to his MBA studies at Northwestern, and a friend who had traveled the back roads of Africa pointed him in the direction of western Kenya. That turned out to be a most fortuitous travel tip.

The *shambas* in the shadow of Mount Elgon set Andrew's mind racing into overdrive. Outside Bungoma, he met two farm families. One was harvesting two tons of maize on one acre. That family was doing well; there was a tile roof on the house, and the children were well dressed and going to school. On the neighboring *shamba*, the harvest was four times less, the kids were in and out of school, and the thatched roof leaked; they had lost one child to hunger.

Two families living side by side, one thriving, the other starving. They brought Andrew face to face with the classic question of development: Why are some so poor and others so relatively rich? The better off family, he learned, could afford seed and fertilizer and had been trained in how best to use it. The other family had none of that. It was his Aha! moment: the difference between the two families was a matter of access to the most basic elements of farming.

"I can help with that," Andrew thought. He had seen the missing link in African agricultural development: getting common technology and knowledge into the farmers' hands. He didn't need to reinvent the wheel of agriculture, which was good because he was neither a seed breeder nor a soil scientist. The vital technology and science already existed, and other people were busy doing research on new innovations. What was needed was a dedication to distribution. That was something he could do; here in western Kenya was the opportunity to put into practice what he had studied.

Andrew returned to Northwestern and used his second academic year at the Kellogg School of Management to develop a business plan for an organization he originally called Little Farmers Renewing Fund before changing it to One Acre Fund. When the next planting season rolled around in February 2006, Andrew worked with several Kenyan agriculture advisors to provide better quality hybrid seeds and a judicious amount of fertilizer—the equivalent of a Coca-Cola bottle cap per plant—to about forty families, and then to train them in the better farming methods. It cost Andrew seven thousand dollars of his own money. At harvest time, those smallholder farm families doubled and tripled their maize yields. Their hunger seasons were considerably shortened.

Andrew marveled at the possibilities. He narrowed his focus to three points: affordability, accessibility, and training. This became his mantra: reach as many people as you can, have a meaningful impact, and do it cost effectively. He latched on to two other words as well: scalability and sustainability.

He was thinking big from the outset. He didn't just want to serve one village; he wanted to serve the continent. The hunger and agricultural neglect he saw was so great that it was impossible for him to think small. In previous work with a big drugstore chain, Andrew had conducted new product trials. If a product was successful in one set of stores, then that product could be scaled up for an entire network of stores. Now he was thinking: Why not do the same for farm services? If it worked for forty farmers, why not for forty million?

To do that sustainably meant building a funding model different from most NGOs, which received money from various sources and then freely provided their services. Andrew began with a traditional strategy to raise capital to buy the seeds and fertilizer: he hustled to win the backing of a number of social enterprise foundations, catching the attention of funders such as Echoing Green, Mulago Foundation, Pershing Square Foundation, the Skoll Foundation, and the Kellogg entrepreneurship center. But he also knew that philanthropic funding alone wouldn't sustain his scaling-up ambitions. Those funds could expand and contract with the up-and-down rhythms of the global economy or a family fortune, leaving the recipient organization at the mercy of forces beyond its control. So One Acre decided to provide the seed, fertilizer, and farming advice in the form of a credit, which the farmers would pay off in the months leading up to the harvest. The credit amounts were about $50 for a half-acre and $100 for a full acre. Andrew believed the farmers would readily pay off their loans once they saw the benefit of the services. And then One Acre would plow the money back into supporting the farmers. It was the principle Leonida demonstrated with the buckets and water in the church: if we provide a service, and you are happy with it, you will pay us back, and we will stay around to provide you with even better services.

One Acre's founding philosophy was simple: if our farmers succeed, we succeed. And to best succeed, Andrew believed, One Acre needed to be based amid the farmers, not in some office building in a far-off big city; agricultural development work completed in the concrete jungles often struggled to find its way to the fields. Customer intimacy was something Andrew had learned in management school and it became a principle he particularly cherished. The best way to learn from your customers, and to serve them, is to live with them. So One Acre set up shop in Bungoma.

BUNGOMA is a fairly shabby town, a hot and sweaty place about one hundred kilometers north of the equator and about thirty kilometers east of the Uganda border. Bungoma County, which includes the surrounding countryside, was the third most populous in the country with nearly two million people. No one seemed to know for certain how many people lived in Bungoma city, not even the civic authorities. The ethnic violence unleashed after the disputed presidential election of 2007 triggered a wave of displaced people who fled the turmoil in other big cities and rural areas to the east and south. Many came to Bungoma because, as any Luhya person will tell you the moment you first shake hands with them, "We get along with everyone." During the violence, Bungoma, they said, "was the peaceful place." And apparently the peace seekers had kept coming, swelling the population beyond anyone's ability to count it.

The electricity grid was overwhelmed; blackouts were common and random in occurrence. During the day, in the dry season, an oppressive heat gripped the city. In late afternoon on most days, a cacophony of shouting and singing rose from dozens of churches and from the open field by the railway tracks; relentless evangelists with bullhorns filled the heavy air with their exhortations of confession and redemption. On weekend and holiday nights, music thumped from the bars and discos until the following dawn. Two paved roads, running parallel to each other a block or two apart, dissected the city center. They were lined with a chaotic array of concrete and cinderblock shops. Most of the restaurants offered exactly the same menu: beef and rice, beef and chips, beef and *ugali*; repeat the same sequence with chicken; add lima beans and kale to taste (or not). A dated feel permeated the town—buildings that were newly constructed in the past ten years had a dilapidated look, as if they originated in a much earlier era. Most storefronts were faded, chipped, or cracked. Even the shops that sold paint cried out for a fresh coat.

No one would mistake Bungoma for a tourist destination. The airstrip had been abandoned. Cows grazed and kids played soccer where airplanes once took off and landed. The construction of a new wing of the Tourist Hotel had long ago ceased and was now just an eerie concrete shell.

Bungoma itself didn't even hold the illusion that it was a tourist mecca. It didn't bother with any of the trappings. In fact, the odd *mzungu*—a wanderer, commonly used to refer to a generic European or white person—who stumbled into town, and who suddenly had an urge to send an old-fashioned correspondence to the outside world, would be forced to embark on a quixotic journey to find a postcard. An Anglican priest from England recalled that his search took him from shop to shop, with each apologetic shopkeeper certain that the next store they were recommending would have postcards. Finally, he wandered over to Hetpur Bookshop, which nobody recommended but looked intriguing to the priest, mainly because it offered a veranda and shade. His hopes soared when the shop girl remembered seeing postcards once. She disappeared to remember where. After several minutes she returned with a handful of extra-large postcards. With a triumphant grin, she fanned them out as if she held a royal flush. They depicted the famous images of Kenya: lions, elephants, giraffes, buffalo, and those *National Geographic*–like photos of bare-breasted women in traditional tribal settings. Each card said *Jambo* (hello) and *Karibu* (welcome), and they were all faded and disfigured to some extent with assorted splotches and flecks of dirt. The writing on Hetpur's outside wall announced that the shop had been in business since 1961, which may have also been the year the postcards first arrived shiny and brand new. The priest put aside the topless scenes, even though they were the least splotchy ones; he reckoned that a greeting conveyed on such a card wouldn't go over well with his parishioners. Instead, he settled on some of the mottled animal cards. He left Hetpur's—slogan: "the cheapest, the best-stocked"—feeling oddly victorious.

That One Acre was based in this rural backwater and not in the pulsating, cosmopolitan capital of Nairobi, which was home to the vast majority of NGOs operating in Kenya, represented a different kind of development ethic. In Bungoma, there were no fancy headquarters, no cushy living quarters, no hip restaurants or watering holes, no flotilla of new vehicles. There were very few trappings of do-gooder-dom for Andrew and his young colleagues.

The One Acre expatriate staff of about a dozen lived in a grouping of small cinderblock bungalows on a rutted dirt path off one of the paved roads, about a fifteen-minute bicycle ride from the city center (riding on the back of taxi bikes, called *boda-bodas*, being the most common form of transport in Bungoma). Andrew's office was in his spartan bedroom; he decorated the walls with fertilizer price charts. The showers were Rube Goldberg contraptions of pipes and hoses with an ever-present danger of getting an electrical shock while turning on the tap. Toilet seats wobbled and pinched, if indeed the toilets had seats. Vehicles rumbled and wheezed. Salaries were miniscule compared to what graduates from top universities in the United States and Europe could command in private business. Malaria and intestinal disease and man-cating potholes were ever-present dangers.

But Bungoma and One Acre was the place they all wanted to be. Hundreds of applications came flooding in for each job opening. Andrew's typical day was a traffic jam of staff meetings, visiting farmers, phones calls with donors, interviews with those job applicants, a quick jog around the neighborhood, wolfing down dinner with the staff while wearing a miner's headlamp during the power outages, then late-night computer work and phone calls with people in the United States. He and his colleagues worked to balance their ambitions while scaling a steep learning curve about both Africa and farming.

None of them were expert agronomists or scientists who majored in seeds or soils. They were development activists, social entrepreneurs, and business professionals a few years removed from college, eager to add something new to the world. Many had been working for other NGOs, mainly writing reports that collected dust on shelves. In Bungoma, they could see the impact of their work in action, be it in better storage practices, new composting methods, or alternative crop varieties.

They were the boots on the ground, the foot soldiers, working with the smallholder farmers who were to be the intended beneficiaries of initiatives being launched by the White House, the Bill & Melinda Gates Foundation, and the World Bank, which had finally rediscovered agriculture after the 2007 global food crisis and was stepping up its rural investments. Billions of dollars were suddenly being marshaled to end hunger through agricultural development. The Alliance for a Green Revolution in Africa (AGRA), a Nairobi-based innovation of the Gates and Rockefeller foundations, focused donor interest on the potential of African farming. Those dollars were financing African scientists and local seed companies to come up with the new seed, soil, and storage technologies tailored to Africa's geography and climate. One Acre wanted to make sure that vital work got into the hands of the smallholder farmers who needed it most.

The One Acre staff formed an innovation team, searching for the latest science and technology and best practices, and then exploring how it all could be delivered and put into play on the *shambas* in an efficient business manner. They crunched the numbers and examined the cost-effectiveness of new developments, such as weather-based crop insurance and solar-powered lights and fortifying maize flour with vital micronutrients during the grinding stage. They made mistakes, like introducing passion fruit cultivation to the farmers; it turned out the process was too complicated, too risky, and too foreign to their farming habits, so One Acre pulled back. But the question always in the air was, "How can this be done better?" They asked each other, and, most important, they asked the farmers. At any given time, more than twenty new products or services were in research and development, all aimed at bettering the farmers' access to life-improving agriculture methods.

ONE OF THE THINGS the farmers regularly requested was greater crop diversity to spread income throughout the year, lessen reliance on maize, and boost family nutrition. Planting different crops in the different seasons would also help with soil vitality.

This had Seth Silverman on the road to the town of Kitale early in the New Year. His hands tightly gripped the steering wheel as the vehicle rattled over a series of nasty potholes on the main road that headed north from Bungoma. It was a white-knuckle trip, with vehicles veering all over the narrow washboard surface. But this journey, and the possible outcome, was why Seth had joined One Acre after graduating from Stanford University and working briefly on sustainable energy and climate politics with the Natural Resources Defense Council in Washington, DC.

Seth was in search of a better bean seed. Kitale, a main city in the highland grain belt, was the home of the country's most prominent seed companies, which mainly concentrated on maize. But One Acre was hoping these companies could help produce a bean seed that would have better yields in the soils around Bungoma.

"That we still can't get better bean seeds to smallholder farmers . . . ," Seth was saying before putting his thought on hold as he negotiated around a sputtering truck. "It's an outrage," he continued about the elusive bean seed. "It seems something we ought to be able to do."

One Acre farmers, who intercropped beans with the maize and also planted beans separately in a second growing season, were using seed varieties that had been developed in the 1980s. Their yields were on a steady decline, and they were ever more susceptible to a deadly affliction called root rot. Beans were important for adding protein to the farmers' diets, cash to their budgets, and nitrogen to the soil. Surely, there must be a better bean out there. Seth had spoken with breeders supported by AGRA and the International Center for Tropical Agriculture (CIAT) and other international seed centers. He was hoping to find the bean seed by July so the farmers could plant it in August during the second growing season.

The first stop in Kitale was Kenya's Agricultural Development Corporation (ADC), a quasi-government outfit that had grown some seed for One Acre farmers the previous year. "We have twenty-eight thousand members this year," Seth told ADC's technical manager, Samuel Bundotich, indicating One Acre was looking for even more seed this year.

"Are you an NGO?" Bundotich asked, sounding skeptical. "What is your growth strategy in Kenya?" He was testing the seriousness of One Acre and the young man across the table. Seth was in his twenties; Bundotich was more than twice that.

"The denser our coverage of an area, the lower our costs of operations," Seth told Bundotich. He explained One Acre's mission of getting the best available technology into the farmers' hands.

Bundotich nodded, praising One Acre's ambition. "The smallholder farmers are the key," he said. "We say we are an agriculture country; 80 percent of our economy depends on agriculture. And 80 percent of our farmers are small scale. So if you want to make the greatest impact on the economy, that is where the focus should be. If the farmers don't get the seeds, they can't succeed."

"Exactly," agreed Seth. He pulled out a preliminary contract he had drawn up should One Acre find a suitable seed for ADC to multiply. "We'll be under pressure to get beans to our farmers by July," he said. He was wondering when ADC could start cultivating the seeds.

"Depending on the weather, beans should be ready by the end of July," Bundotich said. He returned to the importance of smallholder farmers increasing income by increasing production. "Someone who has money, they can get food, get a mobile phone, send children to school, get electricity. Otherwise, they just sit."

Then he veered off on a popular Kenyan tangent: politics. "Too many politicians want people to remain ignorant, so they won't challenge them," Bundotich said, leaning back in his leather chair. "The people wait for someone to tell them what to do."

Seth was waiting to sign a contract. Bundotich said he would take it under advisement. Politics.

The next stop, on the other side of Kitale, was Western Seed Company and founder Saleem Esmail. Western, which supplied maize seed to One Acre, was a growing alternative to Kenya Seed Company, a government-related enterprise that dominated the country's seed business. Esmail welcomed Seth to his office, which overlooked the company's storage warehouses. As they settled into their chairs, Esmail, behind his desk, said, "I must warn you, we don't have a bean breeding program."

Esmail, an entrepreneur himself and a veteran of the vicissitudes of African agriculture, took the position of wise and cautious advisor to his young guest. Esmail had seen many well-intentioned NGOs come and go over the years, and he regarded new ventures with a certain suspicion. He told Seth, sometimes in a lecturing tone, that there can be a frustrating time lag between getting new seed varieties from the breeders to the seed companies for production, that official certification of new varieties was an onerous process, that seed markets were unreliable. Several times Esmail began a statement with, "I must warn you."

Seth knew that Western Seed's focus was on breeding and then multiplying maize seed for farmers to plant. He had come to try and convince Esmail to get into beans. "I see us working together to invest in a commercially viable value chain that can overcome the hurdles of getting bean seed to farmers," Seth said. He explained that One Acre would seek to find the germplasm, or the breeder seed, and that Western could then multiply that seed in its fields. One Acre would then buy the seed in bulk from Western and supply it to the farmers. One Acre, he said, could provide a market of tens of thousands of farmers.

That got Esmail's attention. "I understand you have the farmers, you have the need, the farmers will use beans for food and to sell for cash. That's important. The missing gap is the right germplasm and the multiplication. It's a tough one; you've got to get the right material. Everything else is just detail."

He suggested that Seth talk to the scientists at the Kenya Agricultural Research Institute (KARI) in Kakamega, another main city in western Kenya. They had both heard about a bean breeder there, Reuben Otsyula, who had developed a variety that was resistant to root rot. But the bean was bottled up in bureaucracy and had yet to reach seed companies and farmers. "It's a matter of talking to the breeder himself," Esmail said. "The goal is to get the research out of the labs and into the fields with the farmers. You really need to have a serious chat with KARI."

Seth said he had tried to reach Otsyula and would redouble his efforts. In the meantime, he wanted to know, could One Acre count on Western to produce bean seed?

"We're interested," Esmail said, leaning forward in his chair, putting his elbows on his desk. "But it's got to make commercial sense for us. It takes a lot of courage for me to say we're interested in beans because we're focused on maize."

"If we can crack this nut," Seth said, "and get it right, it could be a model for other projects."

Esmail insisted Western would need additional funding to expand to beans. "Let's be honest," he said. "We're in a high-risk business, and we're in a risky environment." He fixed Seth with a firm stare. "Look, you draw up a strategy and then come back. Let's see how fast we can get the seeds into farmers' hands. The poor farmers, it's not an easy life."

The old, wary African hand seemed to realize that he sounded terribly pessimistic, even too stern, so Esmail offered some parting encouragement to his visitor. "We've got to provoke initiative, provoke creativity, provoke the science. You've really got to do it. At the end of the day, you'll open up some possibilities. You'll do it. You'll find a way."

"That's the hope," Seth said.

Esmail agreed. "That's the goal."

AT THE BUNGOMA WAREHOUSE, the two Andrews—Youn and Wanyonyi—were checking off their hopes and goals as they watched the maize seed and fertilizer fill up the trucks.

One Acre's top priority was to make sure their farmers got what they needed on time, in the right amount, and at the right price. By moving out the seed and fertilizer in late February, One Acre assured that the farmers would have their ingredients by the time the rain began falling. They had moved up the distribution a week earlier than the year before; then, the rain started early, and some of the delivery trucks were mired in the muddy roads. There was more than enough seed and fertilizer to fill the orders of the farmers; Wanyonyi had wisely stockpiled extra supplies to cover for any broken bags or any spoiled seed that would turn up during inspections. And by buying in bulk like that, One Acre was able to deliver significant savings to the farmers.

Wanyonyi reported to Youn that One Acre was able to save the farmers at least 16 shillings for every two-kilogram bag of seed (he had paid an average of 216 shillings, while the retail price on the day of distribution was 232), and 500 shillings per fifty-kilogram bag of fertilizer (2,700 shillings compared to 3,200). "It adds up," he said. "For these very poor farmers, it's a huge savings."

Youn smiled broadly. His strategy from the outset was to gain strength by increasing numbers. "We consolidate the farmers, giving them leverage," he told Wanyonyi. "Left on their own, the farmers don't have much power. We want them to be empowered to change their own lives, through their own work, not through handouts."

In the past, farmers would save seed from the harvest to plant the next year. But the hybrid seeds performed best when purchased anew every year; the burst in yields produced during the first year of use decreases with every subsequent year. Once the farmers saw the increased yields, they were eager to buy the new seeds every year to get the better harvests. The production gains far surpassed the increased cost of annual seed purchase.

"The farmers are very astute people," Wanyonyi said. "They know what works, and they will pay for it."

"Our greatest hope," Youn added, "is to prove that farmers in rural Africa with transactions of less than one hundred dollars, less than fifty dollars, can actually be profitable customers. We'd love for for-profit companies to come into this."

It was an odd business principle for an entrepreneur who so admired the distribution practices of arch-capitalist corporations like Coca-Cola and McDonald's. But One Acre wasn't out to dominate and monopolize the market, as the game plan of a for-profit company would dictate. The need to serve smallholder farmers was so great that Andrew Youn fervently hoped others would join in, particularly the traditional farm service companies that had so long ignored them.

Two fully loaded trucks slowly pulled away from the warehouse dock. Andrew Youn giddily hopped into One Acre's battered white Toyota van and followed them. He was eager to see the seed and fertilizer arrive at the distribution site where farmers were eagerly gathering. "In our grandest dreams," he declared as the van headed out of Bungoma, "we do think we can actually move the needle in Africa."

THE NEEDLE WAS CERTAINLY moving at the Baptist Church Elgon View, a sturdy brick structure that doubled as a private primary school in Kabuchai, a thirty-minute drive from the warehouse. Hundreds of farmers from the surrounding area milled around the churchyard or sat on the pews that had been moved outside. When the trucks and the One Acre van arrived, kicking up plumes of dust on the dirt road in front of the church, the farmers burst into singing and clapping. It was late morning, and the sun was nearing its zenith in a blue, cloudless sky, scorching everything below.

Alighting from the van, Andrew was greeted joyously by the One Acre field officers and a swarm of farmers. He shook hands and patted backs, a smile glued to his face.

"This is very gratifying," he told the farmers. "It's always a very renewing thing to see every year."

Andrew slowly made his way through the crowd and eventually found a sliver of shade under a skinny tree. He sat on a low, wobbly stool and opened his laptop. Even in this remote setting, he was connected to the Internet with an external modem from Safaricom, one of the prominent mobile communications providers in Kenya that was aggressively expanding into the rural areas. Andrew clicked on a spreadsheet. Numbers. He would follow the numbers as One Acre made good on its promise to the farmers to deliver their seeds and fertilizer in advance of the planting season. In the numbers, as well as in the crowd, he found inspiration.

"What inspires me is when these farmers have a chance to improve their lives," he said to his One Acre colleagues. "We change the odds only slightly. Seeing them unlock the human potential, and seeing what is possible in their lives is very inspirational."

Andrew knew that on their own, many of these farmers would need to walk or pedal a bike for hours to reach farm supply stores on the main, paved roads. Once there, the shopkeepers would often tell them that their preferred maize seed variety or fertilizer was in short supply, or that prices had soared as the planting time neared. Fake seed and stale, impotent fertilizer often found its way into the market to trick farmers desperate for anything to plant.

On this day, the farmers had the seed and fertilizer brought to them. None had to walk more than thirty minutes to reach the church. They already knew the price; it was fixed in their credit contracts. And they could rely on One Acre's quality control to avoid being cheated.

Rasoa Wasike had walked ten minutes down the dirt roads from her house to the Baptist church. It was an often-trod path. Her two youngest boys attended the church school, and she volunteered there as a cook, her smile beaming through the smoke in the little kitchen out back. And it was a favorite gathering site for One Acre field officers. Now, as the trucks arrived, Rasoa, wearing a long blue dress, her hair in braids under a red headband, quickly hopped into action. She organized the farmers into their One Acre groups as they waited to receive the seed and fertilizer. She was a natural leader, unafraid to take charge.

"Distribution day is a new beginning for all of us," she told her fellow farmers. She knew almost all of them; many were her neighbors.

Her group, the Kabuchai Women Self-Help, was expanding to four subgroups this year. One was made up entirely of newcomers like Zipporah Biketi, who watched wide-eyed as the trucks were unloaded.

"It really is a new day for me and my family," Zipporah told Rasoa. "It is like a dream come true."

Zipporah's family was among the poorest in the area. Her mud-and-sticks house was smaller than most: a sitting room, bedroom, and cooking room all squeezed into little more than three hundred square feet. The roof made of brown and brittle thatched grass was an indicator of deep poverty, one step below families who lived under metal roofs. Zipporah's three oldest children—ten-year-old Samwel, seven-year-old Cynthia, and four-year-old Tabitha—attended the government primary school; they could no longer afford the modest fees at the Baptist school. The government school didn't provide meals to the pupils during the day. That morning, Zipporah had sent her children off to school, more than a half-hour walking distance, with just a cup of thin tea—no milk or sugar—for breakfast. The youngest child, little David, followed his mother as she did her work on the *shamba*. His nagging cough announced his presence.

Zipporah's husband, Sanet, was a livestock trader. He would buy a goat or a couple of chickens or a calf, and then by working the various area markets hope to turn a profit. Business was slow. Sanet, who was thirty-four, didn't have the money to buy an animal to begin the process. Their only other source of income was the milk of their two skinny cows.

Together, Zipporah and Sanet farmed one acre of land, but most of that had been planted with sugarcane for the past three years. When the cane company came to harvest the crop, Zipporah and Sanet didn't reap anything. They had joined two other farmers when they went into sugarcane; the company provided fertilizer and other essentials for the crop on credit, which would be paid off at harvest time. The two other farmers had sold their harvested cane independent of the company, ignoring paying back the credit. When the company harvested the Biketis' crop, it deducted the entire credit from their revenue. Which left them with nothing.

"What a waste of land. Three years growing sugarcane, and then nothing," Zipporah complained to her husband. "If we had planted anything else, we would have something for our family."

The Biketis were counting on One Acre to begin their climb out of such abject poverty; they had seen the improvements of Rasoa and other members of the Kabuchai Women group. Over the past year, Zipporah had also been curiously following the activity on a neighboring *shamba*, one she walked past several times a day on the way to the Kabuchai market. She and the other neighborhood farmers believed that half-acre of land was cursed; nothing much had ever grown on it, despite valiant efforts. Now Pastor Isaiah Wekesa Makandayi of the King Jesus Faith Ministries Church was working the plot. Zipporah watched as he planted in precisely measured straight lines, adding just a small scoop of fertilizer, and dropping just one maize seed per hole. It looked like backbreaking work, all the bending over to make sure the fertilizer and seed were deposited properly. It took the pastor and his friends all day to plant the half-acre field. Openly laughing, Zipporah and Sanet had considered such effort to be a waste of time, particularly on that plot of land. And then they watched the pastor patiently pull weeds throughout the growing period. It was methodical, tedious labor.

Zipporah and her neighbors scoffed at the pastor's work. They dismissed it as silly, childish behavior, the work of a dreamer.

But the pastor's maize grew strong and tall. Zipporah was astonished. She watched the pastor harvest. It was no laughing matter. He reaped eight bags of maize on the half acre. The curse had been broken. "A miracle," Zipporah told her neighbors. She asked the pastor what he had done, what prayers he had offered. Yes, he said, it was a miracle. A miracle of better inputs and new information and hard work. He was a One Acre farmer.

Zipporah and Sanet, meanwhile, had struggled to scrape together enough money at planting time to buy seeds and fertilizer. It was their effort that had turned out to be laughable, pathetic. They had planted just one quarter of an acre, scattering the seed over lightly dug furrows, and they had their usual paltry harvest: one-and-a-half bags of maize.

It didn't even last into the New Year. By November they were down to the final forty kilograms. Then Zipporah's father died, and, as is the local custom, she and her siblings had to provide food for the funeral guests. She took her last bit of maize and shared it with others.

Now, in late February, the Biketis were deep into their *wanjala*. Since November, Zipporah had been buying maize on the market. Sanet began selling bricks he fashioned from the *shamba*'s clay-like soil. Every shilling they could scrape up was being spent on food. In December and January the maize price had remained about 25 to 30 shillings per *goro-goro*. But in February it jumped to 55 shillings. Such a large increase so early in the year made all the farmers nervous. How high might the maize price climb this year? Fifty-five was a price more common in April or May. For Zipporah and her family, the breakfast of plain tea had become standard fare.

Zipporah waited nervously to receive her seed and fertilizer at the Baptist church. She was overjoyed to be a One Acre member; without the early delivery of the farm inputs on credit, she wouldn't be able to plant her full acre this year, and the *wanjala* would be unending. Still, she wished she had joined a year or two earlier; her children wouldn't be suffering so much now.

Rasoa called the new members of Kabuchai Women to the back of the trucks. Zipporah's mood brightened considerably as she hurried to find a place in line. She joyfully lifted two twenty-five-kilogram bags of fertilizer and one ten-kilogram bag of seed from one truck and lugged them to a shady area under a tree where men with motorcycles waited to help the farmers haul their loads home. Zipporah handed a ten-shilling coin to one driver, and he strapped the fertilizer bags on the back seat of his bike.

Then Zipporah, who had been named after the wife of Moses, hopped on top of the fertilizer. Holding tight to her bag of seed, she sped off down the dirt road, to her expectant family and, she hoped, to better times. Her exodus had begun.

FRANCIS WANJALA MAMATI pumped Andrew Youn's hand in an enthusiastic welcome. "Thank you for coming back to see us," he told One Acre's founder when he spotted him at the Baptist church.

Francis hadn't known if he himself would be back this year working with One Acre. He was running very low on food and money. He desperately wanted to receive One Acre's seed and fertilizer and extension advice, but he didn't know if he would be able to pay back the credit, even with One Acre's unhurried repayment schedule. He had been laid low by a cultural tradition that was the direct opposite of Zipporah's obligation. Zipporah gave up all her maize in grief. Francis gave all his maize in celebration. On December 17, his eldest daughter had gotten married.

He was happy to see her marry; the husband seemed like a fine young man. But in Kenya, the wedding feast supplied by the bride's family was a community affair. Four hundred people flocked to his homestead at the base of a magnificent rock formation that had been sculpted by centuries of wind and rain. It seemed that everybody within shouting distance of his *shamba* had come—and shouts carry a long distance in the placid countryside, particularly when they are picked up and distributed by the wind. Some had been invited, some hadn't been; the prospect of free food in a land of chronic hunger was alluring. Some of the visitors Francis didn't even know. But he couldn't turn anyone away. He recalled a Biblical parable of a marriage feast where all were welcome. Now the multitudes were descending on his home. They were all his guests. And they came to eat.

Francis and his wife, Mary, devoted their entire maize surplus to the celebration, cooking *ugali* and *githeri* and selling a portion to buy other food. They were determined that the feast be abundant and the fare memorable. Kenyans weren't reluctant to complain about the quality of the food or any perceived stinginess, even at funerals. So Francis and Mary went all out. He reckoned the entire affair—wedding dress, transport to the church, the feast—cost him twenty thousand shillings.

Francis was a very gracious, gregarious, and welcoming man. And that, it seemed, was part of his problem. He'd give you the shirt off his back, even if that shirt were dirty and ripped across the shoulders, like the checkered one he wore at the input distribution.

At fifty-three, Francis was a relative relic in Kenya, where life expectancy was in the mid-fifties. His age gave him a certain wisdom. He was reflective and a good storyteller, be it about the rhythm of the seasons or about chasing the monkeys that once lived in the rocks around his homestead. He and Mary had nine children.

Francis had only a sixth-grade education, but he had seemed to make the most of it. His English was quite good, though he sometimes rummaged around in his mind to find the proper phrasing. He had worked for the government's livestock department for many years, spraying cows for ticks, before taking an early retirement. With a retirement bonus, he bought the three acres of his homestead, which included the majestic rocks, and became a farmer. Ever since, he had been trying to grow enough to feed his family. Many times his efforts failed, and he lived up to—or, rather, down to—his traditional name, Wanjala.

His fortunes changed in the late summer of 2009. He joined the One Acre Fund just in time for the bean-planting season. He accepted a credit of eighteen hundred shillings for the seed and fertilizer needed for one-quarter of an acre, and he followed the One Acre instructions to perfection. Three months later, he sold his bean harvest, 158.8 kilograms, for eighty shillings per kilogram. It was such a remarkable, and profitable, experience that the figures were etched in his mind. He had never before had his harvest weighed. He had never even sold beans by the kilogram before; he had simply sold his harvest to middlemen who came by his *shamba*. They scooped up his beans in a container and paid him about forty-five shillings. Francis reckoned their container could hold about two-and-a-half kilograms, which came to less than twenty shillings a kilogram. He always had the unsettling feeling that he was being cheated. But there were no other buyers, and he had no alternative. Until the end of 2009, when One Acre bought the bean harvest of Francis's ten-person group—named Muyai, after their village—and was able to negotiate a far higher price than the farmers had ever received individually. Francis was astonished.

Suddenly he saw the possibilities of farming to make a living, instead of merely farming to live, and he started to think big. Five large avocado trees and one mango tree grew wild in front of his house. He envisioned building a fruit and vegetable business around them. He talked about one day constructing a greenhouse and growing tomatoes and chili peppers. Along with the maize and beans and some bananas, these market crops would help him pay for his two oldest daughters to go to the local technical college to study fashion design. He wanted all his children to at least finish high school. He wanted them to dream big, beyond the farm. If there was one thing he could give his children, it was education. His farming would prepare that gift.

Since the wedding, he had been pruning back his ambitions. He had received four cows from his new son-in-law as a dowry, and they would help him rebuild assets. But he feared he would have to drop out of One Acre and borrow maize seed from a neighbor and forego the use of fertilizer, which would mean lower yields. He could see the trap door of poverty opening wide.

On Input Distribution Day, though, Francis was back at the Baptist church, waiting in line for maize seed and fertilizer. He and his wife had decided to make their maize harvest their top priority for the year, and somehow they would come up with the money to pay off the credit. The potential for improvement—the opportunity to get his dreams back on track—was too great to pass up. He had discovered that potential with his first One Acre bean harvest, when his income was seven times greater than his expenses. If he wanted to beat back the *wanjala*, to conquer his own name, he figured it was better to be *in* One Acre than *out*.

As he waited with his fellow farmers, hovering around the delivery trucks, Francis kept his eyes trained on the western horizon, toward Mount Elgon. Drought was gripping large swaths of northern and eastern Kenya, and it was still dry and hot in the west. The newspapers were speculating about the drought extending to parts of the country that normally received good rain, like western Kenya. The local weather forecast was indicating that the dry season would stretch into March, and indeed Francis noted that the first rains were already delayed compared to last year.

Francis studied the hazy, blue sky. Last year, he remembered, he had planted on March 1. That was less than a week away. Wisps of white were beginning to appear over the hills in the distance. They were barely clouds, but Francis tried to be optimistic. The rains were near, he said. They would come in from the west. The winds would pick up speed and carry the precipitation. Francis strained his rail-thin body to catch a hint of a breeze. Nothing yet. One to one-and-a-half weeks, that's what Francis predicted. That's when the rains would come.

As the distribution of seeds and fertilizer continued, the One Acre field manager for the Kabuchai area called for a prayer. Francis and his neighbors bowed their heads. From among the farmers sitting on the pews on the church lawn, a minister stepped forward. It was Protus Kamlet, a member of the One Acre group Yetana—"To Help Each Other." He removed his red baseball cap and tucked it under his right arm. With his left arm raised toward heaven, he prayed: "Dear God, shower us with the rain so that the work we do now won't be destroyed by the sun. Bring peace for our seeds and for our people to work together. Bring the rains so we won't be visited by hunger yet again."

"Amen," whispered Francis Hunger Mamati. "Amen."

CHAPTER 3

WAFULA

(The Rains)

Leonida sighed as she peered out her door toward Mount Elgon. The air was so clear that, with just a hint of haze high in the sky, she could see far into the distance. No clouds anywhere. Another beautiful day. She shook her head in despair.

Where were the rains? The so-called long rains that would steadily fall for three months or so and produce a good harvest, where were they? They were late, at least compared to last year. The farmers needed the rain—a good three days of it to soak the soil—before they would begin planting. Leonida stepped out into her yard and scanned the sky in all directions. Nothing but blue. Returning to her house, she reported her forecast to her husband: "No rain today."

It was the morning of March 2. Last year, she planted her maize on this day. Now she worried that she had mistimed her land preparation. The soil that she had paid dearly to be plowed not once but three times was drying and turning hard again.

Her anxiety for the rains to come, to begin planting, grew as the food stocks in the house dwindled. The sooner the planting, the sooner the harvest and a fresh injection of food. Leonida walked across her parched yard to her kitchen hut and returned with a reed basket containing several large sweet potatoes—the white variety common in Africa, not the vitamin-A rich orange variety that is a staple of American Thanksgiving tables—and a few chunks of the cassava that she had grown. It was all that was left of her food. That and the bag of maize perched on the chair in the corner of the living room.

When the last of her homegrown maize had been consumed in mid-February, Leonida sold four chickens to buy the ninety-kilogram bag at a cost of about two thousand shillings—a price already more than 50 percent above what she received when she sold her own maize back in January. It would last through the end of the month, Leonida calculated. To stretch her food as far as she could, Leonida was rationing portions at breakfast and lunch and restricting the maize to dinner only, and then only a few bites for everyone. The meals were getting monotonous and unhealthy—a relentless dosage of starch. Today, sweet potatoes and tea for breakfast; for lunch, just sweet potatoes; for dinner, *ugali* plain.

Sweet potatoes and cassava—a bland, underground tuber also known as *manioc*—were regarded in Kenya and throughout much of Africa as the poor man's food. They were often the last defense against famine. Maize is what the Luhya people preferred to eat, two or three times a day if they could. Porridge, *githeri*, *ugali*, roasted on the cob. For Leonida and her family, such meals were now becoming delicacies, rare treats, as the bag of maize emptied and the market price increased and the *wanjala* neared. They knew that soon they would likely "pass through" entire days without any-thing to consume beyond a cup of tea. "Pass through" was Leonida's phrase for how she and her family would endure these times of great deprivation, as if they would travel across another dimension. The longer the rains delayed, the longer the hunger sea-son, the time of deprivation, would be.

A balanced diet with vegetables, fruit, meat, and dairy was a for-eign concept on many *shambas*. It was certainly something Leonida's younger daughters had never known. Leonida wrapped her arms around Dorcas, who was standing silently at her side. "She's so very thin," Leonida told her husband, Peter. "She's not strong because I have no more food to give her. She's trying to read—A, B, C, D—but how do you learn when you aren't strong?"

Peter gingerly shifted one of the wooden chairs to sit beside his wife. He could see her anxiety and offered words of encouragement. "You work so hard to feed us," he told her. "Without you, we wouldn't eat. You are very strong. You push me forward."

Peter was battling a new round of malaria; he was moving slower than usual. The treatment, a regiment of tablets, cost six hun-dred shillings. Leonida retrieved the last of the shilling notes she had stashed under the tablecloth of her living room table. That was where she kept the cash she used to whittle down the One Acre credit bit by bit, pay school fees, buy some food, cover emergencies. Peter's malaria treatment was one of those emergencies; it was an unexpected expense, putting more pressure on their ability to buy food.

Their homestead was bone dry and as hard as concrete. The grass in the yard between the structures was grazed to the dirt. Fod-der for the cows was scarce; the stock of greens and cornstalks stored in one of the round, thatched huts was dwindling. The stream—Malaria—was a five-minute walk away; it was difficult enough to carry water for cooking and washing several times a day without hauling water for the grass, too. In the midday heat, not much stirred. Even the chickens seemed too lazy to peck at the ground.

Leonida had been helping other farmers with their land preparation for fifty shillings a day. The trickle of money from the milk was thinning. With less grass to eat, the cows gave less milk. Even with his malaria, Peter had to lead the cows further from the *shamba* each day to graze.

Leonida had been hoping to plant one acre of maize this year. She had harvested the sugarcane that had been growing on a half acre of her land and would now be sowing maize. But she had just learned that the half-acre she had rented last year wouldn't be available again; the owner wanted to use it himself. It was a disappointing discovery, because expanding crop size was the simplest way to increase production and income.

"A half-acre will have to do," Leonida told Peter. She added a caveat: "As long as it rains abundantly when it does rain, it won't affect the harvest, just push it back."

Dreading the prospect of an extended hunger season, Leonida once more looked to Mount Elgon. Still clear. "No," she declared, "no rains today."

AS THE CALENDAR TURNED to March, all eyes turned heavenward. The weather, particularly the chance for rain, became the overriding interest of the day. Every day. It was every farmer's preoccupation. Obsession, really. The prayers were fervent, the speculation rampant.

The Lutacho farmers looked to their field officer, Kennedy Wafula, to provide the forecasts. After all, his name was "rain." As March began, he was sagging under the burden of bearing bad news. "I'm afraid the rains aren't near," he would say as he made his rounds.

Older farmers helped with the prognostications. "First comes the wind from west to east. Then the temperatures rise. It gets hot. At night it is difficult to sleep," Agnes Wekhwela of *Amua* advised. Now in her eighth decade, she had plenty of experience reading the signs. "Then comes the mist, which means the rains are near." Sensing the anxiety of her neighbors, she offered some assurance: "If you plant in early March, you can't fail. You will get a good harvest."

Pressed for a prediction, Agnes said, "The rains should come in the next week." Then she quickly retreated. "I don't know," she said apologetically. "That is God's work!"

The farmers of western Kenya were deeply spiritual. Being solely at the mercy of the elements such as rain and bearing all of the risk of a very risky business bred a profound fatalism. They had no control over so many things of importance to them; their response to all possibilities was, "It will happen if God wills." This led them to be close observers of nature, studying the signs that indicated God's will in motion.

"It will rain when the new moon comes. That will be next week," volunteered farmer Geoffrey Sitata at one of Kennedy's meetings with new One Acre members. "Of course, the new moon stuff is only tradition. It's not scientific."

But that didn't stop him from continuing to rattle off cultural harbingers of rain. "Many birds will be singing in the morning. And tree frogs croaking at night," he said. "The heat will be great. And trees will begin to flower. You will see."

The entire country was straining to see the appearance of these traditional totems that would herald the onset of the long rains. They looked for the agak, ogungo, and kowach birds, and scoured the omukuyu, olwa, and mikuyu trees for signs of flowering; they watched for the vunza marere snake to come down from the trees, for red ants to emerge from the ground, for cattle to run in all directions. With the drought spreading in the eastern and northern parts of Kenya, good rains and a good maize harvest were vital in the breadbasket regions that included the Western zone and the nearby Rift Valley and the old white highlands where the colonial settlers from Europe had once farmed huge swaths of land. Farming directly contributed 26 percent of the country's gross domestic product, and maize alone contributed 12 percent. More than 90 percent of Kenya's farmers grew maize; it was the most important food security crop. And maize depended on rain. Drought in the breadbasket regions would be devastating, a huge calamity for Kenya and for East Africa.

The nation turned its longing eyes to the signs of nature. When, oh when, would the tree frogs croak?

THE NEXT DAY, March 3, dawned clear, hot, and silent—no chorus of song birds or frogs, just the usual cackling of roosters. Michael Hudson, One Acre's director of new programs, was up early to visit the organization's One Village project just west of Bungoma. One Village was an innovation to increase the efficiency of the training and extension work by involving all the residents in a particular location; the denser the membership, the more farmers a single field officer could reach. It was seed and fertilizer distribution day for One Village, and an opportunity to sign up new members. A DJ played upbeat dance songs and shouted over a loudspeaker, "Come, come, pick up your seed and fertilizer. Come and register with One Village."

A few dozen villagers who had gathered under a canopy of trees at the Nang'eni Glory church welcomed the caravan of trucks with singing and dancing. Soon, dozens more farmers flocked to the scene as the music spread. Then, the distribution began. One of the farmers stepped forward with a prayer of thanksgiving for the seeds and fertilizer and a plea for the rains to arrive soon and then stay steady. Then Henry Wanyonyi, a preacher and farmer who had become a One Acre field manager, asked all the farmers to stand and follow his motions and words.

He raised his hands toward heaven and wiggled his fingers. "Rain, rain, rain come!" he shouted. The farmers stretched and wiggled and chanted, "Rain, rain, rain come!"

Then they all reached and wiggled to the left. "Rain, rain, rain come!"

And then to the right. "Rain, rain, rain come!"

And then behind their backs. "Rain, rain, rain come!"

And then to the ground. "Rain, rain, rain come!"

It was a rain dance of sorts, an incantation that was at once hopeful and desperate. They were summoning the rain from the heavens to the earth. With their wiggling fingers, it was as if they were trying to grab the rain and channel it into the soil. It was a ritualistic hedge to the opening prayer, an attempt to cover all bases and appeal to God and then to the Gods of rain—just in case they were different.

"Rain, rain, rain come!" the chant continued. It was the opposite of the children's rhyme: "Rain, rain, go away, come again some other day." The farmers' version would be: "Rain, rain, come and stay, stay for day after day."

When the stretching and wiggling and chanting finished, Michael spoke to the farmers. "Can I have one promise from you today?" he asked. "No planting before the rains." One Acre staff members knew that the longer the rains delayed, the greater the temptation would be to plant the seeds they were about to receive in *anticipation* of rain. That would render them useless; they needed to be planted in moisture.

"No planting before the rains," Michael repeated. The farmers nodded and murmured their promises.

As if on cue, the wind picked up and conjured a dust devil that danced across the parched field near the church. "You see," one of the farmers said with great excitement, "that's a sign from God that the rain is coming."

"When?" the others demanded to know.

The farmer studied the swirling dervish. "Three days," he declared with confidence.

The dust devil raced to the end of the field, veered onto the dirt road, and spun out of sight.

ON MARCH 4, nine days after his "week, week-and-a-half" prediction of rain, Francis Mamati was sweating up a storm. It was sunny and hot, with only a few strands of white interrupting the blue above. Gusts of wind felt like blasts from a furnace. Francis had been working on a tiny plot of land high in the rock formation that embroidered his homestead.

Like a sure-footed goat, he had scrambled up the rocks, using a *jembe* for balance. As the first incline gave way to a small plateau, Francis ducked into a cave for a brief rest and a bit of shade. These rocks were once the preserve of the Bong'omek people who had migrated to the Mount Elgon area from Egypt. They lived in the caves until a severe drought in 1720 led to famine, killing many people and forcing the Bong'omek to move down to the plains around what became Bungoma. Ever since, the rocks retained a sacred aura. Francis often came to his cave to contemplate and pray for rain or sunshine or whatever the crops needed to avoid another famine in the area. It was a solitary place. The floor was moist clay, the low ceiling a flat sheet of rock. Light poured in through the opening, which offered a spectacular view of the valley below and a troubling glimpse of the impact of the lingering dry season. Heat mirages shimmied over the plain. Brown was overtaking green. Water pans had dried up. Francis hoped everyone down there was praying for rain as well.

Exiting the cave, plunging back into the intense light and heat, Francis continued to climb. Rivulets of sweat ran down his face. He reached a terraced sliver of land sandwiched between two rocks. He was determined to plant maize anywhere there was a swath of soil on his property, beyond the acre that would be covered by the One Acre supplies. Before beginning to hack away at the soil with his *jembe*, he dropped to his knees and stretched his arms heavenward and rendered a supplication in Swahili.

"God, have mercy on us. Provide us with the rain, for when it rains enough, the dirt will easily break and make our work easier. And the seeds will germinate and push up through the soil. Hear my prayer, dear God."

Francis returned to his feet and stood silent for a moment. Then he raised his *jembe* above his head and swiftly brought it down, slashing through the air. The blade sliced through the soil and made an abrasive sound as it clashed with stones. Francis bent deeply, picked out the stones, and tossed them aside. Then he slashed again with the *jembe*. And again.

By planting in every nook and cranny of his property, Francis was hoping his family would be able to harvest as many as twenty bags of maize. If he would be so blessed, he would set aside fifteen bags to feed his family and sell the other five for cash to pay school fees, buy clothes and other necessities, and cover medical costs that would surely arise.

As he dug with his *jembe*, Francis pondered how Mother Nature had seemingly become more capricious. It was difficult to time anything according to the weather these days. Francis had caught various soundbites from the contentious climate change debate. What he heard left him thinking that even the experts didn't know which way the wind was blowing in regards to predicting coming weather patterns.

In fact, on that very day, a news report from Nairobi featured fresh research from America that concluded climate change would bring increased drought to the East African region in coming years. That contradicted predictions of increased rainfall in East Africa from another panel studying climate change. Whether from too little rain or too much rain, the International Maize and Wheat Improvement Center (CIMMYT) was predicting that maize yields across Africa would decline drastically over the next decades, perhaps by up to 65 percent for every rise in temperature of one degree Celsius.

More drought? More rain? Francis, toiling on the frontline of the debate, was already seeing both. The rains were less predictable, often lengthening the dry season. And when they came, they were often more intense and more punishing than he remembered. He had no doubt that the climate was changing. He reckoned that Kenyans were cutting down too many trees to use for cooking fires, making charcoal, building structures. Trees, he believed, were a major enticement of rain. He had observed over the years that the rains were more regular in areas with plenty of trees.

Francis had begun nurturing a grove of eucalyptus trees beside his house. If managed properly, he believed, those trees could help his land retain water and also be a source of income as he culled them for sale and then replanted. He also planned to begin planting hardy Napier grass for his few dairy cows. He explained the strategy to his wife, Mary: "If we have grass, when drought comes I won't feel so worried. At least we'll be able to feed the cows and we'll have milk."

Francis was preoccupied by the prospect of drought; he was particularly distressed by the growing hunger in the northern part of
Kenya, where the World Food Program was feeding some two million people. Forecasters were saying it might be East Africa's worst
drought in sixty years. He and Mary would often discuss the news as
it came across the radio. "So much crying, so much hunger," Francis
would say. He worried it would spread to western Kenya, if the rains
truly did delay for much longer. "I can't understand why this northern part of Kenya can't receive rain yearly," he said. "What is the
problem? I think in the U.S.A. there is no drought."

Drought was indeed also spreading across the western United
States, particularly ravaging Texas. But that news never came
through on Francis's radio. It would have likely given him a strange
comfort, knowing that Kenya was not alone in its parched misery.

It was nearing noon and the sun was bearing down from the
clear blue sky, raising the temperature close to 100 degrees. The sen-
sible thing would have been for Francis to put down his *jembe* and
head for shelter. But rather than retreat to the shade of the cave or
his house, Francis insisted on hacking away at the soil, to do all he
could to put himself in the best position when the rains finally came.
The old saying of midday toil in the blazing sun—"only mad dogs
and Englishmen"—needed to be amended to include smallholder
African farmers like Francis.

"You don't give up," he often told Mary and his children. "As a
farmer, you struggle to succeed, not to fail."

RASOA SOUGHT a brief respite in the shade of a line of trees bordering her field, but only to prepare a lunch of boiled bananas for
her boys. She had been turning her soil with her *jembe*, though with
no rain in sight she wondered if it would be better to leave it undisturbed to preserve whatever moisture remained in the ground

rather than have it baked away by the sun. But then she would have to act quickly to ready the land for the planting when the rain did begin. Farming was like gambling, she thought, rolling the dice on the weather. When would it rain?

She prayed and held fast to her faith. Some of the writings on the walls of her house were simply references to certain Bible passages. Ruth 1:16–17, she had scribbled beside the door; on another wall, Jeremiah 29:11. Ruth is about a journey to Bethlehem; Jeremiah spoke about "thoughts of peace, and not of evil, to give you an expected end."

Rasoa's expected end to her journey was a thriving business on the farm. She hoped to rent or buy more land to grow more maize as a cash crop, and to diversify into other products such as tomatoes and onions. She intended to buy more milk cows. And she also dreamed of opening a small kiosk near the well-trod path beside her homestead. There she would sell daily necessities: soap, sugar, kerosene, telephone calling cards, and her homegrown vegetables. Crops, cows, and a kiosk—three income streams that would pay for her boys' education and quality-of-life improvements.

To realize this vision, Rasoa planned to save a little bit every week. But that was becoming more difficult every day with the rapidly rising price of maize, which turned her focus from her future plans to daily subsistence. She sat on a bench beside her field, peeling bananas from her own trees. She cut them into small pieces, which fell from her hands into a pot of water. When the bananas filled the pot, she carried it to her cooking hut and set it on three stones nestled into the fire pit. Smoke saturated the hut; the only light came through a tiny window. The temperature rose with the flames. Rasoa seemed unaffected; she lingered in the smoke, crouching by the fire, stirring the bananas, adding salt, until it all began to boil and turn to a mash.

Rasoa removed the pot from the fire, letting the mash cool before the boys came home from school for lunch. She doused the embers and stepped outside, squinting in the bright sun. There was little relief, though; it was like she had walked from a blast furnace into a sauna. Rasoa, sweat beads forming on her forehead and neck, strolled to the far end of her *shamba* to gather some Napier grass and weeds for her new calf. Her 401(Cow) investment needed feeding like her boys. As she intended, the cow's name, One Acre, had her thinking back to when she sold her maize. It was barely two months, and the maize price had escalated to fifty-five shillings per *goro-goro* from thirty shillings. When she sold, she didn't think the price would go that high, and certainly not by the first days of March.

Had she made the right decision, to sell the maize and buy the calf? The grass was dying, there was less for One Acre to eat. The higher maize price was squeezing her husband's salary from his job as the local M-Pesa agent. Accordingly, Rasoa was cutting back on maize consumption and relying more on her bananas and cassava. But her growing boys needed regular helpings of *ugali*. How high would the price of maize rise, she worried, if the rains didn't arrive soon? Surely the market would know that the harvest would be delayed if the planting was late.

Rasoa patted One Acre on the head and looked heavenward. Not a cloud in sight. She shrugged. "So we wait," she said to the calf. Her smile was there as usual, but its radiance had dimmed a watt or two.

THAT NIGHT, a small shower sprinkled over Bungoma. Was it the start? The next day, March 5, thunder rumbled through a stifling heat. At times, the growling rolled on for several minutes. At 4 p.m., the sky over Bungoma darkened from all sides and with an electric clap the heavens opened and poured down a heavy dose of rain. It lasted for twenty minutes, and then moved on. The One Acre staff wondered, was that the dramatic start of the *wafula*?

As darkness descended at the One Acre headquarters, a chorus of tree frogs began singing as fervently as a Gospel choir. The frogs were invisible in the dark, and they wanted to keep it that way. Their singing softened as footsteps neared and then grew louder again as the intruders moved away. Above, the new moon appeared as a thin reddish crescent. The signs of nature, the harbingers of rain, were coming together.

A brilliant galaxy of stars surrounded the moon. This was one of the most wondrous sights of rural Africa. In the deep, dark nights, with little ambient light and minimal pollution, the stars looked so much brighter and more abundant than perhaps anywhere else on earth. But when waiting for the rains, the appearance of the sparkling constellations was cause for consternation and cursing. They signaled that the clouds of the afternoon had thinned and moved off, indicating that rain likely wouldn't return for many more hours, perhaps until the clouds began building again the next afternoon. The day's heavy but fleeting burst of rain wasn't enough to begin the countdown to planting.

The next morning, March 6, a few clouds gathered early. Chirping birds seemed to be particularly active. One Acre's Kenya operations manager, Nick Handler, circulated the regional weather forecast by a government agency: rain on Sunday and Monday, three or four millimeters each day, then no rain for Tuesday and Wednesday. "Take it all with a grain of salt," Nick advised. Even if the forecast came true, it wouldn't be enough to start planting. When the rains come, they need to be prolonged, and constant, virtually all-day rains, every day. Good soakings. Sprinkles of three or four millimeters wouldn't do.

By early afternoon, a blanket of gray clouds covered the sky, and thunder registered from all directions. A few showers fell in Bungoma. Not much. Temperatures dropped, breaking the heat. Overnight, the rain picked up intensity, pounding Bungoma, making a racket on the metal roofs at 3 a.m. The thunder hovered, groaning on uninterrupted for four or five minutes at a stretch.

It was three days since the appearance of the dust devil.

DAWN ON MARCH 7, however, introduced yet another day of clear, fresh skies. As the sun burned off the morning haze, a gorgeous blue stretched across the land. It was a beauty and color that existed only in Africa's palette. The farmers, however, would have preferred an ugly gray from London or Moscow or Seattle, and the rain to go with it.

At the Encouragement Center, a community hall in the town of Webuye, at the foot of the Lugulu Hills, several dozen One Acre field officers gathered for their weekly meeting. They all reported that there had been very little weekend rain, if any, on the *shambas*. It seemed the heavier rain had concentrated on the city of Bungoma. The few scattered sprinkles in the rural areas were only a tease, raising hopes but certainly not enough to start the countdown to planting. Even in the Encouragement Center, encouraging news was hard to come by.

Patrick Keya, One Acre's district manager, began the meeting with a jolt of enthusiasm. He had been working with smallholder farmers for many years. Before joining One Acre, he had been an extension officer for Farm Input Promotions Africa, an NGO that introduced farmers to better seeds and agricultural practices and had helped Andrew Youn develop One Acre's extension methods.

"We don't want to waste the moisture *when* it comes," Patrick said. His pointed use of "when", not "if," was meant to chase away any doubt in the room that the rains would eventually arrive. "So the fields must be prepared properly. Let's make sure that tomorrow is a big day in the field, to make sure that all the farmers are prepared for planting."

Then he started another incantation, summoning the rain.

"Rain, rain, rain, rain," he said, waving his arms above his head.

"Rain, rain, rain, rain," came the response from the waving field officers.

"The rains are coming this week, and then the planting next week," Patrick boldly told them. "That is my faith."

It was a rare and impressive gathering, dozens of Africans coming together to improve agricultural production. And they came to the Encouragement Center not just to talk abstractly about boosting yields and incomes but also to strategize with enthusiasm and great conviction.

"Be sure to review planting techniques with your farmers, be ready to answer all questions," Patrick exhorted. He reminded the field officers that the rains could be deceptive. Beware of false starts, he warned. One downpour could be followed by several days of baking sun. A farmer who would plant after that one teaser downpour would likely see the seeds wither and go to waste. Patience was always a virtue in Africa, and never more so than in the weeks and days before the planting commenced.

"Wait," Patrick urged, repeating the fundamental message; wait for at least three consecutive days of rain, so the soil will be well saturated. The army of farmers needed to hold their fire.

"Planting should start when?" Patrick asked the gathering.

"After three days of good rains," the gathering replied.

Before the field officers went out to spread the word, there was a final prayer and another calling of the rains.

"Rains come, rains come," went the chant. Arms waved, and eyes lifted upward. "Rains come."

With the sun beating down outside, it was all they could do.

AT LEONIDA'S *shamba*, up the hill from the Encouragement Center, other worries shifted her focus from the skies. Out of the blue, Gideon had been sent home from school. The principal had banished him until he could return with more money. His appearance at the *shamba*, close to tears, shocked his parents.

The ten bags of maize used for the tuition payment at the beginning of year had bought only two months of education. Leonida didn't have any other assets that could raise a large sum of money. So she sold a goat—her last one—for one thousand shillings, and early the next morning at five, Gideon set off back to Milo High with his father, the two of them balancing on the family's rickety bicycle. They also carried that morning's milk. Gideon cycled the thirty kilometers to the school, and Peter, still weakened with malaria, pedaled the way back, walking the uphill sections.

Leonida was outside her house, barefoot and chopping wood for the kitchen fire, when Peter returned. He said Gideon was happy to be back in school but nervous that he wouldn't be staying for long. Leonida shared the worry. "Soon he'll be sent back home for more money," Leonida fretted. "We don't have much left to sell."

She was constantly juggling assets, making decisions on what to buy, how long to hold it, when to sell. After selling the goat and sending money to school, there was nothing left under her tablecloth for emergencies. "Not a single shilling," Leonida told Peter. "We don't even have soap to wash with."

Leonida sat at her living room table, her head in her hands. "With the school fees, life has become so hard," she said to Peter. And those fees would only be going higher as her two middle daughters, Jackline and Sarah, entered high school in the coming years. Her goal was that they go to boarding schools as well, for the greater attention and discipline. She sighed heavily. "It is only the necessity to pay school fees that keeps us hungry."

Dorcas and her orphan cousins came home for lunch and quietly sat on chairs in the living room. A few minutes later, Sarah and Jackline returned as well. The older two girls started the year as boarders at Lutacho Primary, about two kilometers away, but when Leonida couldn't afford the fees, they become day students, which meant they came home for lunch. On this day when they entered the house, the kids found no food.

"This lunch we are going without," their mother told them. Sarah and Jackline wandered outside. The boys stayed sitting. Dorcas walked to the table and rested her head on her mother's shoulder.

"She is always hungry," Leonida said. The night before had been particularly hard.

"Mother, I want more food," Dorcas cried after finishing her small portion of *ugali.*

"We have no more," her mother said.

The thought of her daughter's tears brought Leonida back to thinking about the rains. "I'm asking God to give us rain," she said. "If we can plant, the price of maize won't go up so high."

Already the price had risen so much that buying another bag of maize was no longer possible. The previous purchase cost her four chickens. The next would likely be six or seven. Peter had set up a perimeter defense of straw baskets around the remaining bag of maize on the corner chair to keep the chickens from pecking away at it. One persistent hen had toppled the biggest basket and was trapped underneath. Peter lifted the basket to free the chicken, and as he stooped to check the other baskets he found a freshly laid egg. "That's seven shillings," he said, holding the egg aloft. That was the going market price.

He put it aside in a dresser drawer with other eggs. Despite their struggle for food, Leonida and Peter had no thought of frying, scrambling, or poaching the eggs. Better they be returned to the chickens at brooding time for hatching; a couple of months later the chicks would be ready to sell. The money would be added to the household emergency stash for medicine or school fees. As with the eggs, there would be no thought of eating the chickens. They were far too valuable to be sacrificed for the pleasure of a single meal.

With the girls home for lunch—or no lunch, as it turned out—Leonida walked with them to Malaria stream to fetch water, a chore they sometimes repeated as many as six or seven times a day. They were lucky; it was only several minutes away. Some farmers trekked half an hour or more to this water source. The water came from an underground spring. A few years ago, the hospital in the town of Webuye built a system of three small pipes to establish a steady flow. Before the pipes, the water rose to the surface and formed a swampy breeding ground for mosquitoes. The malaria patients had crowded the hospital, stretching its resources. The engineering reduced the incidence of malaria marginally; the water, though flowing better at the source, still stagnated a bit further downstream and still produced plenty of mosquitoes. And although Leonida's family and most of the neighbors slept under bed nets to protect from mosquito bites overnight, they were exposed while milking the cows and biking to market and walking to school and cooking and doing homework in the pre-dawn and evening hours.

On the walk back to her *shamba*, balancing a bucket of water on her head, Leonida faced Mount Elgon. Light clouds were gathering. Neighbors making their way to the river wondered if the clouds might bring rain.

"Not today," Leonida said.

WHILE THE RAINS indeed stayed away from Lutacho that night, they paid a visit to the Kabuchai area on the other side of the Lugulu Hills.

It was a short rain but with enough force to come streaming through Zipporah's thatched roof, into the bedroom. There was one lone bed with no mattress, just a thick green-and-red-striped blanket tucked into the wood frame. A shabby mosquito net hung limply to the side. The rain fell near the foot of the bed, leaving a puddle on the dirt-and-dung floor. Zipporah and her husband, Sanet, and little David scrunched closer together to avoid the drops. The three older children slept on the unpadded wooden furniture in the living room.

For the Biketi family, the rains were both joyous and vexing. In the fields, they saturated the thirsty soil. But on the homestead, they poured through the roof. Last year, the rains washed away their mud outhouse.

With the sun bearing down from a blue sky on the morning of March 8, the rain of the previous evening appeared to be just a tease. It wasn't enough, Zipporah said, to begin the countdown to planting. While Sanet kept an eye on the sky, Zipporah was keeping a lookout for butterflies. Since the time she was a girl, she had been told that the rains would come when butterflies began fluttering as a group, switching fast from one direction to another. She hadn't spotted any such group maneuvers yet. But she claimed not to be worried, believing that the rainy season would begin within days. She often told her children, "When God created man, He put him on the earth to survive." So the rains won't fail, she said, not in western Kenya.

What was worrying her, though, was the dwindling food supplies in the house. She was regretting not joining One Acre last year, when she could see how well Pastor Isaiah was doing on the neighboring *shamba,* the one she thought was cursed. Since November, and her father's funeral, they had been going day-to-day with food. She felt she had no control over the nutrition of her children.

She would like to prepare four kilograms of ground maize every day for her family. Just a month earlier, that would have cost sixty shillings. Now it was up to 130 shillings. That was forcing her, like Leonida and Rasoa, to become even stingier in rationing meals and portions.

The three older children arrived home from the local public school shortly after noon and were told by their mother there wouldn't be any lunch beyond a cup of tea. That was what they had for breakfast. The children turned away silently, without complaint, and sat outside in the shade of the house, sipping their tea, until it was time to walk back to school. The littlest, David, stayed in the house, clinging to his mother. He wore yellow overalls that hid his distended stomach. He was still coughing badly. Zipporah felt his forehead and detected a fever.

"He's sick," she told Sanet. "Today he has refused to eat. He may have malaria."

Treatment for a child cost about two hundred shillings at the medical clinic, which was a fifteen-minute walk through the fields. That would be enough money for two nights of *ugali* for the whole family. Would that help David more, his mother wondered? Would eating a good meal be more beneficial than malaria tablets?

She decided on the treatment, but Sanet doubted if they had the money. "Every shilling we have goes to food," he said.

Sanet had already seen his business of livestock trading come to a halt. "I need a stake to get going," he told Zipporah. Cash was important; for instance, he might start the day buying goats at one market, trade the goats for a cow on another market, and then, at a third market, sell the cow for more than he had originally paid for the goats. At least that's how it was supposed to work. "Sometimes I lose money," he said. Zipporah rolled her eyes. "It's a risk," she sighed. Like Rasoa, she felt she was living the life of a gambler.

Their main income, besides Sanet striking it lucky on the livestock market, was the milk from their two dairy cows. And that was drying up in the heat. With little to eat, the cows produced just two liters of milk a day, less than one-third of their rainy season production. The Biketis, with a leaky thatched roof and struggling to nourish their children, were much like the poorer of the two families that first got Andrew Youn thinking about the inequality and hardships of African farming.

Zipporah couldn't sit still in the house during an afternoon with no food. When the children returned to school, she followed the cows to the rocks that rose up behind the *shamba*. The rainwater from the night before formed little puddles in the pans and crevices. Zipporah came to collect some water for cooking and washing clothes, and the cows came to drink.

The view of Mount Elgon from the rocks was spectacular, particularly in the late afternoon sun. Stretching out beyond the house, beyond the one-acre rectangular field waiting for the rain and the seeds, was a vast plain of smallholder *shambas* separated by lines of trees and bushes. It was as if God had spread a quilt with brown and green patches over the earth. In the distance, the land rose in an emerald swell, washing up the slope of Mount Elgon. It was lush and verdant, even in the dry season; now, as the days got hotter, evaporation from the forests and rivers below created a mist that hovered over the peak, producing an array of shape-shifting shadows. This spot on the rocks, with the breathtaking view, was a spiritual sanctuary for Zipporah and Sanet. They often came here to think, and to pray. It was like Francis's cave, except this was an altar open to the sky.

On display were both the majesty and misery of Africa. It was difficult to reconcile the poverty and humility of the thatched homestead with the richness and grandeur of the scenery. Zipporah and Sanet were among the poorest on earth, but their perch on these rocks, and the view from the crooked windows carved out of the mud walls of their house, would be the envy of the richest. Few people could look upon this scene and not ponder, at least fleetingly, building a house here and having this expanse as their front yard for their remaining years on earth—the few being those with little sense of awe and wonder.

Sanet joined his wife on the rocks. A butterfly, yellow, green, and black, flittered past. Zipporah spotted it. It was flying solo. She was looking for a group.

Sanet missed the butterfly. He was studying the gathering clouds and was gaining optimism. Puffs of white earlier in the afternoon, the clouds were growing darker.

"I think it will rain tonight," Sanet confidently proclaimed.

It didn't.

Nor did it rain for the next three days.

WHILE THE FARMERS waited for the rain, Kennedy continued making the rounds in Lutacho, hosting practice planting meetings. As he navigated his bike over the rutted dirt roads, he carried a planting string and small bags of seed and fertilizer, as well as instruction leaflets, which advised, "Fertilizer and seed mixed together will burn the seed. Plant slowly and carefully and you will harvest many bags of maize." A series of pictures then showed that the few granules of fertilizer portioned out by a tiny, red plastic scoop and placed at the bottom of the hole must be covered by a layer of dirt before the maize seed is dropped in.

The *Amua* farmers gathered for a practice planting on the morning of March 11. Blue skies, a clear day. The mist had lifted from Mount Elgon. The farmers wondered, "What did that mean?"

"The rain isn't near," Leonida said. "It means we are still waiting." Every dawn was like Groundhog Day. Look outside. Check the weather. See the blue, clear skies. Sigh. Worry. Pray. The constant vigilance heightened the anxiety.

In the cool early morning hours, Leonida had been out in her field, attacking clumps of hardened dirt with her *jembe*. Then she tidied up a bit to join her neighbors for the practice session in a field across from the Kenya Assemblies of God church. They unfurled the planting string and deployed the sticks that measured the distance between rows. They practiced the teamwork: two farmers wielding their *jembes* to dig holes, one following with the tiny scoop of fertilizer, one pushing some dirt on the fertilizer, one dropping a seed in each hole, one filling in the holes. After thirty minutes of meticulous practice, they declared their readiness to plant for real. They were confident that by working together they could plant one acre a day. Their expectations for a good harvest were high.

Agnes Wekhwela said she would be happy with twenty bags on one acre. Esther Burudi was counting on twelve to thirteen bags on a half-acre. Beatrice Arinyula, wearing a black knit cap with white stitching on the front that spelled out "Obama," was aiming for fifteen bags on a half-acre. Alan Kuvati figured he could get eighteen bags on three-quarters of an acre. Elizabeth Namasaka said twelve bags on half an acre would be good for her, as did Alice Barasa and Margaret Lumunyasi. Leonida proclaimed her hope for twelve bags on a half-acre, twenty-four bags on one acre if she was able to rent another plot of land at the last minute.

Then came the obligatory prayer for rain. The farmers gathered in a circle and lifted their voices and hopes heavenward. Someone asked the question on everybody's mind: What if it doesn't rain? What if the drought ravaging other parts of the country extended westward?

"It must rain," Agnes declared, unwavering in her faith. "God knows who we are. God knows where we live."

BUT DID OTHERS in the earthly realm know who they were, where they lived? A large group in Washington, DC, apparently didn't—and didn't seem to want to. Republicans in the House of Representatives were charging hard to slash the budget, particularly foreign aid, waving a party report that called for a drastic defunding of the U.S. Agency for International Development. The plan was unveiled by the Republican Study Committee, a convening of 165 self-identified conservative House members, as part of a broad proposal to cut $2.5 trillion in federal spending over ten years. USAID had established a Bureau of Food Security to implement President Obama's Feed the Future initiative, which would greatly benefit smallholder farmers such as Agnes and Leonida and their *Amua* and One Acre colleagues. Kenya was one of Feed the Future's focus countries. Under the Republican plan, that initiative and those ambitions would likely be killed.

The plan to wipe out USAID funding wasn't given much chance of passing, but it was setting the tone of budget cutting—and revealing a deep, ideological divide. Foreign aid was a top target, even though it amounted to less than 1 percent of federal spending. The Republicans, especially the newcomers to Congress, argued that they had come to Washington to do the people's will, which was to severely cut back on deficit spending. But polls of the American people consistently showed that they would support spending as much as 10 percent of the budget on foreign aid. This would mean, one prominent Democrat pointed out, that if the people's will was indeed to be followed, foreign aid should actually increase by tenfold.

Battle lines were hardening in the fight over the fiscal year 2011 budget bill. The resolution passed in the House cut food aid programs by up to 50 percent and slashed about 30 percent from agricultural development programs that aimed to prevent future food crises so people wouldn't need food aid to begin with. Republicans argued that if there wasn't money for programs that benefit Americans, there shouldn't be money for people in foreign countries, either. Democrats countered that foreign aid was a crucial deployment of America's "soft power," and top-ranking voices in the Pentagon, including Defense Secretary Robert Gates and top military commander General David Petraeus, strongly supported development spending and USAID funding. They insisted that bread, and particularly bread made from crops grown by smallholder farmers in the developing world, was far better than bullets.

Their global security argument in the budget turmoil was buttressed by the ongoing Mideast turmoil. People were in the streets shouting down oppressive governments; food shortages and soaring prices were near the top of their grievances. In North Africa, governments in Tunisia and Egypt were toppled. President Obama, cautioning against further unrest, said countries should stop trying to deny those who had a "hunger for freedom."

South of the Sahara, the farmers of western Kenya were hoping the president would reorder those words and, in defending Feed the Future and agricultural development aid from budget cuts, embrace all those seeking "freedom from hunger." On his *shamba*, up in the cave, Francis Mamati continued to pray for rain, adding a few special words for President Obama, asking that he keep his focus on the farms of Kenya and Africa so that there would be no place where people were dying of hunger.

ON SUNDAY MORNING, March 13, puddles—glorious puddles!—dotted the deeply rutted roads of Lutacho. There had been rain overnight, a downpour actually, albeit brief. As Leonida walked down the dirt path past her house to the market area, she stepped carefully to keep the mud off her Sunday best outfit—a crisp white dress with a pink circle pattern. Dorcas was also very proper looking in her church clothes—a pink dress embroidered with yellow and red flowers with green stems. Still, they wouldn't have complained over a splattering of mud; better that than the coat of dust they wore throughout the dry season. Leonida hoped to see more rain, a longer downpour, that evening.

She and Dorcas were not on their way to church but to visit Gideon at the Milo Friends Boys High School in Webuye. The second Sunday of every month was parents' visitation day. It was a highlight for Leonida, a chance to visit with Gideon, and to check on her investment. Their first stop was the nearby Lukusi market, a cluster of tiny ramshackle shops. Leonida carried a sack filled with goodies for Gideon. She wanted to add a bottle of orange juice and cookies.

Leonida was well acquainted with the journey to the high school. She rarely missed the monthly visits, and there were other times when she consulted with the principal over tuition fees. In the town of Lugulu, the dirt road met up with a paved highway that carried travelers straight down a hill. At the bottom, the road ended in a T-junction with the main national highway that ran from Mombasa on the Indian Ocean coast clear across the country to the Uganda border. A left turn led to the largest town in the area, Webuye, and then after a kilometer a sign on the right pointed to Milo Friends Boys High School. Ten kilometers down a bouncy dirt road a low concrete wall announced the entrance to the school. The school's ambitions and goals were written in large lettering near the front gate.

VISION: Quality Education for the Future.

MISSION: Commitment to Provide Education While Utilizing the Latest Technology and Knowledge in Child Development for Today and Tomorrow.

MOTTO: Education is the Key to Success.

That was Leonida's motto, too. It's why she favored this school for Gideon.

Leonida greeted the security guard at the gate and walked into the school's tidy courtyard. Other than nine cows grazing on the lawn between the concrete barrack-like buildings that housed the classrooms, the place was empty. Leonida and Dorcas wandered the grounds, peering into classroom windows, looking for some sign of life. Suddenly, the silence was broken by some indecipherable exhortations rolling in from the distance. It sounded like the Sunday morning preaching from one of the many country churches. The visitors followed the feverish sounds to the back of the school and discovered they were coming from the assembly hall. Now the exhortations were clearer, something about students and parents and teachers. They were high-pitched exclamations, a woman's voice perhaps. Entering the hall, though, Leonida saw a man holding a microphone pacing the stage. Francis Wanyungu, motivational speaker extraordinaire, was hitting his stride.

"Do you want to succeed?" he asked the students, his voice trembling at a higher octave. The students, sitting in neat rows of wooden chairs, shouted, "Yes!" They were dressed in white, gray, and green uniforms, boys wearing slacks and a sweater and a tie, and the girls (there were a handful of girls, despite the name of the school) wearing a blouse and skirt.

One of the boys in the back saw Leonida and Dorcas enter and insisted they sit in the front. He ushered them to the first row, right beneath the stage, in direct range of the fulminations. Wanyungu didn't skip a beat as they settled onto their chairs.

"Success belongs to the student. Success belongs to no one else," he shouted. "What should the student do? One, believe in yourself as the owner of success. Believe that success is yours. Be confident in yourself. Two, invest your energy, invest your passion, and invest your effort into your success. Don't be lazy, work with all your energy. Three, persevere and endure."

Wanyungu told a story of a mother who couldn't afford to visit her child at school. "Now," he said, "the student of that parent will say, 'I will work hard because I don't want to fail *my* children. I will work hard because I don't want to be the parent who can't afford to visit.' Was it a lack of desire of that mother? No, she didn't have the ability."

A boy sitting behind an electronic keyboard at the edge of the stage pounded a few dramatic notes to punctuate the story. He was like the piano player sitting beside the screen of the old silent movies, heightening the dramatic tension with his music.

Leonida was clapping and cheering along with the students. She liked this message. Succeed, work hard, and make something of yourself.

"Another day we will talk about breaking the poverty cycle by hard work, by patience, by perseverance," Wanyungu promised. Then he immediately proceeded to talk about it. "My father told me I used to suffer from fear of high places. I had the biggest problem crossing bridges. My father told me, 'If you want to cross the bridge, don't look into the water. Look ahead to where you are going.'" Wanyungu's lesson for the students: "You don't focus on the afflictions you have, on your poverty; you focus on where you are going."

Where Wanyungu was going now was clear. Don't let the poverty of your families slow you down. Overcome. Wanyungu, himself the son of poor smallholder farmers, reached back to his own life, and to passages and parables from the Bible.

"Somebody sent you to Milo. Like Jesus, who said, 'I do the will of He who sent me.' Who sent you? Your parents! Are you performing the will of those who sent you?"

A suspenseful chord exploded from the keyboard.

"When I was in school," Wanyungu said, "I thought of my mother, and I read. I thought of my brothers and sisters, and I read." Sweat poured down his face. "My mother came to visit me in high school. She came in a green dress, the same dress she wore when she cut sugarcane. The guard at the school thought she was coming to beg for food. 'That is my mother,' I said. 'My *mother.*'"

The keyboard player leapt from his chair and leaned into a higher octave.

One night, Wanyungu recalled, there was a disco at his school. But rather than dance, he said, "I went behind a building and hid, and I read. How can I dance when my mother and brothers and sisters are at home hungry? My mother is the one who sent me to school."

Leonida was spellbound. She marveled at Wanyungu's words. It was as if they were meant specifically for Gideon and her.

Now Wanyungu shifted targets, from praising mothers to warning about girls. Boys, he said, beware of girls. Don't let your success be derailed by sex. Stay focused on your goal of education. The students squirmed in their seats, each word thundering from the stage ratching up the discomfort.

"Do not spend your strength on women," Wanyungu shouted into his microphone. The keyboard player pounded a note of alarm.

Wanyungu feverishly rifled through the Bible, quoting from the Book of Proverbs, as if he had written the words himself. "Don't spend all your time on women. They have destroyed kings. Look what happened to Samson. Sex is sin. It destroys your energy; it sucks your potential. How will you have a vision when you have a woman around you? The girl says to the boy, 'I love you.' And then she goes back to reading. But the boy, it takes the boy one week to get back to the books!"

"You go to college, and then you come back home and say to the girl, 'You remember our love for each other in high school? I have come back to marry you now.' We aren't saying women are bad and you should never get close to them. We are talking about measured time."

Wanyungu had hit top gear. His exhortations had sucked the air out of the building. The heat intensified. He wiped the heavy sweat from his brow. He squeezed the microphone. He was at one with the keyboard player, producing a rhythm of soaring rhetoric and electronic foreboding.

"Bad company kills success. Proverbs 13:20. Avoid idleness. Idleness brings poverty. Diligent hearts will succeed. Proverbs 13:4. A hard worker will get what he desires. Walk with your hands ready to work. Don't walk with your hands in empty pockets. Rest, slumber, sleep, they lead to poverty."

Sweat dripped through his black suit.

"You want to succeed?" he asked the students.

"Yes," they shouted.

"Avoid too much sleep, avoid too much idleness, avoid too much rest. You want to succeed? Avoid idleness. Work hard. Save time."

Wanyungu called for a prayer, but it sounded like the grand summation to his sermon. "I should achieve what my mother and father sent me to do," he pleaded on behalf of the students. "Read, study, work hard, get good grades. Make up your mind, believe that you can and you will. If you come from a hard background, if you don't have anything, let your background challenge you to work hard. When you think of poverty at home, work hard. It is through your books that you will deliver your parents and brothers and sisters. Love your studies, love your mother, build your future. Stick to your mission that you were sent to this school by your parents to achieve."

"Amen," he said.

"Amen," the students echoed.

"Amen," Leonida whispered.

Whew, it was over. Wanyungu was a puddle of sweat. The keyboardist feverishly played a spiritual. Leonida rose with the students in a standing ovation. This is why she had sent Gideon to this school. This is why he will succeed. He was on a mission from home, from his mother.

Leonida left the hall, blinking in the bright sun, soaking up the fresh air. She greeted the principal of Milo, Albert Mutambo, and he invited her into his little cubbyhole of an office. His desk was crammed between files and storage boxes and trophies for academic performances and sporting victories in soccer, field hockey, and rugby. The shelves and cabinets were stuffed with documents accumulated over the years since the Quakers, who were prominent educators in Kenya's western province, established the school in 1972.

Outside the office window, in the central courtyard, was a large concrete slab that had been overtaken by grass and weeds and the grazing cows. It looked like an abandoned basketball court, but Mutambo explained that it was supposed to be a block of administration offices, the central piece of a donor project from about fifteen years ago that also included the construction of a dining hall, some classrooms, and a science laboratory. A few of the buildings were completed, but not the office block, before the funds disappeared. "The money was misappropriated," the principal said. That was before his time, he hurried to add.

His cramped office symbolized the tight squeeze on education in Kenya. Milo High was bursting at the seams with 510 students: 483 boys and 27 girls. All the girls were in their final year. Next year it would be an all-boys school, following the boys-and-girls-don't-make-for-success-in-high-school precept of Wanyungu. They were taught by 28 teachers, 17 paid for by the national government, 11 employed directly by the school. It was the private teachers, supported by the tuition fees that gave the school a higher standing. Milo was ranked third in the Bungoma East district, the principal boasted, a lofty level for a rural school educating the children of smallholder farmers.

"Most of the students come from very poor families," Mutambo told Leonida. "One of our biggest problems is the fee payment. Many students come from sugarcane growers. The companies provide the seeds and fertilizer, and then when the harvest comes they take the cane away and leave little money, saying the harvest is enough to pay off the debt. The company doesn't weigh the harvest on the farm but at the factory. In transit, some of the cane falls off the truck. If the truck has a breakdown, everyone comes and takes from the truck. So the farmers always lose at the weighing. The companies are benefiting more from the farmers than the farmers are benefiting from them. They don't empower families.

"Many of the students didn't do well in primary school, on the national exam. Average marks, most got C grades. Gideon had Bs. We help them succeed. One student came in with C-minus grades, and he left with straight As."

"Thank you," Leonida said, nodding her head.

"Yes, we change them," Mutambo said. "We turn them into top students. You give them the time, and some of the students have a lot of success."

Leonida continued nodding. "Very good," she agreed.

Now, the principal said, about the money.

"This is a boarding school. The school must make meals, provide services. So when the families don't pay, services fail. We can't put up proper infrastructure. We don't have a proper administration building." He cast a disapproving glance around his office.

"We're supposed to have e-learning, be an e-learning school," he said, chuckling sarcastically. A foreign company had donated about twenty computers a few years ago. Now, they sat on tables in a classroom full of dust. Mosquitoes hovered in the dark corners, waiting for warm-blooded victims to enter. Most of the computers looked like they hadn't functioned for quite a while. Even if they had, the technology would be trumped by a wobbly electrical supply that suffered frequent blackouts. The school didn't have a backup generator.

"We don't have proper blackboards," the principal continued with his litany of woes. "We don't have a single projector. We can't teach from PowerPoints. We do it the old-fashioned way. Standing and talking."

He acknowledged that the tuition with boarding—twenty-three thousand shillings a year—was a steep price for poor parents. "For many of them, it is either buy food or pay school fees," he said. "According to the rules of survival, you do the food first."

Leonida, who did the school fees first, listened silently.

The principal continued his long wind-up to her essential question: Why must you keep sending Gideon home for more money? "Our tuition is one of the lowest for any boarding school in the area, but still it is very expensive," Mutambo explained. "For families with income less than ten dollars a month, people living on very small land. . . . " He dropped the thought. "It is the problem in rural Kenya: poverty."

Leonida wondered if there could be any flexibility on the timing of the tuition payments for smallholder farmers? Why must they be due when the price for maize is at its lowest?

"We have the academic calendar," the principal began. "It begins in January and ends in November. When the academic calendar begins in January, that's when people should pay. I know that is when the maize price is low." He shrugged.

"Right now, the government is about to open up the cereals board for purchase of maize," Mutambo continued. The stories in the newspapers on his desk mentioned that the price would be set above two thousand shillings per bag, nearly two times more than what Leonida had received when she sold her maize in January to make the tuition payment. The principal knew the price move was coming far too late for Leonida and most other parents of students in the school. "I wish," he said, "the government could send money to the cereals board in December so the farmers could sell for a better price and then pay school fees. There are a lot of structural problems that don't allow the farmers to come out of the vicious circle of poverty."

Leonida believed the principal was a man truly struggling with a dilemma: an educator who wanted to keep the kids in school, but an administrator who had no money to do so.

"Almost half of the students will drop out during the year. If we are very strict," Mutambo told her. "So many owe money." He shuffled through a folder of papers and then ticked off the cumulative debt of the classes. The Form 4 students, the seniors, owed 2.3 million shillings, collectively. Form 3 owed 2.1 million shillings. Form 2 owed 1.6 million shillings. Form 1 owed half-a-million shillings.

"And they just started!" the principal howled about the freshman class. Less than three months into the school year, and the first-year students, as a group, were already woefully in debt.

"If we were strict—those who don't pay go home—then they would all go home," he said. "We try to work with the parents. We invite the parents to talk and explain why they need to pay.

"Those who graduated last year, if they still owe, we held on to their certificates. That is illegal under Kenya law," he said, smiling conspiratorially. "But what can we do?" Once a diploma was issued, he said, he would have no chance of claiming any of the student's debt.

The principal turned to Gideon's situation. A pained expression seized his face. He said he appreciated Leonida's sacrifices to scrape together the tuition money, and he understood that sending Gideon home would be a big loss for his family and for the school.

"Gideon is in the top ten in his class. He's a house prefect. Gideon just needs encouragement here and there in his studies, and he will be at the top," Mutambo said. "He has an appealing character. When fees are due, he comes to me and says, 'We are organizing.'"

Leonida nodded some more. "We are trying," she said softly.

"Gideon is a student leader," the principal continued. "This year, he will represent the school at the student leadership forum at the provincial level. If he does well, he will represent the school at the national level, in Nairobi."

Mutambo said he was trying to keep Gideon in school. The school needed him. The fellow students needed his leadership. He was the one who raised the flag every morning. But the school also needed the fees.

"I understand," Leonida said. The mother and the principal shook hands and smiled. As she left the office, shuffling sideways to escape the clutter, Leonida hoped the principal understood her needs, as well.

Gideon and Dorcas had been waiting outside in the shade of a large tree. With their mother, they walked to a classroom that served as the chemistry and biology lab. It was a lab in name only. There were no lab materials; no chemicals, no test tubes, no Bunsen burners. No periodic table, no plastic skeletons, nothing to experiment on. There were just sinks. And plain, wooden benches and simple, wooden stools. It was little wonder then that science wasn't included in Gideon's favorite subjects. He preferred history, English, and Christian religious education.

A shy, soft-spoken, respectful boy, with an easy gap-toothed grin, Gideon made clear that he needed the school as much as Principal Mutambo said the school needed him. He wanted to advance to university and study to become a lawyer so he could spread knowledge of the rule of law—and thus, fair treatment under the law—to the far reaches of the country. His mother didn't have the opportunity to pursue her dream of law enforcement as a police lady, so he would as a lawyer.

Gideon figured there must be a shortage of lawyers in Kenya, based on a general disregard of laws throughout society. But he also knew a law degree required many more years of schooling, which meant many more years of tuition fees. So he had a backup plan: agriculture engineer. In that profession he could aid the discovery of better ways to grow crops and raise animals; he could help farmers reduce poverty through agriculture.

But he didn't want to be a farmer himself. Too much work, he figured. He had watched his mother struggle as a farmer for many years. It was hard.

He told his mother he was grateful for her commitment to send him to school. He knew that one day it would be his responsibility to help his sisters, Jackline, Sarah, and Dorcas, make it through high school.

Gideon was a sturdy young man, wiry yet athletic. But every time he was sent home for more fees, he felt a little more stooped from the weight of expectation. It was a double burden: missing work in the classroom and failing his family. That is why even during school breaks he preferred to remain in his school dormitory. Home was a reminder of his family's heavy sacrifice.

School was where he felt most comfortable. From the moment he arrived, he began performing much better than in primary school. In the lower grades, the teachers mainly fed the students information. But at Milo, the students were challenged to think for themselves, to achieve goals, to be successful. He liked that; he set ambitious goals.

With his mother and sister, Gideon walked through an open door into his homeroom, which he shared with fifty students in the Form 3-A class. There they studied math, geography, history, religion, English, Kiswahili, and agriculture business. Simple desks with chairs faced the front wall, where a clock with a Jesus face kept time above a well-worn blackboard. Also above the board a slogan had been written on the wall: IT NEEDS A HAMMER OF PERSISTENCE TO DRIVE THE NAIL OF SUCCESS.

"That's our class motto," Gideon said proudly.

There was also a special math blackboard covered with little squares to work on graphs and charts. "Failing to Plan is Planning to Fail," was written above that board.

"I like that one, too," Gideon said.

He then led the way to the residential area behind the classrooms where several cinderblock dormitories lurked. Inside, the dorms were divided into a number of cubicles, each with six bunk beds. Each boy had a metal footlocker, which served as closet, dresser, and safe. Gideon, the prefect of his dorm, bunked in a back cubicle. Written above the lone window was another slogan: "Use Common Sense."

A group of boys whose parents hadn't come to visit peered in through the cubicle's doorway. Leonida opened her bag and quietly pointed out each item to her son: a handful of quince fruits, a bag of twelve scones, a bunch of bananas, a couple of small sweet potatoes, a bottle of orange soda, and two packets of cookies. She hugged Gideon and slipped him two hundred shillings. The other boys didn't see that. He stealthily shoved the money into his pants pocket and stashed the other goodies in his metal chest, which he then secured with a padlock.

It was lunchtime, and the dorm residents scurried to retrieve their plates and spoons and forks from their footlockers and then hurried over to the hall where motivational speaker Wanyungu had raised their appetite for success. *Githeri*, maize and beans, was on the menu.

Gideon said he, too, must go, and he walked with his mother and sister back to the center lawn between the classrooms. They shared a family hug. Gideon hoped to see them again next month on family visit day and not before at the *shamba*. He dreaded the prospect of being sent home for more money. Leonida, too, hoped she wouldn't see him at home. He belonged here. She would send as many shillings to the principal as she could.

It was late in the afternoon when Leonida returned to her *shamba* and continued the vigil for rain. She stood outside her house, on soil still moist from the downpour the night before, and scanned the horizon. Clouds were forming in the direction of Mount Elgon. Thunder rumbled in the distance. "You can tell," Leonida said, "the rain is close."

LEONIDA WAS RIGHT. At last, the rainy season arrived. Those clouds from Mount Elgon settled over the area on both sides of the Lugulu Hills and ushered in soaking rains that would last for hours at a time over the next couple of days. The water, so long awaited, introduced a glorious freshness across the countryside. The rains washed away the anxiety and despair; in came a new optimism carried by the same winds that brought the clouds. Here, now, clouds and wind and rain and gray were associated with hope and rebirth, rather than foreboding and gloom.

Everything that had a dusty, stale, humid burden was liberated, renewed. The oppression of drought was toppled by the democracy of rain. A revolution, a true green revolution, spread across the land. The parched soil absorbed the water like a sponge, and brown quickly turned to green. Tree frogs croaked, birds chirped, trees blossomed, and swarms of butterflies flitted here and there. All the harbingers of nature came to pass.

The first drops settled the dust of the long, dry season. The torrent that followed created an oozing, brown-red wonderful mess of mud. As they walked, men folded up pant legs, women hiked up long skirts. Bicycle riders of all ages gleefully raced through the puddles, spreading out their legs like kids cruising down a steep hill. Barefoot was the daily fashion, more so than before. Cars bogged down in the mud, potholes expanded with every drop. Dirt roads became largely impassable, except by motorcycle drivers skidding over the bumps and holes like moguls skiers.

There was a new burst of activity on the *shambas*. The livestock became livelier, eagerly devouring the new, green sprouts. Chickens pecked more aggressively at the bugs in the soil. And the farmers rushed to their fields to take advantage of every drop. With their *jembes* they turned over the soil, breaking up clumps, making it receptive to the rain.

For the One Acre farmers, the three-day countdown to planting finally began.

ON MARCH 17, a restless Sanet Biketi was up before dawn at his *shamba* in Kabuchai. He rose from his stark, wooden bed and stepped carefully to avoid the bedroom puddle beneath his porous thatched roof. Grabbing his *jembe*, he walked outside twenty yards to his field and stood alone in the quiet dark. The big day had arrived. There, in solitude, with the sun poised to poke above the horizon, Sanet raised his arms and voice in prayer. "Almighty Father," he said, "take control of the planting and the growing. Thy will be done."

Zipporah stirred in bed. She lingered for an extra minute until she, too, began her day with a prayer. "Thank you, Father, for the new day you have given us. You have given us this day to plant. Bless all those who are coming to help us. Give us the strength to complete the planting in one day."

Sanet hauled out the fertilizer and seed, which he had kept in a corner of their living room. He and his wife had chosen the 513 variety from Kenya Seed, which was widely desired by farmers because it matured early and permitted a second crop to be grown after harvest. By 8 a.m., Zipporah and Sanet were joined by ten other farmers from their One Acre group, and they began to plant according to the One Acre method. They unfurled the planting string and worked meticulously as a team. For long stretches there was little talking as everyone concentrated on the task of digging the holes, sprinkling in the tiny scoop of fertilizer, covering with soil, dropping in a seed, and filling the hole.

It was the same routine that Zipporah had ridiculed as "childish" the year before when she watched Pastor Isaiah plant the supposedly cursed land nearby. Now, as she began her first One Acre season, Zipporah understood that there was nothing silly about the disciplined planting work. When she finally stood up straight to survey the progress on her acre—arching her back and wiping her brow—she despaired that they were only about one-third of the way finished. And it was already noon.

"We're not going to complete this in one day," she muttered to herself. It was a significant worry. The next day, she and Sanet and the others would move on to help plant the land of another group member. And so it would go for more than a week until all members had planted. If her acre wasn't completed today, she fretted, when would she have time to finish?

In the afternoon, the planting became more routine, and the pace increased. By 5 p.m. the Biketis's acre was finished. "God is faithful," Zipporah declared.

Now, with the work done, it was time for song. Zipporah, a praiser in her church who would often lead the congregation in singing, encouraged the farmers with a beautiful soprano voice. "He's a miracle-working God," she sang. "He's a miracle-working God. He's Alpha and Omega. He's a miracle-working God."

THE RAINS CONTINUED. On March 18, the *Amua* group began planting. Rasoa planted on March 19 in a morning drizzle. On March 20, a Sunday, Francis's group rolled out their planting string. Also on that day, the men with their team of oxen were back at Leonida's *shamba*, replowing her half-acre, turning over once more the tough soil where sugarcane had grown. Leonida wanted the soil to be as loose as possible, so the planting would be easier and the new maize shoots would have less resistance poking through the earth. The plowing began at four in the morning and finished at ten. Then Leonida went to church. In the sermon, the pastor preached from the last words of the Book of Matthew: "And lo, I am with you always, even unto the end of the world." And the prayers turned from please rain come to please seeds grow.

THE SEEDS, every farmer knew, were the game-changers in their lives. They knew the hybrid seeds, delivered fresh each year, were capable of doubling or tripling yields above those attained from the traditional varieties that they had customarily saved from their harvests and reused year after year. They knew the names of the seed varieties—selected for their performance in soil types and altitude ranges—as well as they knew the names of their children. And they talked about them just as fondly.

"I'm planting Kenya Seed 6213," Francis told a group from One Acre who had come to check on the planting. "We chose this seed because it is released recently, so we know it is the latest technology. It grows tall and strong." As he did each time he received visitors, Francis scurried to move several chairs from his house to the shaded area beneath one of his avocado trees. There, he held forth on the value of seeds.

He acknowledged that hybrid seeds cost more than the traditional varieties. But he said it was well worth the cost to attain the higher yields from the hybrid vigor burst. Someone mentioned that some people in the United States and elsewhere in the rich world—those clinging to a romantic notion of African farming—believed that annual seed purchases trapped African farmers in a cycle of higher expenses. Francis laughed derisively and shook his head.

"You mean they would rather we be trapped in a cycle of hunger?" he asked. "We will all pay more for seeds if they give us much better harvests. Who wouldn't? It doesn't cost anything to be hungry. Starvation is cheap! You mean these people would rather we not spend money and be content with low yields?"

He fixed his visitors with a pained look of incredulity.

"We've come to discover that the seed you save in your house and use year after year doesn't perform as well as the hybrid seed," he explained. "One, it is too easily attacked by disease; no changes have been made to resist new disease. Two, the cobs are smaller than with hybrid seed."

"Look," he said slowly, choosing his English words carefully, "life is going on. There is new technology in the world. So you should follow the technology rather than hold on to old customs that are leaving you hungry. We look forward to our better harvests."

The farmers' embrace of better seeds was similar to their swift and eager adoption of cell-phone technology. The phones themselves cost money, plus the farmers had to constantly purchase the calling minutes and also pay to recharge the battery at a shop with power. These were recurring expenses, just like buying new seeds, but none of the farmers would be willing to go back to life without phones. The phones connected them to a wider world; they became the means of banking, of communicating over long distances. It was an expense they happily accepted. Improved seeds were the same.

The value of seeds had been a key revelation of farmers across the world as agricultural transformations spread from country to country. The One Acre staff was familiar with a graph circulated by Joe DeVries, the head of the seed program at the Nairobi-based AGRA. The brightly colored graph was titled, "The Impact of the Introduction of Hybrid Maize Seed on Maize Yields in the United States." It showed that from 1865 to the 1930s, maize yields were stuck on a steady line at 1.5 metric tons per hectare (about 2.5 acres). In the 1930s, the line takes an abrupt upward turn and continues on a relentless forty-five-degree ascent through the end of the century. By the year 2000, U.S. maize yields had soared to near nine metric tons per hectare. A thick, red arrow pointed to the inflection point in the 1930s: "Start of adoption of hybrid seed."

That's the point where Africa was in 2011, nearly a century behind U.S. maize yields, but at the moment when production was beginning to increase with a wider adoption of hybrid seed. While farmers in the United States had moved on to the next generation of maize seed technology—genetically modified organisms, or GMOs—that technology hadn't been accepted in sub-Saharan Africa beyond South Africa. Most farmers in Kenya and elsewhere on the continent hadn't ever heard of genetically modified seed; Francis and the other One Acre farmers would shake their heads in bewilderment at the mention of GMOs. But they were pioneers in the use of hybrid seed. African seed breeders estimated that less than 20 percent of African maize came from hybrid seed in 2011. In some countries, it was less than 5 percent. In Kenya, the percentage was beginning to rise to perhaps 50 percent, as AGRA's support of Kenyan breeders and local seed companies began to get the latest seed technology into the hands of the smallholder farmers.

But with this increase came another problem: seed shortages. The supply, it appeared, couldn't keep up with demand. Zipporah, Rasoa, Francis, and Leonida were able to plant as soon as the sustained rains arrived because One Acre assured that they had received the seeds they wanted in the right amount and on time. But as they were beginning to plant, other farmers in western Kenya and the Rift Valley were still scrambling to obtain their seeds. Reports of seed shortages in various locations were followed by reports of near riots by farmers.

"What is usually a relatively smooth and simple process became a nightmare," Sylvia Mwichuli wrote in a blog post. She was one of Joe DeVries's colleagues at AGRA, in charge of communications. Although she and her husband worked in Nairobi, they maintained a farm near Kitale, the very home of the big seed companies. They normally planted about thirty acres of maize. But as the planting season neared, they couldn't get the 614 variety they wanted from Kenya Seed. They waited with scrums of farmers at the agro-dealer shops. They called everyone they knew at Kenya Seed, even accountants. Nothing. The rains were falling, the planting season had arrived, time was moving along.

"I could not find any seed in any of the shops, and despite queuing for long hours with thousands of other farmers, could not find appropriate maize hybrid seed to buy," Mwichuli wrote. "The frustration among both small- and large-scale farmers in my hometown was palpable!"

Anger spread. Smallholder farmers, scraping for every shilling, were paying two hundred shillings or more for the journey into town to try to find seed, only to be turned away. They slept outside the shops and gathered at the gates of the seed companies. Rumors proliferated that seeds were sold to neighboring Sudan, to be used in the fertile southern region that had declared independence after decades of fighting with the north. Kenya Seed claimed there was unexpected heavy demand for seed. The farmers didn't want to hear any excuses. They were in the breadbasket region; how could there be no seed?

"None of us could believe what was happening, and the government's response, that unexpected demand had exceeded supply, did little to calm our nerves!" Mwichuli wrote.

With the rains falling and the soil ready, farmers were forced to buy whatever seed they could find, even if it wasn't the right kind suited to their soil and elevation. Mwichuli and her husband bought seed meant for the Kakamega region, far to the south of Kitale. They planted only ten acres, one-third of their potential. Some of their neighbors, larger farmers like themselves, planted only two acres. Some planted only a half-acre.

"Now we are waiting with our hearts in our mouths and fingers crossed," she concluded, "hoping to get a reasonable yield."

In Bungoma, Andrew Youn scratched his head over the paradox: while drought choked crops in some parts of the country, farmers in the rain-blessed regions couldn't plant because of seed shortages. It was the kind of illogic that reminded him of his original proposition: "We can do better than that."

MARCH 23 DAWNED sunny and cool in the Lugulu Hills. It was Leonida's turn to plant, exactly three weeks after she had planted the year before. Seven *Amua* members came to her *shamba* to help with the work: Agnes, Alice, Elizabeth, Margaret, Alan, Esther, and Beatrice, who was once again wearing her Obama knit cap. Leonida prepared a breakfast of tea and *githeri* to fuel them for the day of hard labor. They asked God to bless their handiwork and the seeds.

It had rained the night before, so the soil was nice and soft. Not too hard, not too muddy. "Just right," Leonida told her friends. She wore a purple sweater against the morning chill and wrapped a yellow-and-blue scarf around her head. Within minutes, her bare feet would be coated with a layer of dirt. The *Amua* farmers formed two teams of four for the planting. Hole digger, fertilizer scooper, dirt coverer, seed dropper/hole filler. They would rotate the duties as they went along. Leonida and Beatrice started off digging with their *jembes*, working from opposite ends of the row, walking backward until they bumped into each other in the center. The teams were efficient and steady, well-practiced in the task of planting.

In mid-morning, while Leonida was wielding a *jembe*, digging the holes, a man from the village approached. He had come to seek the assistance of the village elder. Leonida chided him. "If you come to my *shamba* on this day you must come with your *jembe*, and you must work," she said sternly. "I can't leave the *shamba* to help you. You must help me."

Flummoxed, the man drifted away. And the planting continued.

By early afternoon, as a light rain began to fall, Leonida's half-acre was finished. She joyously thanked her friends for their diligent work and then served lunch. It was a feast of *ugali* and *sukuma wiki* to celebrate and to restore their energy.

Leonida had been conserving her maize, rationing it through the days, knowing she would need it for strength during the planting. In the market, the maize price had soared to eighty-five shillings per *goro-goro*, nearly three times higher than at the beginning of the year. A few evenings earlier, Dorcas announced she was tired of sweet potatoes and refused to eat them again. She went on strike over the repetitive, meager portions. Leonida, realizing the strain on her youngest child, dipped into her reserve and made some maize porridge for Dorcas.

Now, after the planting, the *Amua* members crowded around the tables in Leonida's house. As they devoured the *ugali*, the farmers once again talked of their expectations for the harvest and prayed for the seeds to grow. The planting was complete. It was a day for hope and optimism. Leonida was buoyant, her worries and cares temporarily lifted.

But as her friends trudged home, weary after the hard work, the day of hope and optimism gave way to an evening of dread and despair. The three kilograms of maize Leonida had used to make the *ugali* was her last. The bag on the chair in the corner of the living room was empty.

As darkness approached, with her new crop in the ground and the harvest more than five months in the future, Leonida sat alone at the table in her living room, fearful of the days to come. She opened a diary she was keeping to record the rhythms of the growing cycle.

"From now on," Leonida confided, "I start every day with nothing, except the grace of God."

Her *wanjala* had begun.

Leonida Wanyama at a table in her sitting room, waiting for rain.

Leonida and her husband, Peter, standing outside their house.

All photos courtesy of the author unless otherwise specified.

Leonida (squatting on the right) and other One Acre Fund farmers at their initial training meeting; the women squatting in the front row represent maize sprouts; those standing in the back are weeds holding back their growth.

The *Amua* group practices planting while waiting for the rains.

One Acre Fund founder Andrew Youn with maize drying on the rocks of Kabuchai.

Rasoa Wasike, ready to plant, with her *jembe* and measuring sticks and string.

Rasoa applies a thimbleful of fertilizer to each maize plant.

Francis Wanjala Mamati with his storage shed.

Francis prays for rain before readying his soil for planting.

Zipporah Biketi and her children David, Tabitha, and Cynthia in front of their house.

"I have a farm in Africa. . . " The *shamba* of Zipporah and Sanet.

Leonida visits Gideon at his high school.

Rasoa and one of her 401(Cow) investments.

Francis and Mary dwarfed by their maize.

Harvest day on the Biketi *shamba*. Even the children help with the husking.

Rasoa shells her maize in her living room.

Leonida serves the Christmas feast under the avocado tree.

David Biketi.

GIULIA LONGO COURTER

GIULIA LONGO COURTER

The four farmers.

CHAPTER 4

WANJALA

(The Hunger)

That evening, Leonida stared into a cupboard that was truly bare. Hungry children who had nothing for lunch were coming home from school for dinner. "What will we eat?" she asked herself.

She didn't ask the question in the same way that millions and millions of other mothers around the world would be asking that evening: What, among various choices, will we eat for dinner? Something fresh from the garden or the grocery, or something frozen from the refrigerator, or maybe something off the menu at a restaurant? Leonida didn't have those choices. Her question was not, What's for dinner? But, Is there dinner? Not, What can we eat? But, Will we eat?

Will we eat? That question would be foremost in her mind for the coming months. It hardly seemed possible, but the praying would become even more intense than during the vigil for rain.

Like with the question, "When will it rain?" the answer to "Will we eat?" was, "If God wishes."

Later that night, March 23, Leonida returned to her diary: "God gave us one hundred shillings," she rejoiced. It was from the hand of Peter's brother, a farmer near Webuye, a gift to help out. Peter bought a *goro-goro* of maize for ninety shillings. Leonida and the girls built a fire in the cooking hut and made *ugali*.

In the hunger season, life was stripped down to the essentials of survival. Tea for breakfast, nothing for lunch, tea for dinner and always the question, "Will we eat?" The chronic hunger, the daily gnawing in the stomach that never really abated, prompted a primal focus on food.

This *wanjala* was delivering a particularly vicious one-two punch. Vanishing household maize supplies were followed by rapidly rising prices. The farmers were all buying maize on the market, and as the price rose, they could afford less. During the *wanjala*, Leonida would record a relentless escalation of the maize price:

- 90 shillings at the end of March;
- 95 in mid-April;
- 120 on May 1;
- 130 by early June;
- 150 in July.

That would be five-times greater for a *goro-goro* than the price she received at the beginning of the year when she sold her maize. She had never, ever seen the price of maize rise that quickly, and that high. And it wasn't just maize, it was everything. After the dry season, most varieties of food were scarce and expensive.

Leonida would save up money from the daily milk runs. But that was unsteady income, depending on how well the cows ate; also, both of her cows would produce less milk as the year went on, a characteristic of the gestation cycle of the local breeds. Some days, Leonida or Peter would get a little money from relatives. Sometimes, Leonida asked her pastor for help. Two or three days a week there would be gaps in the diary, when Leonida recorded nothing for dinner. Of those evenings, she noted, "We have a cup of tea and lie down."

IN WASHINGTON, DC, on March 28, Tony Hall voluntarily stopped eating. It was a protest of last resort; he believed it was the only way he could grab the attention of members of Congress and focus their minds on the consequences of the proposed budget cuts targeting global hunger and agricultural development projects. Hall, approaching seventy, was a former congressman, having served the state of Ohio for two decades. He was the former U.S. ambassador to the United Nations food agencies in Rome—the World Food Program, the Food and Agriculture Organization, the International Fund for Agricultural Development. Now, he was leading the Alliance to End Hunger, a faith-based advocacy group that stretched across religions.

He began the fast alongside other generals in the fight against hunger: Rev. David Beckmann, the president of Bread for the World; Jim Wallis, the president of Sojourners, a Christian social justice movement; and Ritu Sharma, the president of Women Thrive Worldwide. They asked people of faith and conscience to join them in creating a "circle of protection" around federal programs benefitting the poor and the hungry in the United States and abroad.

After months of reasoning, pleading, and admonishing by these leaders and their followers, Congress was still proposing to slash 50 percent of food aid to hungry people overseas and nutrition assistance to deeply poor women and children in the United States. The Obama administration's Feed the Future initiative and the Global

Agriculture Food Security Program were on the ropes. The proposed cuts amounted to a 26 percent drop in spending on poverty-focused foreign aid. Hall believed it was time to take the ultimate step of protest: refusing food. "When you face a crucial situation, and all the things you've tried seem to fail, a fast signals an appeal for divine guidance and direction," he told Alliance supporters.

It was the second time Hall resorted to a fast—a solitary, quiet act, to shout out to Congress. In 1993, as a congressman, he fasted to protest what he believed was a lack of conscience in Congress as the House was set to eliminate the only committee that worked with the poor and hungry. His fast stretched for twenty-two days. At first, as the hunger pangs slowed his step and clouded his mind, he felt lonely and wondered whether his action would have any impact. Soon, some six thousand high schools and two hundred universities joined him in fasting. The congressional leadership allowed Hall to establish the Congressional Hunger Center, which had since gone on to train more than five hundred professional hunger warriors.

Now, as the *wanjala* arrived in western Kenya and famine crept across the Horn of Africa, Hall was at it again, ushering in his own private hunger season. "The stakes are even higher this time, as many of the proposed budget cuts will cause even greater harm to vulnerable people than the cuts that provoked my last fast," he said.

The fasters hoped to put a human frame around the budget and make the case that "budgets are moral documents," as Hall said. They sought to take the budget debate beyond the realm of numbers and line items and make it about real people and the common good. Their message to Congress: "Don't balance the budget on the backs of the poor and hungry; they aren't the ones who got us into the fiscal mess, and hurting them isn't the way out of it."

LEONIDA'S BACK was perpetually hurting. One of the cruelest aspects of the hunger season was that it arrived as the work in the fields became more demanding. In the days after the planting, weed control was important to help with the germination of the seeds. Leonida was a stickler for the meticulous practices of the One Acre method, so she was often in the fields, bending deeply, pulling weeds. She recalled the skit from the base training in January, when she was a maize plant trying to push up against the force of weeds. She wanted to make the journey to harvest as easy as possible for her maize.

On April 2, at the break of dawn, Leonida looked immediately to her field. It was a glorious sight. The maize shoots were poking through the soil, taller than her ankles. They formed straight green lines, just like she and her *Amua* friends had planted. The germination was very good. Nearly all the seeds had sprouted; there were very few gaps in the field. The seeds from One Acre had a germination rate of better than 90 percent. Seeds saved from the previous year usually performed much worse. In her past planting experience, Leonida found that maybe only three-quarters of the leftover seeds would grow. They lacked the protective coating against insects that the new seeds had, so they were attacked the moment they landed in the soil.

Since planting day, the weather had been ideal for growing. The rains had continued to fall, softly and steadily, in the first week after planting. But at the beginning of April, the clouds disappeared. The first dry day didn't cause much worry. After the third day, though, the farmers again began fixating on the sky over Mount Elgon. As they met on the pathways to the market or to the stream, they asked each other, "Will it rain? Will it rain?" Those who weren't in One Acre and who hadn't planted yet due to lack of seeds or fertilizer fretted that they had missed the crucial start to the rainy season.

On the evening of April 5, the rain returned with a vengeance. A bad storm rattled the Lugulu Hills. Rain poured, hailstones pounded, wind raged. The young maize stalks whipped back and forth in the storm.

Early the next morning, after milking the cows, Leonida was in the field repairing the damage. She was on her hands and knees, forming little dirt mounds of support at the base of any stalks that were bent or leaning. She hadn't had anything to eat the day before, just tea, and now tea again for breakfast and there would be nothing for lunch. The fieldwork was slow and draining, sapping whatever energy she carried from her breakfast cup of tea. In the early afternoon she retreated from the sun and sat, exhausted, at the table in her living room. She stirred again when the girls returned from school and together they fetched water and wood and lit the fire in the kitchen hut. As darkness approached, Leonida prepared plain tea for her family; they were facing a second consecutive night of going to bed without food. Then Peter returned from his milk run. He was carrying a little packet of sugar and a bowl of *ugali* from relatives in Webuye.

"It was a good day," Leonida noted. "Tea with sugar, *ugali* with sukuma. Like Christmas."

During the hunger season, the fortunes of the farmers and their maize ran in opposite directions: as the maize grew taller and stronger, the farmers grew weaker both physically and financially. On April 7, Gideon called Leonida on her cellphone. It rang to the tune of Rimsky-Korsakov's piano masterpiece, "Flight of the Bumblebee." Gideon needed two thousand shillings to pay for extra instruction for math tests required to move up to the next class.

Leonida had nothing of such value to sell, except a young bull that had been born a month earlier to her black cow. It would be a couple of years before the bull would be much of an asset on the *shamba*, pulling a plow. Until then, it just consumed grass that the two dairy cows needed, and it didn't produce milk. So she sold it for 4,500 shillings. She spent 2,000 for the tutoring, and another 1,000 for a math practice book, a ruler, and a calculator. She added some toothpaste and soap and a bit of sugar for Gideon. He needed to remain strong and successful. With the rest, Leonida bought a new school uniform for Jackline to replace her old, ragged outfit, and new school shoes for Sarah. All the kids needed to be suitable for school so they wouldn't be sent home. And she bought a *goro-goro* of maize and some sugar for the family.

Leonida had been hoping to keep the bull for a while, build up its value, and then sell it to raise money for high school tuition. But it was now that she needed the money. So she sold from a position of weakness, just like she had with her maize at the beginning of the year. It was a matter of necessity, not choice.

In the one choice she did have, she again favored the future over the present, education over daily bread. The farmers had established a resiliency over the years to cope with the hunger season, to survive on diminishing portions and meals. They knew the *wanjala* would end with the next harvest. But their poverty they hoped would end with education.

The demands of the field were unceasing. Leonida planted beans in between the maize stalks. They were complementary crops, the beans adding some nutrients to the soil that the maize needed. The beans would also be ready to harvest before the maize, helping to bring the hunger season to a close. She also finished planting early maturing varieties of maize on some strips of land beyond her half-acre plot of the One Acre maize. And she planted cassava. Then, too, there was the weeding, a constant task. Leonida often started the fieldwork at 8 a.m., after the pre-dawn household chores and, fortified with only a weak cup of tea, worked through noon when the heat drove her into the shade.

On April 14, she began to top dress her One Acre maize with nitrogen-based fertilizer. The One Acre farmers had been taught to whittle a sharp point to a stick and use that to poke a hole four inches deep into the ground next to every stalk. It took some exertion, leaning on the stick, pushing it into the rugged soil. Then they were instructed to measure out a tiny portion of fertilizer with a thimble-like scoop and to bend deeply to add it to the hole. Push, bend. Push, bend. Leonida repeated this for every stalk, hundreds of them. When they could, the *Amua* members helped each other, so Leonida repeated the wearying routine on other *shambas* for the better part of a week.

During the hunger season, the *shambas* presented a giant paradox: while hunger mounted, the food ripened. There was plenty of food growing, but none of it would be ready to eat for several months. Leonida had maize, beans, cassava, potatoes, and sugarcane growing; pumpkin vines were beginning to spread; mangos, avocados, and bananas were growing big on trees but wouldn't be ripe until late June or July. The farmers would just have to make it through. On the days without food, Leonida reminded her family, "God is our leader."

As the meager meals slowed Leonida's work in the field, so did the lack of nutrition slow the learning of her children in school. The principal of the Lutacho Primary School, who was in charge of 850 students, had sympathy for Dorcas and the orphan boys, and a number of other children whose parents were struggling to provide enough food, and allowed them to stay in school during the lunch break and have a meal, even though the parents didn't pay for half-day boarding. But Jackline and Sarah were still walking the two kilometers in each direction, coming home for a lunch that on most days wasn't there and then going back on an empty stomach.

Whenever they entered the school grounds, they saw the school's ambitions painted in big letters on the side of the administration building:

MOTTO: Hard Work Begets Success.

MISSION: Educate Boys and Girls to Overcome Challenges in Their Lives.

VISION: To Succeed by Working Hard.

The *wanjala* mocked those goals. Both Jackline and Sarah complained to their mother that it was difficult to work hard in school on just a cup of tea. They were good students with ambitious plans. Jackline hoped to be a nurse, Sarah a teacher. They both wanted to go to high school, and Leonida dearly wanted that, too. It was a particularly important year for Jackline, who was in the eighth class and would be taking the tests at the end of the year to qualify for high school.

On the days they returned home for lunch and were told by their mother that there was nothing to eat, they turned with a quiet fury and headed outside to sit in the shade of the avocado tree. Hunger didn't relieve them of their chores. They were up before dawn, getting out of the bed in their kitchen hut and starting the fire for tea. They washed dishes and tidied the yard. They began the trek to school before 6 a.m. After school, there were more chores to do: fetching water and firewood, helping with dinner if there was any, washing up afterward. Then there was homework around the kerosene lamp. Work seemed to be all the girls knew; they had never watched television or gone to a movie.

At Milo High, Gideon's studies were plagued by the daily dread that he would be sent home for more money. The worrying, and the pressure to succeed, was taking its toll. At the end of March, Leonida had been called to the school because Gideon was sick with a stomach problem. He wasn't eating properly; he was dehydrated.

She took him to the Webuye hospital, where he stayed for four days before coming home for a few days to rest. He was exhausted. Then later in April, he came home with malaria—headaches, joint pain, loss of appetite, severe sweating. Peter carried him on the back of the bicycle. At least his school absences for illness kept the principal from demanding more tuition payments. But Gideon feared that he was missing too much class time and falling behind.

The unexpected expense of the health treatments put an added strain on Leonida and her family. In fact, the *wanjala* had the entire country on edge. From various parts of Kenya came reports of protests over the escalating costs of food and fuel. Chants of *"unga"* (flour) interrupted the public speeches of politicians. Demonstrators were camping out in front of government offices. The Consumer Federation of Kenya actually sued the government in High Court over rising food and fuel prices. It accused various ministers of violating the consumers' right to be free of hunger, which was enshrined in the new constitution. The federation said the ministers were duty bound to come up with policies that would provide enough food of acceptable quality for every citizen. Instead, there were seed shortages, fake fertilizer, inefficient markets, horrible infrastructure—results of policies that restricted, rather than expanded, agricultural development. Kenyans, particularly those in rural areas, expected very little from their politicians, most of whom showed up every five years seeking votes and then never returned until the next election. The *wanjala* deepened the feeling of abandonment.

Instead, the farmers relied on each other to survive the hunger season. Thus, as individuals became hungrier and poorer, so did the broader community. As Leonida ran short of money and food, so did those in the community she turned to for help.

At the local pharmacy, a small storefront in the Lukusi market where Leonida obtained the health treatments for her family, Janet

Nekesa Kundu was running out of medicine. Most of her customers were farmers, and the farmers were uniformly out of cash, so she provided treatments to them on credit. But if they didn't pay for her services, she wouldn't have the money to restock her shelves.

Janet was the closest thing to a doctor in the Lutacho area. After high school, she attended a medical training center in western Kenya and began studying to become a nurse, but she could stay only for one year because her parents couldn't afford the tuition. She had been a good student, a fast learner, so she got a job assisting a doctor at a pharmacy in a bigger town for several years. She watched his every move, studying the patients' symptoms, learning about the treatments. After she married, she took out a loan from a bank that worked with women entrepreneurs, and she opened her own pharmacy. She stocked the store with medicines, and she bought a stethoscope. She was what the Kenyans called a "dispensing chemist."

Now the *wanjala* was pushing her to the limit, too. Working behind the wooden counter in her store, she treated a steady stream of patients—at least ten a day with malaria, nearly that many with pneumonia or other respiratory illnesses, and a few daily cases of severe diarrhea and children with worms. With her stethoscope, she offered a cursory diagnosis—she had no other equipment, not even a standard blood pressure gauge or a microscope to analyze blood and confirm her hunches—and then handed over some medicine. More often than not, her patients offered an effusive "thank you" and then left her store without paying the full cost, if indeed they paid anything.

Janet was thirty-four but stooped by the burdens of her patients. She felt she couldn't turn them away if they didn't have any money. Where would they go? The government clinic in the area didn't have much of anything in the way of treatment beyond some mild painkillers. She hated to send people to pharmacies in other villages or to the hospital in Webuye because she feared she would lose them as customers. And she worried about what kind of treatment they would receive in those places. But mostly, she felt a responsibility to those who came into her shop. They were her friends and neighbors, like Leonida. She lived among them in the same type of mud-and-sticks house, and she struggled with her crops just as they did. If she didn't help them when they first showed signs of malaria or pneumonia, they would delay treatment and likely end up in the hospital for a longer, and costlier, stay. She couldn't refuse treatment; she asked them to pay what they could.

"The calling of being a nurse is to treat, prevent, provide information. You are there to render service, first, before you charge them," Janet told Leonida, reassuring her that it was fine this time if she didn't have the money for Gideon's malaria tablets. She would put it on her tab.

Leonida thanked her and lowered her head in reverence and guilt. "I have a balance to pay, Gideon has a balance, Dorcas has a balance, Peter has a balance," Leonida said. "I'm sorry, but I just can't sit with a sick child. I must seek treatment."

She promised to pay off her debts, bit by bit. Janet told her any payment would be welcome. Janet had a monthly rent of five hundred shillings to cover, a loan payment was due, and she needed to restock her shelves. "But I don't have any money myself," she said. "My patients, like Leonida, they have my money."

Janet managed a weak laugh and then clapped her hands in resignation. Leonida smiled sheepishly. "Thank God we have you here," she said. Janet offered some sympathy. "This *wanjala* is very difficult for all of us."

Leonida walked to the big Kenya Assemblies of God church a few minutes from the pharmacy. It was the mother church to the smaller parish church near Leonida's house that often served as host to One Acre meetings. Leonida wanted to thank her pastor, Reverend Jackson Fukwo, for his kindness to her family. She was running a tab on her pastor and church as well.

"I would like to help more," Pastor Fukwo told her, "but the church doesn't have much." He said the Sunday offering might bring in one thousand shillings after the harvest, but far less during the *wanjala*. "It is difficult to preach about giving when nobody has anything to give."

He himself has had to diversify from preaching to support his family of six children. In the Kenya Assemblies of God ministry, every pastor is dependent on his congregation's members for income. When they don't have anything, you don't have anything. So, a couple of years ago Pastor Fukwo opened two little shops in the market—a general store and a clothes boutique—though he knew boutique was too fancy a word for a shop in a shanty. He also sought to boost income from his farm; he was one of the initial One Acre members in Lutacho but dropped out when he didn't have enough time beyond his work with the church and the shops to help out on the *shambas* of other members of his group.

But as pastor, he helped them by sharing whatever money he and the church had. Fifty shillings here, one hundred shillings there. That is why the church, an ambitious cinderblock and brick structure, was still a construction site four years after the congregation began building it. Except for rows of wooden benches to accommodate the 180 members, the church was hollow inside. Wires hung from the ceiling, waiting for the congregation to be able to afford electricity. The floor was just dirt—not even a dung covering—which made dancing in the aisles difficult. There was a permanent cloud of dust. Without a loudspeaker system, Pastor Fukwo had to shout mightily to address the people in the back rows.

And yet, the parishioners came with arms outstretched and empty hands. Including Leonida. "This year, the *wanjala* is very bad," the pastor told her. "We are breaking records for the maize price. We have so many people come to the church for help. Everyone has to have enough to eat. When there is enough to eat, people are content in their home, and that is good for a pastor."

Also good for a pastor was how such deep poverty drove people closer to the church. "When you are so poor," he said, "you can lay here for a whole day praying to God. Because whether you live or die, there is nothing for you to do but pray."

But, he feared, this *wanjala* would even overwhelm heaven. "I pray for so many needs of my people," he told Leonida, who enthusiastically nodded her head. "If we get one from God, we are happy."

LEONIDA WAS CERTAINLY overwhelmed. On top of her worries to meet her family's demand for food, school fees, and medicine, another money worry arrived. She and Peter were called to the chief's office; there was a demand that they turn over part of their land. Another woman in the area was claiming she had purchased it years earlier. Peter said he never sold the land, and he had the deed to prove it. His signature wasn't on any of the sale documents the chief produced. Peter suspected his identification card had been copied and then used to sell his land without him knowing it.

The chief's office had first raised the land issue on the last day of 2010, but Leonida figured it would go away. Disputes over land were frequent; corruption was rife in the Kenyan government from the federal authorities down to the local administrators, and land ownership was often at the center of scams and swindles and political intimidation. When the case persisted, Leonida and Peter dug in their heels; they weren't about to give in. They reported the case to the police and the courts. And then they went to the top, filing a complaint with the Land Commission in Nairobi and the anti-corruption office.

Leonida embraced a copy of Kenya's new constitution, which guaranteed property rights and the sanctity of transactions. She had mobilized her neighbors to vote in the constitutional referendum the year before. She knew the law. "The chief's office has nothing to do with land anymore," she told Peter. "It is an outmoded system. The constitution is what protects us."

It was proving to be a costly battle. It took money to travel to Webuye and other cities to make the claims and hunt for documentation. It was money that could be spent on food or put aside for school fees. But land was very dear to all Kenyan farmers, particularly the smallholders; it was uncertain land rights that had held back agricultural development in many African countries, including Kenya. Without the certainty of land ownership—if local leaders could confiscate property on a whim—farmers were reluctant to make improvements on their *shambas* and take on the risks of new seeds and planting methods and credit.

This was a battle Leonida believed she had to wage for her family, for her neighbors, and for all smallholder farmers. It was one more drain on her money and her strength, one more hunger season worry, one more burden to carry on her back. She sat at a table in her living room, reading documents, confirming her rights. Leonida buried her head in her hands and turned to her husband. "It's all so stressful," she said.

ON APRIL 24, Easter Sunday, Tony Hall ended his fast. By then, more than thirty-six thousand people, including twenty-eight members of Congress, had joined him. The support came from a diverse coalition of NGOs and from faith-based organizations be they

Christian, Jewish, or Muslim—more than one hundred groups in all. They amplified the quiet protest of fasting by raising a clamor that put protecting domestic and international poverty programs at the center of their lobbying. The Circle of Protection group, as the fasters came to be known, stormed Capitol Hill. They told Republicans who were intent on whacking international aid and Democrats who weren't rising to its defense that they were acting counter to American values. Suddenly, members of Congress who thought foreign aid could be cut without creating as much as a whimper of protest were hearing from constituents who cared. Bread for the World organized a massive letter-writing campaign in church basements across the United States. More than eighty thousand appeals, many of them handwritten, arrived in Washington. They contained a simple message: It is wrong, morally and religiously, to focus our budget cuts on the people who are already hurting and make them hurt more. Please find better ways to cut our national deficit.

Hall declared a victory of sorts. "We softened the blow of proposed cuts in the fiscal year 2011 budgets," he wrote to fast supporters. "Things were not as bad as they could have been, though there were serious losses as well." For instance, Republicans had proposed cutting the long-standing international school feeding program named for its champions, former senators George McGovern and Bob Dole, and other food aid programs by 50 percent; in the end they were cut 17 percent. Other international health and development spending was barely touched. Domestically, programs benefiting poor children and their mothers were reduced 7 percent; Hunger-Free Communities Grants weren't renewed.

The 2011 funding for some agricultural development programs held firm with prior year spending. But the Global Agriculture and Food Security Program (GAFSP) was hit. President Obama had sought $408 million to make good on U.S. pledges to fund the agriculture development priorities of poor countries. Congress approved only $100 million. Some activists looked at the glass as being one-quarter full; at least the program got something. Others saw the glass as three-quarters empty; GAFSP was down to a last gasp. In its first year, the program had funded projects in only eight countries amounting to $321 million, far below ambitions. Nearly twenty countries, most of them African, that had prepared agriculture investment plans deemed worthy of support were turned away for lack of funding. One of those countries was Kenya. GAFSP was running out of money before it could really begin reversing the decades of neglect of agricultural development, and with the United States pulling back on commitments, it was doubtful that any other countries would contribute to the fund.

One country, China, was doing the opposite of the United States; it was increasing its foreign aid, particularly in the realm of agricultural development. Here was the yin and the yang of global development spending. Three days before Hall ended his fast, the Chinese government, through the Information Office of the State Council, issued its first-ever white paper on foreign aid, trumpeting annual increases of nearly 30 percent since 2004. Those increases were coming off a small base, but they signaled a rapid escalation, especially in Africa, which had received nearly half of China's foreign assistance in 2009.

China began aiding African countries in 1956. Over the next decades, the report noted, it built the Tanzania-Zambia Railway and many other railways, roads, and major infrastructure projects around the continent. In 2000, the Forum on China-Africa Cooperation was initiated. In the first decade of the new century, the Export-Import Bank of China reportedly extended more money in loans to the countries of sub-Saharan Africa than did the World Bank. Going forward, the white paper stated, China would make "agriculture, rural development, and poverty reduction in developing countries priorities of its foreign aid."

China pledged to establish thirty demonstration centers for agricultural technologies in other developing countries, dispatch three thousand agricultural experts and technicians to those countries, and invite five thousand agricultural personnel to China for training. The white paper talked about constructing irrigation and water-harvesting systems, supplying agriculture machinery and farm implements, nurturing fisheries and dairies, and conducting research and development. "China," it said, "has been increasing its aid for agriculture and grain production in particular. In recent years, food security has become a global issue."

This was China's version of the Obama administration's Feed the Future initiative, but with one significant difference: China's foreign aid would "impose no political conditions." Unlike U.S. development aid to Africa, which was often funneled to countries promoting democracy and free markets, China's funding would remain blind to the political and social forces in the recipient countries and ignorant of human rights abuses. In some instances, China's aid was propping up repressive governments, such as in Sudan and Zimbabwe, while increasing China's political and business positions in those countries; Sudan's oil was vital to fueling the industrial expansion inside China. Also, China was emerging as one of the leading forces in the "land-grabbing" phenomenon, which was introducing the prospect of a new kind of colonialism in Africa. Rather than taking out precious minerals or oil or timber from the continent as had historically happened, these were efforts to exploit Africa's soil, sun, and water. China, India, South Korea, Saudi Arabia and a few other countries were facing their own limitations on arable land and water—and thus limitations on their own agriculture production—and were moving into Africa to grow food. They were snapping up large tracts of land, often to the detriment of nearby smallholder farmers. The question spreading across the continent and unanswered in the white paper was: Are these aid projects and investments in agricultural development meant to feed Africans or to feed Chinese back home?

What became clear, though, was that China's foreign aid white paper signaled a full-scale advance in Africa and on the global food security front while the budget debate and debt crisis in the United States had many calling for a retreat.

And it had Tony Hall sounding an alarm as he ended his fast. Efforts needed to be doubled for the 2012 budget fight, he wrote in a blog post to supporters. The proposal by Congressman Paul Ryan, a Republican from Wisconsin, he said, "is even worse" than the 2011 actions. It called for deep cuts across the board in non-defense spending, which would include indiscriminate whacking of U.S. poverty reduction programs and foreign aid projects. "This goes beyond responsible budget cutting," Hall said. "The proposal literally targets poor and hungry people, asking them to carry the burden of decades of fiscal irresponsibility in Washington."

On Easter Sunday, Tony Hall made a peanut butter sandwich and began eating again. But before he did, he reminded his supporters that "millions of people here in America and around the world will not have the same luxury. They will continue to go hungry."

"NOTHING FOR LUNCH TODAY," Zipporah Biketi told her husband, Sanet, on a sunny May day as they met on the pathway beside their field. She was returning home from a One Acre meeting in Kabuchai village, and he was inspecting the maize, which was now a foot taller than they were. "For dinner, rice," Zipporah added.

"With vegetables?" Sanet asked hopefully.

Zipporah shook her head. "Plain."

Sanet had asked about the meals because he was hungry. He was waiting for Zipporah to return to their house to cook lunch. The day before, they'd had no dinner. Breakfast was a weak cup of tea, no milk or sugar. Sanet was losing weight, his shirt hung limply off his shoulders; he said his wife and children were looking thinner, too. He scrunched his face when he heard that rice was on the menu. "This family of ours isn't used to rice," he said. "It's a light food, compared to maize."

But rice was cheaper than maize, 70 shillings for a *goro-goro* compared to 120. Prices were rising on many daily necessities. A kilogram of sugar was up to 110 shillings, from 80; a liter of kerosene was pushing 100 shillings, up from 65.

"Life now is very hard," Zipporah told her husband. "We are passing through hard times."

The rising prices made this the most desperate *wanjala* in anyone's memory. Zipporah and Sanet had been depending on milk sales from their two cows. But, as with Leonida's local breeds, their milk was drying up after the cows produced calves. Zipporah and Sanet made some bricks in a dirt pit on the edge of their *shamba*, but sales were slow, as few people were building anything. Sanet's large, extended family—his father had nineteen children from two wives—shared whatever anyone had, but that wasn't much. And Sanet's animal trading business had pretty much come to a halt. He couldn't count on much daily income.

"No one is buying cattle, everyone is struggling to afford maize," Sanet explained to his wife. "Life has gotten very expensive. The season isn't very favorable."

At the house, the two oldest children, Samwel and Cynthia, were home from school, sitting on the hard dirt outside the door, reading books, waiting for their mother to come home and cook lunch. The kitchen fire was cold, but they were still expecting something. Their mother had yet to tell them there would be nothing. Tabitha

Nanjala, who had just turned five with no celebration, was in the house, sitting on one of the hard, wooden chairs, her head resting against the back. She had an upset stomach. Little David Wanjala was still coughing, his belly still bloated.

A mild strain of malaria had plagued the family. The rains were still proving to be a double-edged sword. They were vital to keep the maize growing, but they also bred mosquitoes. Everyone was talking about how this was one of the worst mosquito—and thus malarial—years they had known. The *wanjala* piled on; the lack of food weakened the body's defenses.

Also, with the rain came the leaks in the bedroom. There was no money to spare for thatch roof repair. Sanet had given up trying to fashion temporary patches. "I'm exhausted with it," he told Zipporah.

All the tribulations were testing their faith; Sanet was beginning to feel like the Biblical Job who suffered affliction after affliction. He had been reading the Bible in their house while waiting for his wife. He found some encouragement and now offered it to Zipporah. "The Bible says we should appreciate everything, in good times and tough times," he said. "We should come with a thankful heart."

They were certainly thankful for their maize. It was growing strong and tall, green and lush. In fact, it was the healthiest thing on the *shamba*. The roof might have been leaking, the fire in the kitchen was often cold, but their maize was the envy of their neighbors. It dwarfed anyone passing by.

"When I am in the field, I hear what people are saying as they walk past. They are commenting very positively. They say it's very good, it looks nice," Sanet said. "I'm very proud of our maize. It is better than I could have imagined."

He was happy they had planted an early maturing maize. The yields might be a little lower than the longer-maturing strains, but the harvest would come quicker, meaning the *wanjala* would end sooner. Sanet and Zipporah were anticipating that their maize would be ready in late July. Sanet said the way it looked now, they could expect to harvest twenty bags.

If, Zipporah cautioned, the weather remained good. "We need moderate rains and moderate sun," she said. After the slow arrival of the rains, the weather had been ideal. Not too wet, not too dry. She wondered, was it asking too much for that to continue?

"We have played our part," Sanet said. "The remaining part is God's work."

ELSEWHERE IN KABUCHAI, Rasoa and Cyrus couldn't believe their eyes every morning when they stepped out of their house. The maize seemed to add a couple of inches every night; by the end of May, it was nearly ten feet tall and beginning to sport the sandy-blonde tassels on top. "I think we will have our best harvest ever," Cyrus told Rasoa. "Maybe fifteen bags."

For them and their three boys, the *wanjala* so far hadn't been as bad as their neighbors had been experiencing. Cyrus had his salary from the M-Pesa shop, and Rasoa had been hired to distribute a water purification contraption called LifeStraw to her neighbors. Vestergaard Frandsen, a European company that made disease prevention products, had hired twenty-one people in the area, mostly women, to hand out and demonstrate the filters. They were paid 700 shillings a day, 3,500 shillings a week. They would work through the month of May. Rasoa, always active in the community, eagerly leading any health-awareness campaigns, was a natural choice. But she knew the timing was a stroke of luck, coming as it did in the middle of the hunger season.

The company was looking for saturation coverage, so Rasoa and the workers were presented with two blue T-shirts emblazoned with the slogan "Drink Clean Water," a motorcycle helmet, and a

Samsung smart phone and dispatched throughout the region. Rasoa and another woman shared a motorcycle ride to reach villagers on the far side of Kabuchai. She entered the house of Jennipher Wafula and was immediately recognized. Rasoa had never met the woman before, but Jennipher knew her; she had a 2011 One Acre calendar hanging on a wall, the one featuring a photo of Rasoa and her three sons. There was also a calendar from 2009 commemorating President Obama's inauguration, with photos of the president and his wife and daughters, and George Bush and Joe Biden and Hillary Clinton. "Obama Conquers the World," it said.

Rasoa hung the water purification device from a ceiling hook. She then demonstrated how to backwash the filters and how to pour in water at the top so it could trickle down through a thin hose and drip into a clean bucket as drinking water. Finally, she opened the smart phone and recorded the size of the household, a cell-phone contact number, and the GPS location of the house. As she left, she fished a blue marker from her bag and wrote the date of the visit on the wooden frame of the door.

She would install dozens of purifiers that day. Back in her own house that evening, Rasoa and Cyrus sat together on their barren, wooden furniture and discussed what to do with the 17,500-shilling windfall from LifeStraw. They would buy some food, for sure. They needed better furniture and another bed since the boys were getting bigger and couldn't share for much longer. But Rasoa also pressed to buy another calf, and Cyrus agreed. It would add to their 401(Cow) savings.

"If we just buy furniture, we'll just sit on it, and that's it. It doesn't contribute to our future," Rasoa told Cyrus. "But another cow will give us more money over the years."

Three days later, Cyrus came walking home with a calf he bought at the regional cattle market in the town of Chwele. It was brown with a white band on its tail. It was a crossbreed, which was a better milk producer than the local breed, perhaps up to five liters a day better. That would have made it more expensive than One Acre, the calf they had bought in January, but Cyrus got this calf for the bargain price of sixty-four hundred shillings. There was a veritable herd of cows for sale at the market, Cyrus told Rasoa. People were selling off their assets, cows included, to buy maize, which was now approaching 150 shillings per *goro-goro*. They knew they were benefitting from others' hardships during the *wanjala*. Rasoa named the calf Vestergaard, after the company that hired her to distribute the purifiers.

With the remaining money, she bought new school uniforms for the boys; the old ones were ripped and faded, and she hated to see her children go to school in rags. She bought some maize, and she bought a bed. There wasn't enough left for new living room furniture, so she bought some foam cushions for the old chairs. She also paid off the remaining balance of her One Acre credit, and she put aside the bit of money that remained for a solar lamp that One Acre was selling for seventeen hundred shillings. It was a product that the innovations team believed would improve the farmers' lives.

Rasoa enthusiastically agreed. She never liked the smell of the kerosene lamp and worried that one day the boys would set it too near to a blanket or tablecloth and the house would go up in flames. The little daughter of one of her friends had a scar on her scalp from the time her hair braids were caught by a lamp's flame. The solar lamp would also provide better light for homework studies. And Rasoa figured it would pay for itself by eliminating the cost of kerosene and providing an outlet to charge her cell phone. Local shops charged ten shillings to recharge.

Electricity was a distant dream. There were wooden poles holding up overhead electricity wires less than one hundred yards from her house, running along the dirt road between the village market and the government primary school. But a connection to her house was prohibitively expensive. Rasoa calculated it would cost 7,000 shillings to wire her house and another 35,000 shillings to connect to the public grid. Then there would be the monthly bills for however much electricity they would use. And so, the small, red, plastic television sitting on a chair in the corner of her living room remained mute. It was once connected to a car battery, and the family would occasionally gather around to watch the news or sporting events like American professional wrestling or Chuck Norris movies. But that battery had died in December and a new one was too expensive. At five thousand shillings, it was a luxury.

Rasoa welcomed the new cow with a bundle of Napier grass. Cyrus, who closed the M-Pesa shop for a few hours, walked beneath the electricity wires to the Kabuchai public primary school at the end of the road. He was the chairman of the school board; Tim, his oldest son, still attended there while the two younger boys were at the Baptist school. When the year started, they hadn't had the money to send all three to the private church school with annual tuition of about five thousand shillings. At the public school, the fees were minimal throughout the year, but so was the education. Cyrus conceded the education gap; his middle son, Arnest, who was in the fourth grade at the Baptist school, was doing the work of sixth graders at the public school.

The public primary school had nearly eight hundred children and sixteen teachers, twelve of them paid by the government and four paid by the parents, though those four often went months without receiving any money, particularly during the *wanjala*. The school had nine more outhouses than teachers. Everything from pencils to blackboards was in short supply.

The school board was meeting to discuss how to help pupils who suffered particularly during the hunger season. They talked about a new school lunch program for those who wouldn't get anything to eat at home, or perhaps having the better-off families provide an occasional meal for the hungry kids at night. Cyrus suggested that maybe the school itself could join the One Acre Fund next year and grow its own maize.

The principal said that every day fifty to one hundred children stayed home because they were hungry. His name was James Wanjala. Principal Hunger, born during the *wanjala* of 1956. "My name," he told the board in a bit of gallows humor, "is the very problem we now face."

FRANCIS WANJALA MAMATI was lost amid the towering maize stalks on his *shamba*. "Over here," he shouted to his wife, Mary, who was coming to join him for a day of work in the field. Normally, Francis did the farming alone while Mary looked after the smaller children and the household chores. But this was a particularly busy time, the end of May, time for the third weeding and the second top-dressing with a bit of nitrogen-rich fertilizer.

It was as if Francis were standing in a thick forest of trees, so tall and lush was the maize. He, too, like Sanet, could hear strangers admire his crop as they walked on the path past his field. "No, this can't be possible," one said. In comparison to their neighbor's patch, the maize of Francis and Mary and their eldest son, Geoffrey, who was also a One Acre member, did beggar the imagination. The neighbor's maize looked anemic, scrawny, stunted; it was already turning yellow.

"You see the difference?" Francis pointed out to Mary as they began the weeding. "That's how we were for so long. If One Acre could have been here many years back, we'd be much farther ahead.

Instead, it's like we wasted our time. We could have chased hunger very far from our community and from Kenya."

He had high hopes for a good harvest, maybe twenty bags of maize total from the two half-acre plots, but he still scoured the sky with worried eyes. The ideal weather conditions of May—plenty of sun with intermittent rain—needed to hold through June. Drought at the time when the maize tasseled would be disastrous. It had happened a few Junes back, so Francis remained vigilant and prayerful, particularly with the drought continuing its advance through other parts of Kenya. "If God can provide rain in moderate amounts, we will be happy," he told Mary.

They had fortified themselves for a day in the field with a breakfast of tea and biscuits. So far, they were maintaining their energy during the *wanjala*. For lunch, to keep them going, they were expecting rice and potatoes. And for dinner, to recover their strength, *ugali*.

They didn't have to skip many meals. Geoffrey, who was thirty and running his own business, was making sure of that.

Francis, who made it only to the fifth grade, had insisted that his children would get high school educations. Geoffrey had been a good pupil in primary school and had many offers to attend high school. But money was tight at home; his father had just left his government job and the farm wasn't yielding much. Geoffrey dropped out of school for a year, but Francis told him not to despair, they would find a way. Together, they convinced a school to give him a spot and a little scholarship money, and Geoffrey became one of the top students. He graduated in 2001, when he was twenty. After school, he traveled to the big city of Mombasa on the Indian Ocean coast and began working with a friend in a textile business. Together, they dyed clothes in imaginative colors and designs. Geoffrey saw the possibilities of life beyond the farm.

He liked the business world. As gracious and hospitable as his father, Geoffrey was good with both people and numbers and he began seeking experience for a career in the restaurant business. He married well; his wife, Jacklyne, was an excellent cook who taught him the ways of the kitchen. He believed she was heaven sent, to help him build his business. They saved their money and dreamed of working together. In 2008, they opened a café in the Kabuchai village, next to a strip of shops that included the M-Pesa, a general store, and a butchery. Geoffrey named it J. Mamati Cafe—the J honoring Jacklyne, who had the idea of offering a fine, simple meal. Within two years it was a thriving business, specializing in breakfast and lunch for travelers and local workers; a small menu featured beef, chicken, or fish stew with beans and assorted vegetables for twenty or thirty shillings. The specialty of the house became "Mamati's *chapatis*," a kind of tortilla made of wheat flour.

Early every morning, Geoffrey and Jacklyne lit the charcoal-fired stove and took turns spinning and flipping the flat, circular *chapatis* until they were a crisp, golden brown. At meal times, with smoke billowing out of the kitchen, the dining room came alive with guests filling the twelve chairs jammed around five knee-high tables. Even during the *wanjala*. Geoffrey worried he was losing business as people looked inside the room, saw there were no empty seats, and turned away. So a second, larger J. Mamati was under construction a short walk down Kabuchai's main dirt road. Geoffrey and Jacklyne had big plans. Eventually, Geoffrey envisioned, Jacklyne would manage the restaurants while he worked on starting a textile dyeing business like the one in Mombasa.

It was this growing business empire that supported the Mamati clan through the *wanjala*. Geoffrey set aside a couple hundred shillings every day to provide food for the family. He helped to pay for the school fees for his younger brothers and sisters. When illness struck, he bought the medicine. Francis was enormously proud of his son. Things were beginning to work as he had planned. The climb out of poverty began with education, he believed. Geoffrey would show the way for his siblings. The second oldest son, John Willy, worked as a building superintendent in Nairobi; he often sent money home to his parents. The two oldest girls were at design school in Bungoma.

Geoffrey, who built a small house on the family *shamba*, talked often with his father about how the farm could become a family business. It matched Francis's dream to grow vegetables in addition to the maize. Already, they had a "treaty," as Geoffrey called it. The father would grow tomatoes, which the son desperately needed as stock for his stews. Instead of Geoffrey having to buy from a vendor, they would keep the money in the family. They could do the same for potatoes and beans and bananas, all things that Francis liked to grow.

"We are lifting Wanjala from your name," Geoffrey told his father with a laugh. "Now you will be known as Wekesa, the harvest."

THE DEVELOPMENTS on the Mamati *shamba* were precisely what Leonida wished for her family. The children, with their high school educations, would get better jobs and help her through the tough times.

But on June 2, a call interrupted that dream. It was Gideon. Principal Mutambo had told him that he once again would have to leave Milo High and return with money if he wanted to continue his studies. Leonida didn't even have the two hundred shillings for him to get a bike ride back home; she told her son to stay with relatives near Webuye.

Where would she come up with the tuition money? She still owed twenty thousand shillings. That amount was impossible, but maybe, she thought, the principal could be persuaded by another down payment. She and Peter did a quick assessment of their options. Their oldest son, Francis, had gone to Kakamega to live with relatives and try to find work as a carpenter in the city, but he hadn't earned any money that he could share. The only asset on the *shamba* of any great value that they would be willing to sell was their remaining calf. They asked around. The best offer they got was for fifteen hundred shillings. It was a ridiculously low amount, but offered in the knowledge that desperation was growing in the hunger season and people needed cash. Leonida was determined not to let the *wanjala* force her into making bad decisions. Selling the calf for that price would have been foolhardy, for it was worth five or six times the offer. And she wouldn't even consider selling the bigger cows, for then she would have no milk and no income.

Instead, Leonida sold their small radio. She got four hundred shillings from a neighbor. To that they added one hundred shillings from milk sales. On June 4, Peter, clutching five hundred shillings, pedaled the bike to Milo High. There, he met with Principal Mutambo, handed over the money, and said they were working on more. Mutambo said Gideon could stay in school for the rest of the day. That night he would review the situation.

Back on the *shamba*, Leonida's mind was working feverishly. Maybe they could get the principal to write a letter for Gideon to attend the high school in Lutacho. It wasn't the same standard, but at least Gideon would have classes to attend. Last June, Gideon had also been sent home from Milo, and he missed more than a week of class as Leonida found buyers for her tree saplings that she had received from One Acre. This year she had also been trying to sell trees, but there was no market. Who could afford to buy trees when the maize price, now at 130 shillings for a *goro-goro* and rising, was at record highs?

Until the call from Gideon, Leonida had been focusing her worry on paying off her One Acre credit. She had been slowly whittling away at it through the year, but she still owed about half of the forty-five-hundred-shilling amount. Now she sat in her living room, resting her head on the back of the chair. She was tired of the daily struggle for food and money. But here was another big decision: Should she pay the school or pay One Acre?

They were both vital for her future. She so wanted Gideon to finish his studies so he would advance into the senior class at school. But she also needed One Acre to keep improving her farm. In fact, she wanted to expand her participation with One Acre, eventually joining the ranks of what were called "super farmers," those with two acres or more.

Leonida had two thoughts, one of relief, one of regret. It turned out to be good that she hadn't been able to rent the extra half-acre of land for One Acre maize; if she had, the size of her One Acre debt would be double what it was. But she wished she still had the maize from her last harvest; if she sold it now, at nearly five times the price she received in January, she could have paid for two years of high school tuition instead of less than one-half.

While Leonida worried and strategized, Dorcas and Sarah came home from school and walked into the house, followed by a reddish-brown chicken and a tiny marmalade kitten. Then Jackline entered, having first stopped by the kitchen to see what was for lunch.

"Nothing!" she declared firmly to her sisters. The fire was cold.

Jackline, a shy girl who looked like her mother, was feeling the strain of the *wanjala*. It was the time of the year when she needed the most strength for her schoolwork, as preparations began for the tests that would qualify her for high school. On most nights she returned to school for a couple of hours of additional learning.

Leonida walked with her and then met her again after class so she wouldn't be alone in the dark. Jackline knew Gideon's education was draining the family's assets, forcing her to sacrifice, but she understood. She was hoping to follow him to high school next year.

That night, Leonida heard from Gideon. Principal Mutambo accepted the five hundred shillings and would allow him to stay in school. Gideon relayed Mutambo's suggestion: first come up with ninety-five hundred by end of term in July, and then ten thousand when the new term started. Leonida was grateful for the window of time. It helped her make a decision. She would focus on the One Acre payment.

Two days later, Leonida was chopping wood for the kitchen fire when Dorcas and her orphan cousins came home from school early. It was mid-morning. They had walked to school and then were turned around and sent back home. The principal couldn't afford to keep them in school, and continue to feed them, without a contribution from the family. The school itself was running low on food. He had little Dorcas carry the message: bring some money.

"Money, they want money?" Leonida asked her daughter. "Everybody wants money." She laughed sarcastically and shrugged. "That's life. Money is life."

Peter, who was tending to the cows, walked over to see what was so distressing his wife. Leonida continued to vent. "In Kenya, there is no free education. That was just election promises," she said. "The government won't change the time when school fees are due so we can get a better price for our maize. The politicians don't help us. They are there just to help themselves. The common people down here are suffering, and they don't even know."

Dorcas had gone into the house, sat in a chair in the living room, put her head down on the table, and fell asleep. The marmalade kitten climbed next to her and curled up in a ball. These two little

creatures, a kindergartener and a kitten, usually so frisky and full of life, were exhausted. Leonida worried that Dorcas was coming down with another bout of malaria.

Leonida was still steaming over the constant money pressure from the schools when Kennedy rode his bike into the shade of her avocado tree. He, too, had come about money. He reminded Leonida that farmers who paid off their One Acre credit by mid-June would receive a free *jembe*, and the group that was the first to complete all payments would win a female goat. The goat's off-spring, as they came, would then be distributed among the members of the group. Kennedy kept the payment rankings on a blackboard in the Assemblies of God church where he held his group meetings. *Amua* was currently in first place.

Leonida told him about her money woes. Kennedy, wearing a green Gatorade baseball hat, scanned the *shamba* and said, in a teasing tone, "Leonida is a very rich farmer, look at all she has growing here. The problem is she doesn't want to work hard for a profit. She has all these trees to sell."

Leonida, bristling at the suggestion of laziness, shot back that there was no market for the tree seedlings. "Why don't you bring the buyers here?" she asked. "Otherwise, you are just telling a story."

Kennedy softened his tone, encouraging Leonida to find a way to make the payment. He wanted her to have that *jembe*; it would also happen to make Kennedy look good within One Acre if he could report early and full payment from all his farmers. Together, they walked into her maize field and were quickly engulfed by the green stalks and leaves. "It looks pretty good," Kennedy said. He pointed out that a few stalks were under siege from grasshoppers. And he noticed some leaves that were fading green, indicating weak soil. The previous sugarcane crop had

taken its toll on the nutrients, as had been feared. Kennedy predicted Leonida would harvest about eight bags on her half-acre. Leonida said she would keep fighting the weeds and hope for a bag or two more.

Kennedy pedaled away, off to inspect other *shambas*. Leonida set out to visit Agnes, the leader of *Amua*. Agnes had just returned from her field where she had been weeding and smiled broadly when she spotted her old friend. They sat on a bench under a shade tree. Agnes, too, brought up the subject of money. Gently.

"We know it is difficult, we know you are trying," Agnes said. "But if you don't pay, we won't win the goat. It is up to you." Leonida was one of two *Amua* members who hadn't yet paid off the credit. Agnes said once Leonida paid, the other one wouldn't have any more reason to delay.

Leonida felt ashamed and embarrassed. She was a village elder, people looked up to her; she needed to lead by example, not follow. She told Agnes said she would somehow raise the money in the coming days.

"I won't let the group down," she promised.

UNDER THE THATCHED ROOF in Kabuchai, Zipporah decided to sell her calf to pay off the One Acre credit. Sanet, summoning his trading skills in a tough market, engineered a good deal. If he sold the calf directly, he reckoned he would get about six thousand shillings, which wouldn't be enough to cover their eighty-eight-hundred-shilling credit. Instead, he traded the calf to a neighboring farmer in exchange for five sheep. Sanet then took the sheep to a livestock market where he heard they were in demand. He sold all five sheep for nine thousand shillings. Zipporah then paid off the credit at the next One Acre meeting and had enough left over for a *goro-goro* of maize.

Sanet was proud of his trading touch. Zipporah was happy to have one less worry. They could have used the money to buy food during the *wanjala*, but that again would have been robbing from the future. It wouldn't lift them out of their poverty, only prolong it. Now, when the harvest came in, they wouldn't be under pressure to sell any maize to clear the credit. It would be all theirs—hopefully making this their last hunger season. And the maize in the field was looking better every day. The cobs were stretching to full size. The Biketis were optimistic they could reap twenty bags, which would be a miracle in their eyes. Everything was riding on the harvest.

Until then, the daily struggle continued. A couple of nights a week there was nothing for dinner. Like on June 6. That day there had been just rice for lunch. The next morning, they began the day with a cup of tea, no milk. By lunchtime, going on twenty-four hours without food, David was whining with hunger. The mangoes on the neighborhood trees were beginning to ripen; Zipporah found one that seemed ready to eat. It was the size of a baseball. She handed it to David, who attacked it like an apple, biting through the green skin into the juicy yellow pulp. It didn't last long. He asked his mother for another.

Zipporah flinched. "The children, they don't know, they just want to eat," she told Sanet. "Sometimes children don't know the hardships that their parents pass through. Our oldest, he understands that we don't have anything."

Just then, Cynthia came walking home from school carrying a blue plastic bag bulging with mangoes. Zipporah had given her twenty shillings the day before in case she passed any *shambas* with ripe fruit. Cynthia took the bag to the cooking room. When David heard the word "mango," he perked up and ran to greet his sister. He emerged from the house with a mango in one hand and juice and a smile all over his face.

"The younger ones, they just want to eat," Zipporah repeated. David was still coughing. Tabitha was battling malaria. "When you lack food . . . " Zipporah began to say, then dropped the thought.

When you lack food, she knew, your immune system is weakened. Undernourishment was behind most of the illness in the rural areas. It prolonged malaria cases, added to the weakness of pneumonia, sapped strength for fighting off stomach ailments. It was particularly bad during the *wanjala*.

And yet, "We don't see many cases of malnutrition brought to us. People are ashamed," said Carolyne Nganga, the nurse at the Kabuchai Health Clinic, which was just a short walk through the fields from Zipporah's *shamba*. People came to the clinic seeking treatment for malaria, dysentery, and various respiratory infections—even sexually transmitted diseases. They picked up malaria bed nets and family planning brochures. Yet few bothered to take the information about balancing diets, diversifying from the carbohydrates, capitalizing on the nutrients in various plants that grow wild on the *shambas*. Nurse Carolyne believed that mothers were reluctant to acknowledge that their children were malnourished. The other illnesses came from mosquitoes or dirty water or from other children. Seeking treatment for malnourishment would be an acknowledgement of their own failure to properly feed their children.

Where the health workers did see malnutrition was when they canvassed the community house by house. Then they saw plenty of distended bellies. "We tell them how it can be prevented. Use simple foods that are on the *shambas*," nurse Carolyne said. "But they don't do it. They think it won't help."

Janet Kundu had the same experience at the pharmacy in Lutacho. "I educate parents about a balanced died. Fresh fruits, a glass of milk, greens," she said. "But I've come to learn one thing from my customers: they forget to balance the diet. It's all *ugali* all the time."

About one in every three children in Kenya suffered stunted growth, and one in five were underweight, Kenya's Public Health and Sanitation ministry reported in the middle of the *wanjala*. Malnutrition was said to be the underlying cause of 53 percent of deaths among children under five.

Internationally, childhood malnutrition was moving up the humanitarian agenda. The governments of the United States and Ireland, along with a host of NGOs, had launched a campaign called 1,000 Days, the period during the mother's pregnancy to the child's second birthday. Without proper nutrition during that time, when brain development was especially critical, a child would likely never reach full physical or mental potential, costing the family and society dearly.

While Leonida and Zipporah struggled to properly nourish their children, some very big brains were worried about these little brains at a Feed the Future symposium in Washington, DC, sponsored by the Chicago Council on Global Affairs in May. Bill Gates, his voice rising, said, "If you have malnutrition as a child, you never (fully) recover." He pointed out that applied to about 40 percent of children in Africa.

Rajiv Shah, the administrator of the United States Agency for International Development who had once worked for the Gates Foundation and had helped to launch their global agriculture initiative, said this diminished potential of Africa's children should not only rattle humanity's conscience but also outrage its economic sensibility. The consequences of such profound malnutrition reach across borders, he said, as the economic lethargy it precipitates undermines real global growth.

"Thirty years ago, we thought stunting was simply a symptom of children who weren't getting enough to eat—a physical manifestation of scarcity," Shah said. "About ten years ago, we started to get economic data that conclusively showed that a population too malnourished to work suffered long-term economic consequences. Individuals suffered a 10 percent reduction in lifetime earning potential, while countries saw 3 percent annual reductions in their GDP."

Most recently, he noted, doctors, scientists, and development workers began studying magnetic resonance imaging scans (MRIs) of the brains of malnourished children, comparing them with scans of children who had been properly nourished. The brain size of the chronically malnourished child seemed to be smaller, with severely impaired neuron development. "Clear in those images," Shah noted, "is the stark and permanent loss of individual human potential. We could begin to understand that a child suffering from malnutrition at a young age has diminished her lifelong potential before the majority of her life has even begun."

Then Josette Sheeran, the director of the World Food Program, took the stage and forcefully waved copies of some brain scans. She traveled the world with those scans in her purse, producing them with powerful effect whenever anybody needed convincing on the impact of hunger. She said that optimal brain development occurred in the first two years of life, making it critical that young children received the vital protein, iodine, iron, zinc, vitamin A, and fatty acids. Hunger, she noted, was more than a lack of food, it was the absence of micronutrients as well.

Shah had sharpened a fine point on this idea. "Yes," he said, "the world must increase its productive yields over the next decades; that much is clear. But let us remember the true yields of food security. Let us remember the fundamental American value that says everyone should be given the opportunity to fulfill their God-given potential to live a healthy, productive life."

Then he pricked Congress with that fine point: "The next time we debate the necessity of the investments we make in food security, let us remember what is truly lost when we turn away."

TWO DAYS LATER, meeting in Deauville, France, the leaders of the largest industrial countries, known as the Group of Eight, or G8, had a chance to increase investments in food security. They turned away.

French president Nicolas Sarkozy had intended to use the summit to again train the leaders' focus on hunger and food security and to revitalize the commitment the leaders had made at their summit two years earlier in L'Aquila, Italy, when they pledged $22 billion in aid to boost the production and nutritious quality of food in Africa and elsewhere in the developing world. The L'Aquila Food Security Initiative was crafted to reverse the neglect of agricultural development with "sustained and predictable" funding, and "to act with the scale and urgency needed to achieve sustainable global food security" by working with governments in vulnerable countries and regions to develop and implement their own agriculture strategies.

But Sarkozy's hoped-for focus on agricultural development was instead obscured and downgraded at Deauville by the Arab Spring and the world financial and debt crises. The G8 leaders pledged $20 billion to support Tunisian and Egyptian reforms following the revolutions that toppled long-standing dictatorships in those countries. And they said international financial institutions, whose purse strings they controlled, would be ready to inject billions more into the region, even in the midst of the global financial crisis. The Deauville Declaration described the G8's other deliberations under these headings: Internet, Global

Economy, Innovation and Knowledge, Green Growth, Nuclear Safety, and Climate Change and Biodiversity. Then, about two-thirds into the Declaration, the G8 finally got around to agricultural development.

There was no new money and little enthusiasm. The Declaration said the leaders "decided to be even more accountable regarding our respective commitments to development, peace, and security," and were "committed to stand even more strongly side-by-side with the people of the African continent." And, the leaders added, "We will intensify our efforts to foster sustainable agricultural production and productivity with an emphasis on smallholder farmers, including through public and private partnerships and research and innovation." They kicked any action on new money or urgency to a larger summit meeting, known as the Group of 20, scheduled for later in the year.

NGOs closely monitoring the summit assailed the Declaration's high-minded but hollow words, charging that the G8 leaders were failing to keep their promises of two years earlier to end hunger through agricultural development and support of smallholder farmers in the world's poorest countries. The critics focused on the G8's own Deauville Accountability Report, which conceded that since the L'Aquila Food Security Initiative, "G8 countries have struggled to maintain their official development assistance commitments." It acknowledged that only 22 percent of the L'Aquila pledges on agricultural development had been disbursed. That was two years into the three-year commitment.

The ONE campaign, an advocacy movement pushing for policies that would eliminate hunger and extreme poverty, named names in its "Agriculture Accountability" report, following the Deauville summit: "Canada and Italy have disbursed more than two-thirds of their pledges. France, the UK, and the United States need to make substantial disbursements in order to be on track. . . . Meanwhile, Germany, Japan, and the EC (European Community) are difficult to assess because they have not yet reported any disbursements, for various reasons."

The report further charged, "The G8 and other major donors are not approaching agriculture and food security with the urgency they deserve. . . . A major injection of political will and good faith are needed without further delay to leverage support from other donors, recipient country governments, and the private sector."

ONE reminded the leaders that the promises they made were to "real people in peril, real people whose lives and futures depend on better aid for agriculture, food security, and rural development." Real people like Leonida, Rasoa, Francis, and Zipporah.

L'Aquila was President Obama's first major summit on the world stage. He put into action his and Secretary of State Hillary Rodham Clinton's early rhetoric that ending hunger through agricultural development would be one of the prime legacies of his administration. The other G8 leaders had come to Italy ready to pledge $15 billion to a new food security initiative the president had proposed in the wake of the shortages and soaring prices and tumultuous protests of the 2007–2008 global food crisis. But Obama pushed for more and eventually increased the pot to $22 billion. He persuaded his fellow leaders with an emotional appeal straight from his family experience. He reminded them that his father had traveled to the United States fifty years earlier from a small farming village in western Kenya, and that some of his family relatives still lived there as farmers. He hastened to note that his relatives weren't going hungry but that hunger was real and ever-present in those villages. He said the food security initiative was needed to help hungry farmers "become self-sufficient, provide for their families, and lift their standards of living."

THOSE WORDS HAD AN ECHO in that small farming village in western Kenya in June 2011. "The main things as a small farmer are education and feeding yourself and your family," Sarah Ogwel Onyango Obama said as she sat under a sixty-year-old mango tree on her *shamba*. She was more popularly known as Mama Sarah or Granny Sarah, step-grandmother of President Obama and the woman who helped raise the president's father, Barack Obama Sr., near the town of Kogelo.

It was still the same dusty village that President Obama described to his G8 colleagues two years earlier in Italy, except now there was a "Yes We Can Tea Room" and a small building named "Yes We Can Investments." It was near the equator, about a two-hour drive south of Bungoma. The Obama *shamba* was several kilometers outside the village, past the Senator Obama Kogelo Secondary School (Motto: Endeavor to Excel). A man who pointed the way stuck out his palm and asked, "What do you have for me?" Boys with sticks and machetes herded goats down the dirt road—just as Barack Senior once did.

Cows and chickens and sheep and rabbits roamed the yard of the Obama homestead. It was surrounded by maize and Napier grass and banana trees. In this way it was a typical, western Kenya *shamba*. But in other ways, it was very different. A satellite dish sat atop the blue roof of the brick house with the neat, blue window trim. There was electricity and a metal fence with an armed security detail at the gate.

"Agriculture is the main lifeline of this community," Granny Sarah said. "The president's father went to school through the sale of agriculture produce."

Granny Sarah once grew a crop called green grams, resembling lentils, which she sold in the larger town of Siaya to raise money to pay for Barack Obama Sr.'s early education, which eventually led to Harvard. She told the president-to-be about this during his visits to Kenya as a younger man. He hung on her every word. "So Barack got interested in farming," she said, "and he knows how important it is."

In her eighth decade, Granny Sarah walked slowly from her house to a chair under the mango tree. "I am an old lady," she said. "My knees hurt. I need more energy." She had organized a group of seventeen neighboring farmers so they could order seeds and fertilizer in bulk and negotiate a cheaper price. After the harvest, they put aside some maize and other crops to feed their families and then sold the rest to local schools. "One of our main objects is for farmers to have dignity," she said. "When you have to beg, you lose your dignity."

Two large mangos fell from the tree, hitting the ground with a thump, thump. She leaned back in her chair, as if to avoid them, and laughed. She wondered, could America help her group of farmers market such produce? Africa's smallholder farmers and their governments were too weak, she worried, to make a dent in world trade.

"What the government is doing is not enough," she said. "You may find only one tractor for a whole district. Seeds aren't enough. The American government and others, even the European Union, can come in with aid and supplement the work of the African governments."

It was a fairly good description of Feed the Future, though she hadn't heard about it. But, she added, "I hear that Barack's involved in programs to help our development."

She didn't know specifics, but she herself was big on technology and research. Her *shamba* was involved in projects to eradicate the tsetse fly and to control disease and pests that attack maize. "African farmers' problems are more infrastructure-related," she noted. "They need technology." She watched a few white clouds move across a blue sky. "Rains are unpredictable," she volunteered. "We have to cushion ourselves against a drought."

INDEED, ONE OF PRIME GOALS of the L'Aquila initiative and Feed the Future was to increase investment in agricultural research and science. While the *wanjala* and the drought intensified in Kenya, some farmers were beginning to test the potential of two promising scientific advances: a maize variety that would be more tolerant of drought conditions (providing the cushion Granny Sarah sought), and a separate maize variety that would more efficiently use nitrogen in the soil.

In the semi-arid region of southcentral Kenya, farmers reported only three short periods of rain, with weeks of drought in between, since the February planting. Yet in June, Philip Ngolania stood amid a field of maize near the town of Machakos. His maize stalks were thin and anemic-looking compared to the sturdy stalks of western Kenya, yet they still produced uniformly large ears of corn. "Without this new seed, I'd have nothing," he said. "Nothing, like my neighbor."

His neighbor's maize was shriveled and dead, the stalks having toppled in their feebleness; there wasn't a cob to be found. The difference was that Philip had planted the new drought-tolerant seed developed by Kenyan breeders, and his neighbor hadn't. The neighbor, and many of the farmers in the area, clung to the traditional, local maize called *mbembasitu*, which meant "our own maize seed."

"My neighbors, they asked me for my secret, why I have cobs and they have none, and I tell them, 'It is the variety I use.' I'm telling them they must change from the *mbembasitu* to this new variety," Philip said.

The Drought Tolerant Maize for Africa program, which was funded by the Bill & Melinda Gates and the Howard Buffett foundations and led by the International Maize and Wheat Improvement Center (CIMMYT) and the International Institute of Tropical Agriculture, developed that new variety. The goal was for national agricultural research institutes to develop drought-tolerant maize varieties and get them into the hands of 30 to 40 million smallholder farmers on the continent.

"The rain is very little here, but even with a little rain, the seed does well," Philip reported to representatives of CIMMYT and Dryland Seed, a private company that was multiplying the drought-tolerant seed developed by Kenyan breeders. As the late-morning sun intensified, Philip took off his jacket and hung it on one of the maize cobs. The cob and the stalk held firm, refusing to bend—proof that the drought hadn't conquered all.

Farmers, Philip said, needed to adapt to newer technology because "the climate is changing very fast. Ever since I was born, I haven't witnessed drought seasons like this year and last." That would be since 1942.

The drought-tolerant seeds cost Philip 270 shillings for two kilograms. He bought four kilograms. The farmers who used the *mbembasitu* seeds from their previous harvest paid nothing. Philip reckoned he had made the better investment.

"Yes, it's more expensive, but at least I'll have something to eat," he told his visitors. "My neighbor paid nothing and he gets nothing." Philip estimated that he would harvest about four ninety-kilogram bags of maize on his three-quarters of an acre; that would be a meager harvest in western Kenya, but in Machakos it was a miracle bounty given the lack of rain. His neighbor, in contrast, would need to purchase maize on the market for more than three thousand shillings a bag. Next year, Philip confidently predicted, his neighbor would be buying the new seed.

Several hundred kilometers to the north, at the foot of Mount Kenya, other maize stalks were also defying the odds. They were standing tall in a trial field where the soil had been intentionally depleted of nitrogen, one of the essential nutrients for maize.

"If you want to feed the people, you want to give the farmers materials that perform best in their soil conditions," said Charles Mutinda as he waded into a thicket of stalks. He was a maize breeder at the Kenya Agricultural Research Institute in the town of Embu, and the coordinator of KARI's participation in the Improved Maize for African Soils project. The goal of the program overseen by CIMMYT was to improve maize varieties so that they would use nitrogen in the soil more efficiently. The project's lead funders were the Gates Foundation and USAID, with American seed company Pioneer Hi-Bred providing some maize traits to breeders in Kenya and South Africa.

The tricky thing about his stress tests, Mutinda acknowledged, was coming up with varieties that thrived in poor soil without further depleting it. "The fear is that we give farmers materials that actually worsen the soils."

Actually, they could hardly get much worse. African soils are some of the poorest in the world. For generations, farmers tilled the same plots, often with the same crop, year after year. The soil had no time to rest and replenish. The smallholder farmers couldn't afford to let an inch of land lie fallow. Nor did they practice much crop rotation, the method of planting different crops in sequential seasons in order to restore certain nutrients to the soil or to prevent the buildup of pests or pathogens that occur when one crop is constantly grown. Also, African farmers used less than 10 percent of the world average amount of fertilizer.

"When I was young, there was no hunger," Mutinda said. "The land was plenty, there was enough space to plant." The soils weren't under such relentless attack. But as the population has grown, family plot sizes have shrunk. The farmers are under annual pressure to squeeze as much out of the soil as possible. Maize, Kenya's staple crop, has been a notorious taker. Mutinda was looking for maize strains that would give back, or at least take away nitrogen more judiciously; perhaps he would even find a strain that required less fertilizer, which was the farmers' top expense.

"The smallholder farmers," Mutinda said, "need all the help they can get. And Africa needs more food."

USAID was pumping $2.2 million into this project. It was Feed the Future at work. Mutinda, walking through the test fields in a gray suit with a pink-striped shirt, went about his work unaware that this benefactor of his was undergoing its own stress test in Congress. But he did know it would be impossible to conjure up crops for Africa's depleted soils with depleted funding.

MEANWHILE, as the hunger season ground on, One Acre's quixotic quest for a better bean seed was becoming a classic African parable of development breakthroughs bottled up by bureaucracy. The effort to pry the beans from the "innovation valley of death" and from the hands of the "Lords of Hunger"—two epithets often heard across the continent for those who dragged their feet on new attempts to reduce hunger—was proving to be a cautionary lesson for the ambitions of Feed the Future.

Frustration was rising on all fronts of the bean crusade. For One Acre's Seth Silverman, time was running out to find a better bean seed by the second planting season, which would begin in August. But even if it came too late for this year, he knew it was a vital quest for the future. Reuben Otsyula, the breeder who had developed the seed Seth was seeking, was becoming disillusioned that his work wasn't moving from his lab to the farmers' fields. And Joe DeVries, who managed the seed program of the Alliance for a Green Revolution in Africa, was losing his patience. DeVries, an old Africa hand who knew patience was perhaps the ultimate virtue on the continent, had sharply communicated with officials at KARI, where Otsyula worked, pointing out the "non-availability of seed of the bean variety, KK-8." Otsyula's research was originally developed through a collaboration between the Rockefeller Foundation and KARI. A subsequent grant from AGRA continued to support the breeding work.

DeVries noted that several seed companies had requested the seed varieties from the breeder so they could multiply it and make it available to the farmers, but they hadn't received any. He feared that breeder seed was languishing in storage with no benefit to farmers and at high risk of spoiling. AGRA, he said, wasn't funding the breeding activities for the sport of it, but to benefit hungry smallholder farmers in Kenya.

On an early June morning, Otsyula and DeVries met in western Kenya to try and liberate the bean seeds, to get them out to the *shambas*. Seth would join them later in the day.

"We should never assume anything in this business," DeVries told Otsyula. They were having coffee with the director of the KARI Kakamega station. "If the beans don't get to the farmers, then it's like we did nothing." DeVries took off his green cap and ran his hands through his hair, which once was a youthful sandy brown. "The seed problem is the reason for all my gray hairs," he said. His mantra had become: release the varieties.

He noted that One Acre and a private seed company, Leldet, were keen to get Otsyula's bean varieties into the hands of the farmers but had been stymied in their efforts by government regulatory institutions acting as gatekeepers over all breeding material. "It seems strange," DeVries said. "It would seem KARI would want to get behind this."

The director nodded. "The process was slow at headquarters," he said. "We are very positive things will move now." He blamed policy makers at the national level big-footing the scientists. Kenya's new constitution, he noted, put more power into the hands of the local counties, where agriculture was far and away the main livelihood. "The county government has to have a voice, to say here's what we need." He was optimistic. In fact, KARI would soon confirm that it would be releasing Otsyula's beans to Leldet, to begin the process of commercialization.

As he drove with Joe to inspect some trial bean plots at the KARI station in Kakamega, Otsyula unwound the curious odyssey of his beans. He had identified the source of resistance to root rot and bred varieties for the mid-altitude, high rainfall area around Bungoma. They thrived in demonstration plots, and word spread that a better bean had been developed. In 2008, KARI released the seeds, but rather than granting the license to a seed company, exclusive rights were awarded to a small Kenyan NGO. "They never mentioned anything to me about it," Otsyula explained. "I had no idea why they did that."

"I don't know if we'll ever get to the bottom of it," Joe said.

The NGO didn't do anything with the seeds. They weren't multiplied. They weren't made available to the farmers. Otsyula heard that the NGO had scaled back its agriculture activities, that the manager left to get a PhD in America. He didn't know why. He just knew that his seeds were stuck on a shelf. It took a year of legal wrangling by KARI to dislodge the exclusive rights and to then award non-exclusive rights to Leldet, which meant other seed companies could also get in on the action. It would mean more beans for more farmers. Finally, Otsyula could see success.

Through all the frustration and disillusionment, Otsyula had continued working with select farmers to demonstrate the benefit of the little black beans. Not only did they survive disease, but they were tasty. They fetched a good price on the local market, more than maize. And, as an added bonus, they were early maturing, ready for eating in May, long before the maize would be ripe. The beans were said by the farmers to "meet the hunger." They shortened the *wanjala*.

Seth had heard about these "whiz bang" properties, as he called them, and was anxious to see how the beans performed. He joined Otsyula and DeVries on the *shamba* of Rose Tamnai in Chwele, near Bungoma. She had been harvesting the trial beans for several weeks already. The three men marveled at her field, their frustrations melting away.

"You must be happy that your work is finally meeting success," Seth told Otsyula. Seth himself was ecstatic to see the beans in action. He thought of the possibilities.

"This year, we need fifteen tons of bean seed," he said. "Next year, we'll need forty-five tons."

"That's what I want to hear, tonnage," DeVries replied with a big laugh.

Otsyula said the next step was to promote the beans' advantages and build demand.

"Marketing and creating demand for bean seed isn't challenging for us," Seth said. "Our challenge is access to the seed."

DeVries turned to Rose, who seemed overwhelmed by the sudden attention. "Many farmers need these beans," he said. "You have given us confidence. We'll get these beans to One Acre. They will get them to thousands of farmers. You have done a wonderful thing."

IN THE LUGULU HILLS, Leonida, weary and achy, felt another bout of malaria was coming on. Still, she was in a downright giddy mood that had nothing to do with her fever. As Kennedy stopped by for another visit, she came bounding out of her maize field, her *jembe* at her side. "I have paid off the One Acre credit," she proclaimed triumphantly. Her bare feet and hands were covered in the red-brown mud of her field.

She wore the relief of someone who had thrown off a heavy burden. After her promise to Agnes that she wouldn't disappoint her *Amua* colleagues, Leonida had decided to sell some of her chickens and her newly ripe avocados to raise the eighteen hundred shillings she still owed. Her strategy was to knock off one worry—the One Acre credit—and then move on to resolving the next—school fees. Up until then, she was nibbling away at each and eliminating neither. Finally, in the second week of June, her load was lightened a notch.

"My happy is so great," she told Kennedy, who was also beaming.

Leonida's joy was magnified by one other development. While she hacked away at the weeds with her *jembe*, she noticed that the beans she had planted beneath her maize stalks were beginning to ripen. She picked one and put it between her teeth to test the texture. Then she picked some more. They were borderline ready to eat. But in the hunger season, borderline didn't matter. Nor did she care that her beans weren't the wonder crop Seth was seeking; at this time of the year, a little looked like a lot. Leonida harvested a couple of handfuls of beans and laid them out to dry in the sun. They were an array of colors—red, auburn, gray-blue, speckled brown-and-white. That evening, she boiled them and mixed them with some of the maize she had bought the day before with milk money. For the first time since the day she planted, her family ate *githeri*.

It was the beginning of the end of her *wanjala*. Leonida's One Acre maize harvest was still two months away, but now she would have a supply of beans—her homegrown beans—to make up some meals.

"A good day," Leonida summarized in her diary. "One Acre is paid. Food is here. I relaxed."

CHAPTER 5

WEKESA

(The Harvest)

Leonida's respite was short lived.

The morning of June 12 she awoke feeling exhausted, sore, and feverish. The malaria was biting harder. She remained in bed while Jackline did the milking. Once the sun was up, Leonida also rose. After a cup of tea, she walked the thirty minutes to Janet's pharmacy in the market. There was already a scrum of people waiting on the concrete stoop under the rusted-metal awning, most of them also seeking malaria medication. Janet gave Leonida some mild painkillers to relieve the hurt and attack the fever. When Leonida returned home, she learned that Peter, also weakened from a tussle with malaria, had fallen off his bike while making the milk run in Webuye. He scraped his foot badly and was being treated at the hospital.

The rains were a blessing for the health of the crops but a bane for the farmers' health. With all the standing water, malaria was ravaging Malaria. On June 15, Leonida answered a call on her cell phone. It was Milo High with the news that Gideon had fallen ill and urgently needed malaria treatment. The next week, Leonida answered Dorcas's sobs. Her youngest was shivering with a malarial fever. Again, Leonida hurried to Janet at the pharmacy. Janet searched her shelves and gathered a number of tablets. Leonida, clutching 150 shillings, offered to pay. But Janet told her she would add the charges to Leonida's tab. "Buy some food," she told her friend. It would be better for Dorcas, who needed to eat while taking the medicine. Leonida walked to a nearby maize seller. She handed over the 150 shillings for a *goro-goro* and kept her hand out for the change. But there wouldn't be any. The price of maize had hit a new seasonal high, rising 15 shillings from the 135 she had paid a few days before.

At the same time she was battling malaria on several fronts, Leonida was also fighting the village chief's office in the land case. She traveled the region, appealing to higher authorities, often with Pastor Fukwo helping out on the transport cost. Every office she visited asked for money. The land office said it would cost 47,000 shillings to search for the deed. A human rights office asked for 4,000 shillings to take up the case. The secretary of one magistrate said he could help for 8,000 shillings.

"Without money, you can't get help?" Leonida pleaded.

"That is the way it is," she was told.

She left every office no closer to resolving the issue than when she had entered.

One afternoon, as she returned to her *shamba*, Leonida was approached by a woman from a neighboring village. The woman said she had run out of food and was hoping that Leonida, as a village elder, could give her and her five children shelter and a meal for an evening. "No," said Leonida, who herself was depending on the goodness of her pastor and pharmacist. "I'm sorry. We can't afford it."

Leonida, who prided herself on being a good neighbor and a fair elder, felt awful. The wait for the harvest, which was draining their physical strength, was even sapping her kindness.

THE WEEKS THAT LED UP to the harvest were a time of rising nervousness and tension and desperation, as the resources of individuals and society were stretched to the limit. In contrast, the maize on the *shambas* had rarely looked so good. The plump cobs were a source of temptation and neighborhood covetousness. A fully fenced-in *shamba* protected behind high barbed wire was unusual, so hungry passers-by could easily strip off cobs from the outside stalks. The maize was still too moist to grind into flour for making *ugali*, but it was nearly ripe enough for roasting, with the succulent kernels harboring a delicious sweet taste. The only way to stop the pilfering was to begin the harvest and move the cobs into the storage bins, which were closer to the houses and easier to keep an eye on. For the harvest to begin, though, the farmers still needed the weather to cooperate.

The Lugulu Hills had received several peltings of hail; some bursts were so heavy that chickens had been killed and cattle spooked. Maize leaves were shredded in the pounding, and stalks bent in the wind. Leonida, Rasoa, Zipporah, and Francis had all lost some stalks, but so far, by the end of June, the losses had been minimal. Now, the farmers were praying for the rains to taper off so the cobs could begin drying on the stalks.

"Almighty God, you have provided the rains we needed. We are very happy," Francis prayed at the close of a harvest preparation meeting of the Kabuchai farmers at the Baptist Church. "Now as we approach the harvest, bless us with sun and dryness so we can harvest to our full potential and get more bags than ever before. We are at your mercy. Amen."

Farmers everywhere in the world were at the mercy of the weather. The more technologically advanced among them could ward off drought with irrigation systems. And those blessed with farms in the rich parts of the world had long had access to crop insurance to protect them financially from natural disaster. That provided a measure of confidence for farmers to take up new innovations and any added expense of planting. But the vast majority of farmers in Africa had no insurance. In Kenya, only about 3 percent of the population had any kind of insurance, and those people lived mainly in Nairobi or other urban areas. The insurance companies offered protection for the large commercial farmers, but they ignored the smallholders, dismissing them as too poor to pay premiums. Thus, the smallholder farmers had been left on their own to carry the risk of an inherently risky business.

It was another forehead-smacking aspect of African farming that had Andrew Youn looking for a better way. He knew that if One Acre or any other initiative, such as Feed the Future, hoped to boost production by getting farmers to adopt new practices and technologies and to pay for it, they needed to also provide a hedge against some of the added risk. Risk mitigation would also be important to assure the sustainability of One Acre's funding model. If a crop failure left the farmers unable to pay off their One Acre credits, the organization would have to cover the losses by scrounging up more donor funding so it could again purchase the seeds and fertilizer for the following year.

So along with providing access to seeds, fertilizer, financing, and farming extension advice, One Acre added one more item: access to insurance. The Kenyan insurance company UAP and the Syngenta

Foundation for Sustainable Agriculture had just begun developing an innovative micro-insurance program for smallholder farmers called Kilimo Salama, which meant "safe farming." One Acre tailored a similar product to its farmers.

The insurance was included in the One Acre credit package, amounting to about three hundred shillings for a half-acre. The centerpiece protected farmers against drought or deluge, reducing the amount they would have to pay back if a lack of rain or too much rain destroyed the maize crop in their particular district. The rainfall amounts were to be measured by small weather stations, some based at schools, where there were historical records to provide a baseline; each station covered a radius of fifteen to twenty kilometers. There was also death insurance: should a One Acre member die after receiving the seeds and fertilizer, the loan would be forgiven and any payments refunded so the family wouldn't be burdened with the debt. And under consideration, funeral insurance: if a member or spouse died after input delivery, the family would receive a twenty-thousand-shilling payout.

"If you ask people to be more productive, which essentially means to take on more risk and make an investment, take money out of their pocket and spend it on seed and fertilizer instead of school fees, if you ask them to do this and you don't mitigate the risk, it's not very responsible," said Rose Goslinga of Syngenta. "You can't be surprised if the farmer is reluctant."

She was sitting on the porch of the Matulo Girls School (Motto: Brighten Your Future) with her laptop open to a spreadsheet of the weather for the past month. The school, down the hill from Leonida's *shamba*, hosted the local solar-powered weather station. It was a curious contraption, the main feature being a tall, thin metal pole with a rain gauge on top. The rain fell into a spoon, which tipped the water into a measuring cup, which fed the information straight into Goslinga's computer.

"The chance for drought in this area is once every fifteen years," she said, staring at the spreadsheet.

Goslinga had developed her first insurance project several years earlier in Rwanda while working with that country's forward-thinking agriculture minister Agnes Kalibata. It was coverage for tomato farmers with an irrigation system; they wanted protection in case there was a drought that would dry up the river that fed the irrigation pipes. After she moved to Kenya, Goslinga focused on insuring maize farmers. "Maize is simple and measurable: if it doesn't rain, it doesn't grow," she said. "Maize is straightforward."

But convincing farmers of the need for insurance was difficult. "People don't trust insurance in Kenya. To insult someone is to say, 'You are such a broker.' To be an insurance broker is an insult," she said.

But Kilimo Salama's credibility grew after insurance was paid out to hundreds of farmers following a drought in the Mount Kenya region in 2009. "It was a great thing because I paid out to the farmers, but it was also depressing because the farmers lost a crop," Goslinga said.

"That helped with our believability," said Joseph Kamiri, the UAP executive in charge of Kilimo Salama. "Maybe farmers don't know about insurance, but they can relate to severe weather. They've all seen it."

Kamiri himself had a farm where he grew tomatoes and green peppers in a greenhouse, in which, he said, "I control the weather." But he grew only one-quarter acre of maize because his area lacked a weather station and thus was out of the range of Kilimo Salama. He understood the risk-averse nature of smallholder farmers because he himself shared their attitude. "My thinking is that a lot of other farmers plant maize, so I'll buy from them, and I don't have to have the risk of maize farming. A lot of people say that they don't want to do the maize thing, because you spend the money and you might not harvest anything. If I get a weather station in the area, and insurance, I'll go back to growing more maize."

For Leonida and the other smallholders of western Kenya, maize was a primary asset, so they lived with the risk. At a meeting of *Amua*, Agnes Wekhwela said that the insurance provisions of the One Acre credit offered her some welcome peace of mind. She was in her seventies, way past average life expectancy in rural Kenya. "If I die and still have a loan, my family is protected," she said. "And if something happens to the crop, we are protected." Knowing that, Agnes said, helped her sleep better.

Leonida wished that the One Acre insurance could help with the daily disasters in her life: children being sent home for school fees, raging malaria, soaring maize prices. "The insurance doesn't help us along the way with our life, only if there are problems with drought," she said. Being battered on all sides for money as she was, Leonida didn't much see the purpose of paying in advance to cushion a blow that might never happen. Allaying future catastrophes was a luxury when there were so many worries in the present. "I already have enough problems that don't let me sleep at night," Leonida said.

ON A LATE JUNE MORNING in Kabuchai, Rasoa awoke to a terrible shock. She opened the door of her house, ready to begin a day of work in the field, and found one of her calves lying dead at her feet. It was Vestergaard, the calf she had purchased with the money she earned distributing the water purifiers. There was no outward sign of violence or distress. It seemed to be fine the night before when Rasoa returned from visiting relatives. "When I woke up, it was dead," she told her family.

It was a huge blow to their 401(Cow) plan. The death of the calf, which had cost them sixty-four hundred shillings and was being counted on to grow in value and cover future education fees, was like a sudden five-hundred-point drop in the Dow Jones Industrial Average with no sign of a reversal. Rasoa knew it was a risky investment, that living things die, that no investment was safe. But who could plan for the death of a creature so young?

Cyrus was baffled. He suspected the calf had eaten a poisonous insect or plant, or that something had gone haywire in the digestive tract. It was the second time a family cow had an untimely ending. A few years before, one of the Wasike cows was felled by internal bleeding. It turned out that somebody had beaten and abused the cow with a stick. The reason why anyone would do that remained lost on the family. But it raised suspicion that perhaps Vestergaard had been intentionally poisoned. Perhaps by a jealous neighbor? Cyrus tried to banish such thinking from his mind. No, he concluded, no one he knew would do that.

"We must just let it be," Rasoa told her boys, who were stunned by the death. "That's the way it is. Just accept it."

The family gave away the meat to anybody who wanted it. They couldn't bring themselves to eat poor Vestergaard.

A few weeks later, Cyrus would open an account at the Cooperative Bank of Kenya in Bungoma. It was a *Haba na Haba* account—Little by Little—which encouraged customers to start small and build an account, which could later provide the basis for a larger business loan. Cyrus began with a five-hundred-shilling deposit, which would be safe from poisonous plants or illness or who knows what.

He gave a copy of the ID card to Rasoa. "I think this is safer," she said. "I'm very happy now."

ELSEWHERE IN KABUCHAI, Zipporah's and Sanet's maize was looking particularly promising. Amos, their One Acre field officer, had come by for an inspection and predicted they would reap twenty to twenty-five bags. They were delighted to hear this, but they also felt a bit unsettled; it was a wonderful outlook but also problematic. Where, they asked themselves, would they store all that maize during the drying process, after it was picked and before it was shelled and put into bags for longer-term storage? Last year, they had less than two bags to handle.

In late July, Sanet began to build a storage bin. He figured he could do better than the typical round hut made of sticks and a thatched-peaked roof. Instead, he would construct a rectangular shed. For the floor, which would be raised a few feet off the ground to aid air circulation, he would lash together rough-hewn tree poles. The maize stalks, once the cobs were harvested, would form the walls. The roof would be a metal sheet. It would be the first metal roof on the *shamba*.

The thatched roof of the house was now leaking in two places, a new hole having appeared over the living room. But the house would have to wait for its metal roof. First things first. Keeping the maize dry and preventing mold and deadly aflatoxins was the top priority.

"The maize needs to have a better roof because the most important thing is you need to eat," Sanet told Zipporah.

She agreed, "A person can run away when it rains. But maize can't run."

As he worked on the storeroom, Sanet was already thinking ahead, looking toward next year. There would be a national election for president and the parliament, and the feverish campaigning, he reckoned, would distract the farmers from their work. It was a Kenyan political ritual that candidates hit the campaign trail with wads of crisp fifty-shilling notes in their pockets. After giving a speech full of promises, the candidate would walk into the crowd, hand out the money while pleading for votes, and hint that there would be more after the election.

Farmers run from their fields to join the rallies when they hear the loudspeakers mounted on trucks announcing a candidate's arrival. That's where Sanet envisioned his advantage. "People will be working less in the fields," he told his wife. "They get up in the morning looking in what directions the politicians will move that day. They go to Kabuchai or Chwele or Bungoma. They leave their work in the *shambas* to get some easy money. I've done some research. It seems the year after an election is usually tough in the country; there's not enough food."

Zipporah nodded her head. "So, isn't this an opportunity?" Sanet reasoned. "When people are running here and there after the politicians, I will be working hard in my *shamba* to increase production. I might even rent more land so I can make more profit."

He might end up with fewer fifty-shilling notes pressed into his palm, but Sanet believed diligent labor in the field would more than make up for it with greater yields. And with good storage facilities, he would be able to hold their maize until the price hit its zenith.

Zipporah, though, was focused on this season's harvest; for her family, it couldn't come soon enough. On July 25, Sanet's mother gave them five kilograms of *ugali*. It had been three weeks since they last ate *ugali*; maizemeal had become such a rarity during the *wanjala* that the staple food became a luxurious treat. They were surviving on pumpkin leaves and whatever rice and vegetables Zipporah could pick up at the market or pick from the plants that grew wild on their *shamba*. They had also begun to eat some of the beans they had planted with the maize.

But it wouldn't be long now until the maize itself was ready to harvest. "Just one more week," Zipporah told her children as they came from school for a lunch of boiled pumpkin. "One more week until we harvest our maize and we have our own *ugali*."

A grin spread from ear to ear. The harvest was so near, she could taste it.

AT THE END OF JULY, Gideon came home from school, trudging up the hill to Lutacho from Webuye. This time, though, it was for the vacation that followed the completion of the second term. He had made it this far. But he returned to the *shamba* carrying an ominous message. It was a "Dear Parents" letter from Milo principal Albert Mutambo.

"All parents should pay all the school fees for this year," he wrote. "Students whose parents have not paid all the required fees will be sent back home for fees when they report back to school. NO PROMISES."

He ended with an appeal: "Thank you for supporting the school, especially your son/daughter, for paying fees, guidance, and upkeep. Give more support and be hopeful for better results."

"He wants cash, and he means cash," Gideon told his mother as he handed over the letter. He reported that the payment of the nearly twenty thousand shillings still owed was due on September 7, when parents come to the school the day after the beginning of the new term. It would be an especially important time for Gideon and his junior-level classmates, for they would be sitting their exams in late October. The scores on those tests would determine which students advanced to the final year of high school. If a student was sent home and didn't take the exams, they weren't promoted. All the scrimping and sacrificing during the year would have been wasted.

Gideon was happy to be home, assisting his parents and sisters with the daily chores. He looked after the cows, fetched water, and pulled weeds in the maize field. He was also using the break to put a new layer of mud on the walls of the storage hut where he slept.

Dorcas was eagerly helping her big brother, carrying the mud from a pit behind the banana trees. They were both covered in mud from head to foot.

Gideon liked agriculture studies more and more in school. Here on the *shamba* he could study the soil directly and observe the impact of rain and pests; he hung a blue pen on the collar of his ragged, green Billabong T-shirt, in case he wanted to make any notes. At night, by the light of the kerosene lamp, he read assiduously and studied math. He wanted to set an example for his younger sisters.

But being home also brought Gideon into direct contact with the sacrifices that were being made for him to remain in school. They were painful reminders. He knew meals were often skipped at home during the *wanjala*. In school, he came out of his afternoon studies and walked into the dining hall where a warm meal awaited the students every night. Sometimes, he would fast for a day or two in school to be at one with his family on the *shamba*.

On the afternoon of July 28, Leonida and her children were all eating beans and maize out of plastic bowls. Gideon and Jackline also roasted cobs that came from the small, early maturing maize crop their mother had planted separately from the One Acre plot. Leonida had forbidden any premature picking of the One Acre maize because she wanted to precisely measure the yield at harvest time. That One Acre crop was still several weeks from harvest, but she knew even that wouldn't be enough to raise the amount needed to cover the remainder of Gideon's tuition. The day before, Leonida had paid the Lutacho Primary School to keep Jackline and Sarah in class until the end of the year: 60 shillings for Sarah, 150 for Jackline. Now she stared at the letter from Gideon's principal and wondered what she would do. The money pressures for education were relentless.

The next day, another letter arrived. It was from the director of the Kenya Anti-Corruption Commission in Nairobi, housed in an office called Integrity Center. It must be about the land case with the chief, Leonida and Peter thought. They hastily ripped open the envelope. Addressed to Peter, the letter said, "Kindly be advised to seek the intervention of the Provincial Commission Western Province. You may also consider seeking civil redress in a court of law to safeguard your rights over the parcel of land."

The letter concluded with the slogan: "On the frontline against Corruption."

Leonida looked at Peter. "This is our land forever," she exclaimed. They had won. Federal authorities were trumping the maneuvers of the chief's office and the money-grabbing, foot-dragging of local officials. Leonida said they must now remain determined to reclaim the money they had spent trying to resolve the case, money they otherwise would have spent on school fees and food. "This ruined my plans for the children," she said. "This brought anger to our land."

She also determined to pursue one other thing: her own piece of land. It would be in her name, to do with it as she wanted, to one day pass it on to her daughters (girls had been routinely passed over when it came to land inheritance in rural Kenya). It was a long-range goal, as an acre cost about three hundred thousand shillings. Her dream was to have a *shamba* big enough to grow plenty of food to help all those in the village who fell short, especially the widows who had no property of their own after their husbands died. Land, Leonida believed, meant independence and security.

For the moment though, it remained a distant dream. She was still scraping for every shilling to handle the daily realities.

On August 2, the *Amua* farmers gathered with Kennedy and members of other groups at the Assemblies of God church for some harvest training. Rather than sit inside in the stifling heat, they moved the meeting outside to the breezy shade of a row of trees. Kennedy used some cobs from early maturing maize to demonstrate the best ways to dry the One Acre harvest in the sun and how to shell the cobs when ready. Each One Acre member received a simple gray metal sheller—a hollow cylinder with ridges on one end. Kennedy inserted a cob and rapidly twisted his wrist back and forth, spinning the cob through the sheller. The kernels fell off easily. If the maize was too moist, he said, the sheller wouldn't work as effectively; the kernels wouldn't fall so quickly. Then it would be better to shell with bare hands, which was hard on the fingertips. Properly drying the maize, he noted, would make this work easier; it was also important to ward off weevils and mold.

After the demonstrations, Kennedy handed out "maize storage tracking" charts to each farmer. They were to record each time they consumed or sold a bag of maize. It was a One Acre tool designed to make the farmers more aware of how they used their major asset, and how proper storing and patience in selling would allow them to take advantage of higher prices later in the year rather than be further impoverished by them. Kennedy then announced that *Amua* was in the lead for the goat that he would be presenting to the group that first cleared the One Acre loans. His chart behind the altar in the church showed that *Amua* had collectively repaid 46,000 shillings of the 53,750 shillings its members owed. Only one member, Esther Burudi, was far behind on her payments, and Agnes and Leonida were lobbying her and her husband to scrape up the money. The chart indicated that 60 of Kennedy's 158 farmers had cleared their loans; 70 percent of the loan total had been repaid. He was confident it would be close to 100 percent before the harvest began. For the past several years, the repayment rate across One Acre exceeded 98 percent.

Already, new members were signing up for next year. One was fifty-five-year-old Margaret Inyuma, who lived across the dirt path from the church and would be joining her friends in *Amua*. She attended the pre-harvest meeting and explained how this growing season had been a disaster for her. First, she overpaid when she bought seeds and fertilizer on the market; she spent more than eight thousand shillings on inputs for her half-acre, which was double what One Acre members paid. Then, without the group discipline of One Acre, she had planted after the first rain in early March. That rain had turned out to be a tease, so her seeds languished in the soil for a couple of weeks until the rains began in earnest. She hadn't used the One Acre method of planting, instead scattering the seed and fertilizer unevenly over her half acre. Now, as the harvest neared, she said, "I look at the One Acre maize and I look at mine and there is a big difference. Your maize looks beautiful, and mine doesn't." She was expecting to reap only four bags at most. That would be less than half the yield of the One Acre farmers for twice the cost.

"It's very expensive to farm on your own," Agnes Wekhwela said. "And you won't get any better yields."

Leonida told Margaret that she could look forward to better days next year. "Our profit from One Acre is what we *learn*. We have the knowledge," she said to her friend. That was one of Leonida's most fervent beliefs. "Knowledge is power," she often told her children.

As the meeting ended and the farmers returned to their *shambas*, Leonida lingered. She scoured the grass where they had been sitting and picked up all the kernels that had been shelled during the demonstration, furtively squirreling them away in her purse. She didn't do it to be tidy; she did it because the kernels would help to stretch that evening's *githeri*. She was a proud woman, but not too proud to pick up the scraps.

EARLY IN THE MORNING of August 5, in the thatched hut near the rocks of Kabuchai, Zipporah's soft, beautiful voice was all that stirred in the silent pre-dawn darkness. "There is no other like God," she sang in a whisper.

It was just after six on the first Friday of the harvest month. Zipporah struck a match and lit two kerosene lamps, which eerily illuminated the mud walls of her living room like fire brightening a cave.

"Oh God, I'm fine," she sang. "You are worthy of my praises today."

Their early maturing maize variety was ready for picking.

At 6:30, Sanet emerged from the house carrying a machete in his right hand. He was wearing a gray shirt and tattered black pants with white pinstripes. The shirtsleeves were rolled up to the elbows, the pant legs up to his knees. Barefoot, he walked twenty yards to the very edge of his maize field and looked heavenward in supplication. He spoke into the thicket of stalks bowing before him with their heavy, ripe cobs.

"Thank you, Father. This is the day you planned for me to take my harvest," he prayed. "Look after everyone on my *shamba*, so no one gets hurt. Keep us safe. You control everything in this field. Since I planted this maize, you have taken care of it. Now I see the results of your work. I will remember the results of my field."

Just as he said "Amen," he raised the machete above his head and brought it down with a quick, violent slash. Then, in a blur, came a second slash. *Whack, whack.* He cut down two stalks of maize at dirt level and then, *thump*, threw them to the ground. He moved swiftly. *Whack, whack, thump.* Two more stalks added to the pile.

The maize harvest, so long anticipated, had begun.

Inside the house, Zipporah faced the light of her lamps. She said her own prayer of thanksgiving. "We worship you, Oh God, because you are about to unleash a miracle on us. Help us, Oh King of Glory, to realize the work of our seeds. There is none like you upon our earth, Dear Jehovah."

With that, she picked up a yellow plastic jug and hurried to the field to greet her husband. Sanet paused and searched his pockets for a few coins. He gave them to his wife. It was money for milk, for the morning tea. Their own cows, in the dry cycle, had stopped producing milk. Zipporah walked to the far end of the field and turned left for the market, her singing voice trailing in her wake like perfume trailed women in the big cities.

Sanet returned to work, establishing a rhythm of his own. *Whack, whack, thump. Whack, whack, thump.* Chickens followed at his feet, pecking at worms and insects uncovered in the freshly disturbed soil. Roosters crowed, summoning the day's first light. Cows mooed. Those were the only sounds except for the coughing of little David.

Shortly after seven, Sanet paused to check a text message on his phone. Help was on its way. A few minutes later, one of his brothers, Oscar, arrived and immediately set to work with his machete. Another brother, John, soon joined, and then came Job, a friend from church. Together, they formed a chorus of slashing machetes. *Whack, whack, thump* in surround sound.

The Biketi children were at work, too. The oldest, Samwel, gathered sticks, and together with his younger sisters coaxed a fire to life in the cooking room. They retrieved water by lowering a bucket into their well twenty steps from their house. They filled a kettle and began making tea over the red-hot embers. Smoke was billowing out the window when their mother returned with the milk.

Zipporah crouched beside the fire and stirred a pot of beans. She mixed in some kernels of maize from the cobs of the freshly felled stalks. While the *githeri* simmered, Zipporah hastened to the field and joined the harvest.

As the men continued to whack their way through the maize with their machetes, Zipporah and a few neighbor women and fellow One Acre members who came to help began yanking the cobs off the stalks. Then they removed the husks, leaving them in the field so any bugs wouldn't be brought into storage. Whenever a new husker arrived, Zipporah pulled out a paring knife tucked in the band of her skirt and whittled away at the end of a thin stick, forming a pointy end like a freshly sharpened pencil. That crude device made the husking easier. The women poked a hole at the tip of the cob, where the silk formed, and then effortlessly stripped away the husk.

The huskers, too, settled into a rhythm: twist off the cob, poke a hole in the husk, strip it away, toss the cob in a pile. Twist, poke, strip, toss.

By 9:30, nearly a dozen people were working in the field, the men wielding the machetes and the women plying the sharpened husking sticks. They had made good progress, more than half of the one-acre field was cleared. Zipporah retreated to the house and retrieved the pot of *githeri* from the fire. Carrying bowls and spoons along with the pot, she returned to the field and served up breakfast to the workers, complete with tea and milk.

The work stopped and conversations began. While whacking and husking, the farmers had frequently stopped to read the text messages that had been arriving on their phones from the network providers. The cell phone companies were part of a campaign soliciting contributions to a fund—Kenyans for Kenya—that would aid fellow Kenyans desperate for food in the drought-stricken regions of the country. The irony wasn't lost on the farmers of Kabuchai.

"It's not right; we're eating and our neighbors are dying," Zipporah told a group of women who were gathering up the cobs. "Look, here we're harvesting a surplus while others are starving.

Can't the government come and buy from us to feed them, rather than importing maize as food aid?"

Sanet chimed in, complaining that the maize pricing had gone haywire again, once more to the disadvantage of the smallholder farmers. As they harvested, the farmers switched back to being maize sellers rather than buyers. Now, a high price was good for them. But the opposite was happening. As freshly harvested maize entered the markets of western Kenya, the record price that had battered them so badly during the *wanjala* began to plummet, even though ever more relief food was needed to feed those suffering from the drought. In these economics, there was no winning scenario for the farmers. When they were maize buyers, the price was high; now that they were sellers the price was coming down.

Standing knee deep in cobs and stalks, Sanet said, "This maize is going for fifty, sixty, seventy shillings per *goro*, while it should go for over two hundred. There's such demand in this country. We see that in these text messages. But there's lack of a market for our maize; instead food aid maize is being brought into our country. That takes away our market and undercuts our price. If we can have enough of a market and get a good price, we can be successful farmers and we can produce more."

When the *githeri* pot was empty, the work resumed. By 11:15, the field was cleared and the men put down their machetes to join the women with the husking. Sanet retreated to the edge of the field where a neighbor, who was a carpenter, was finishing the construction of the storage shed. The wooden frame and metal roof were already in place. Now, Sanet and his friend used the stalks that were just cut and stripped of cobs to form the walls of the shed. Sanet smoothed the stalks and the carpenter lashed them together, side by side, with string-like threads he tore from the husks.

Shortly after noon, with the sun bearing down through a clear blue sky, Pastor Isaiah Wekesa Makandayi arrived with members of his King Jesus Faith Ministries Church congregation to help fellow parishioners Zipporah and Sanet. It was fitting that the pastor came, given his traditional name—Wekesa, the harvest. And he was the miracle worker who had broken the curse on the neighboring plot of land the year before, which had convinced the Biketis to join One Acre.

There were now thirteen adults and four children husking. Even David and some of his friends were pitching in; they sat on the ground by the house, playfully pulling off the husks and covering their heads and faces with the silks. They laughed like they rarely had during the *wanjala*.

As the piles of maize grew in the field, the cobs were stuffed into large plastic bags, which were then hauled to the storage bin. Sometimes four women were needed to carry a single bag, with a woman on each corner. This backbreaking work would continue for hours into the early evening.

"Work hard so we can produce more food," Pastor Isaiah exhorted the team. "We can be an example of what the Bible says: 'God will bless the work of our hands.'"

He believed that was all that had been necessary—hard work and God's blessing—to break the curse of the field on the other side of the dirt pathway beyond Sanet and Zipporah's *shamba*. In the cadence of a modern-day parable, from a new Book of Isaiah, the pastor explained what really happened on that land:

> The person who was on the land didn't work it properly. He tried and never got anything, and he gave up. That man gave the land to me to farm. I had joined the One Acre Fund, and I followed the instructions I was given. I applied it over all the land. The results of the harvest were so good that the man who gave me the land to

farm couldn't believe it. He said, "Pastor, you have managed to overcome the witchcraft that was there." Now, it's true the land didn't produce anything before, but the man didn't plant well, and he didn't do the weeding. He said, "This land is no good; it's cursed." But the land isn't cursed. I managed to get eight bags of maize from that land that had produced nothing. God did a miracle for me. He helped me to plow well, to uproot the weeds, to make the land green. I used a lot of energy to uproot the weeds. The weeds were the witchcraft. If somebody comes to me and says, "My land is cursed," I say, "Give it to me, or join One Acre Fund to get more knowledge about how to work the farm, to get more harvest." A miracle from God? God came through One Acre Fund to us to give us this knowledge of how to work the land to harvest a greater yield.

The pastor then shifted from the ecclesiastical to the political. "If our government would support the farmers . . . "

His phone buzzed; a new text message arrived. Pastor Isaiah read another plea to contribute to Kenyans for Kenya—the goal was to raise five hundred million shillings in four weeks to aid three million people. The pastor shook his head. "Here we have a good rain, and others in our country have no rain," he said. Then he finished his earlier thought: "If our government supported the farmers, we could really prosper."

In the Kabuchai market, fifteen minutes away by foot, Sanet's earlier price calculations were confirmed. In the general stores, maize was selling for 80 shillings per *goro-goro*, down dramatically from the 150 shillings just several weeks earlier. The merchants, however, were buying the maize from the farmers for just 60 shillings.

Pamela Wangila, a One Acre farmer who also sold maize from her general store, saw the price madness from both sides. "We wish the government could come and buy from us at a higher price rather than importing from other countries and paying transport costs as well as the cost of maize. Here we have a surplus, and this maize is grown here in Kenya, so the Kenyans who eat it will enjoy it."

Pamela was a member of Rasoa's One Acre group; they stood together on the veranda of the shop, trying to make sense of what to them seemed like nonsense. George Masinde, a county councilor of Bungoma, seeing a gathering of two voters, stopped to add his thoughts. He chose a populist tone.

"It's a major concern," he said of the prices. "When farmers go to the government shops to buy government-imported fertilizer at planting time, the price is so high. Now, at the time of harvest, when the farmers can make some money, the government brings in maize and drives down prices. If the government can come and buy with a reasonable price, our farmers can go on and prosper. The government should give our farmers first priority. And if there still isn't enough food to feed the country, then they can import."

Pamela and Rasoa looked at him with expectant eyes. Wasn't he in the government?

The politician shrugged. He reminded them that he was also a One Acre farmer who would soon be harvesting his own crop and wrestling with the falling prices himself. He, too, had been receiving the text messages to contribute cash to Kenyans for Kenya. He agreed it was a horrible tragedy—countrymen suffering while he and his neighbors were bringing in good harvests—but that some good could come from it if Kenyan farmers benefited from supplying the aid organizations. He suggested a better name for the campaign: Kenyans *Feeding* Kenya.

A TWO-HOUR DRIVE from Zipporah's *shamba*, at a warehouse in the large city of Eldoret, food aid was arriving from around the world to feed hungry Kenyans who had been hit by the drought.

Much of it was being rushed to the World Food Program warehouse from the port of Mombasa on Kenya's east coast—the opposite side of the country from Kabuchai near the western border. The bags of food—maize, beans, peas, and a maize-soybean mix—were labeled with the flags of donor countries: USA, Japan, South Korea, and the nations of the European Union.

On a drizzly and chilly August morning, a flock of workers scurried to unload the trucks coming in and to load others going out. It was an urgent transportation shuttle to and from the drought-stricken areas. WFP officials, including one wearing a Santa hat, choreographed the movement with precision. "It's unseasonably cold," said Daniel Onyonge, explaining his Santa look. "Also, it feels like Christmas every day here with the food aid coming in and out."

Some of the food would be bound for the East Pokots region, where 66,000 people were being fed by the WFP; earlier in the year, the number was 26,000. Josiah Bunde followed some of the trucks heading to a smaller warehouse near the town of Marigat high in the central hills. While the people in need of the food aid were suffering through a severe drought, that highland region was having an overdose of rain. On the drive, the WFP trucks sloshed over roads that became fast-flowing streams of water rushing down from the hills. "The water harvesting in Kenya and Africa is terrible. It's quite sad," Josiah said as he watched the water runoff. "Today these people will complain about the mud. One month from now, they will complain they have no water. There should be efforts to collect all this rainwater for the dry times of the year."

At the Marigat warehouse, the constant shuffle of trucks arriving and departing had turned the parking lot into a mud pit. Inside, the scene resembled the One Acre input distribution day back in February. One conga line of strong-shouldered men toted heavy bags of food from the arriving trucks to the mounds of stockpiled food,

while another conga line moved from the mounds to fill trucks waiting to depart. The warehouse belonged to the National Cereals and
Produce Board, just like the One Acre warehouse in Bungoma, but
the international humanitarian NGO World Vision operated this
one. The workers scurried past signs bearing World Vision exhortations such as, "Be the Change You Desire—Promote Peace."

In less than thirty minutes, two trucks just like those that carried
One Acre seeds and fertilizer to farmers in February were filled with
195 bags of maize, 59 bags of peas, and 26 cartons of cooking oil.
Their destination was the village of Kipnai, deep in the bush, where
290 households of farmers and herders desperately awaited deliverance from starvation.

The drive to Kipnai followed a tortuous route once the paved
highway gave way to a wretched dirt road peppered with jagged
rocks. The road, if it could be called such a thing, descended from
the moist, green highlands to parched, unforgiving terrain of scrub
brush, flat-topped acacia trees, and randomly scattered boulders. It
took the WFP drivers, veterans of such jarring misery, three hours to
cover 100 kilometers.

Kipnai was about 200 kilometers total from Kabuchai, where
Zipporah and Sanet were bringing in their harvest. But none of their
maize was included in the shipment. There were yellow split peas
and maize flour and fortified vegetable oil from the United States,
and maize from Uganda purchased by the WFP with donations
from Japan. The trucks arrived at a small, metal-sided shed that was
a house of worship belonging to the Africa Inland Church. *Yesu ni
Bwana*—Jesus is Lord—was written on the sheet metal wall behind
the altar. The church now became a warehouse, as volunteers, most
of them women, unloaded the trucks, staggering under the fifty-
kilogram bags. One of the women wore a red T-shirt proclaiming
"God Is Faithful" on the front, and on the back "All Things are

Possibble." The spelling mistake had likely confined it to a goodwill donation in America or some other English-speaking precinct that then made its way to Africa.

Two World Vision workers hopped on a motorcycle, the one in the back carrying a microphone and loudspeaker. They sped through the scrub brush announcing that food aid had arrived. Scores of people, many of them elderly, emerged from the bush and slowly made their way on foot to the church. They were men and women, heads of households, struggling to feed their families amid the disastrous drought. They were very thin and lethargic, each a story of woe.

"This year, it didn't rain on time, so I didn't plant any maize. No one planted maize," Salina Achau told Josiah from the WFP. She was sitting on a rock in the stingy shade of a thorn bush outside the church. She was cradling a heavily swaddled infant, the youngest of her six children. Salina, who was forty-three years old, was draped in a loose yellow dress embroidered with a red-and-yellow flower pattern. It couldn't hide her protruding shoulders and collarbones. Her limbs were like twigs, her cheeks hollow, her eyes tired.

She would normally plant a half-acre of maize; last year she had harvested nearly five bags. But she had abandoned all hope of planting maize in April when the rains failed. Instead, she sowed some millet seeds, a sturdier grain. "But it all withered and died," she said. There was no end in sight to her *wanjala*.

Salina, like the others gathering at the church, were mainly goat herders. To buy maize and other food beyond what they were able to grow themselves, they would usually sell a goat. But with the drought, the goats had less to eat and they, like their owners, were little more than skin and bones; their market value had dropped to less than one thousand shillings each from more than two thousand. The herders were reluctant to sell their major assets for so little. And given the escalating price of maize, they wouldn't be able to buy much food, even if they did sell a goat.

Salina's family hadn't eaten maize, their staple food, for nearly three weeks, since July 24, she remembered. That maize had been shared among her women's group, which was able to pool money to make a small purchase at the market that was a three-hour walk from Kipnai. "We try and support each other," Salina told Josiah.

Now they were dependent on the support of strangers from places they couldn't even fathom.

"We are told this food is coming from America. Where is that? I don't even know where that is," said Lomong Songor, an old man, a walking skeleton, who had brought his own stool to sit on while he waited for the aid.

Josiah asked him how old he was. "Oh, I can't remember," Lomong said. He rubbed his hands over his face. He thought he was about five or six in 1950 when a local uprising was brutally crushed by the colonial authorities. It was called the Kolowa Massacre. He remembered that.

He figured America was three months distant, because it had been three months since their last food aid distribution. He hoped more food was already on the way. "It will be necessary," he said, "because this dry spell will continue."

The World Vision organizers called for a prayer to begin the distribution. Maria Kachumwo, a fervent member of the Africa Inland Church, stepped forward. She was wearing a tattered red baseball T-shirt from America: "St. Louis Cardinals. PUJOLS 5." She had never heard of baseball or Albert Pujols, one of its best practitioners.

Maria raised her hands. "Thank you, God, for the food and for the visitors from abroad," she said. "Your people are in need of food. We thank you that you have responded."

Then the distribution commenced. The elderly were the first to be called. The rations were, per household member: 6.9 kilograms of maize, 2.1 kilograms of peas, 0.4 kilograms of cooking oil.

After a patient wait, Salina Achau received her food and she lugged it back to the scrawny bush where she waited for relatives to help her carry it home. She admired the USAID logo of two clasping hands that was present on most of the bags. "Imagine being fed by a foreign country," she said. "We are grateful."

Salina imagined that the food was shipped by President Obama, who, she believed, wouldn't forget Kenya. She and her neighbors had celebrated mightily nearly three years earlier when the radio brought the news that Obama had been elected. They slaughtered a cow and had a feast.

Now they had nothing of their own. "It would be good if Kenyans could feed Kenyans," she offered. Then she looked at the parched hardscrabble landscape around her and doubted that could happen. "I don't think Kenya can feed itself."

AS SALINA HAULED her food home, and as the empty relief trucks rolled out of Kipnai, Zipporah and Sanet in Kabuchai were filling up their storeroom with their freshly harvested maize cobs. The drying process—taking cobs out of the bin each morning, spreading them out over the rocks behind the house where they would dry in the sun, and then carrying them back to the bin each night to protect them from rain or theft—would take weeks. The Biketis were immensely proud of their bountiful production, and Sanet believed the farmers of Kenya could take up Salina's challenge for the country to feed itself. But it would take more than them just improving their yields.

Here, between Kabuchai and Kipnai was the great African paradox: feast and famine in the same country, separated by only about 200 kilometers. The only silver lining of the hunger spreading through the Horn of Africa would be if the poor smallholder farmers of Kenya could reap higher prices for their surplus maize spurred by the tremendous demand for food. It is what the normal economics of supply and demand would dictate, and it was what farmers like Sanet so desired. But the market, which should direct the food from the surplus areas to the shortage areas, didn't function normally here. Horrible infrastructure—namely wretched farm-to-market roads—disturbed the distribution, and the influx of free food aid and government imports distorted the supply side of the equation.

It was all more evidence of the need to invest in long-term agricultural development in Africa. And it provided another example of how food aid could be reformed by international donors like the United States to do as the residents of Kabuchai suggested: first buy local food that is available, which would provide incentive for farmers to keep growing more, and then bring in food aid if the local supply isn't enough.

A glimpse of how this would work had been on display at the Kipnai food distribution. Among the hundreds of bags of maize and peas from foreign lands were several bags emblazoned with the words "Purchase for Progress." The World Food Program operated this program, known as P4P. The WFP used cash donations from other countries to purchase food grown by smallholder farmers near the hunger zones. The P4P maize distributed at Kipnai was grown by farmers in the southern part of Kenya. The program was just beginning to organize in the western area. It was the kind of market innovation and incentive that Sanet and Zipporah believed could propel them to prosperity year after year.

The harvest they had just reaped was a good start. Sanet looked upon his full storeroom and at the now empty harvested field just beyond. It was the first bumper crop of their lives and a great relief after their difficult *wanjala*. "For now," Sanet told Zipporah, "we are safe."

TONY HALL, the former congressman who led the fast to protest the proposed foreign aid cuts in the United States, was all too familiar with Africa's feast-famine paradox and the tragedy of needless hunger deaths. He had first witnessed it in 1984, in Ethiopia, when nearly one billion people died in a famine while cheap, surplus food piled up in rich countries. The world recoiled in horror at the dying. It prompted the first Live Aid concert and the song "We Are the World" and global cries of "Never Again!"

Back then, Hall traveled to the feeding camps in northern Ethiopia, where overwhelmed and underfunded humanitarian aid workers and doctors had to pick and choose which famine refugees would receive food and which wouldn't, which might recover and which were too far gone, which would live and which would die. Hall looked at the multitudes who had come seeking salvation and then at the limited resources available to help them. He saw people walk across the bone-dry, barren landscape for miles and miles and arrive at the camp thinking there would be food and blankets and medicine. There wasn't. They just laid down and died.

Those searing scenes of utter hopelessness had haunted Hall and driven him to become a champion of the hungry ever since. They propelled him through the April fast, and now they brought him back to the Horn of Africa in August, to Kenya this time, to again see, feel, and smell the need for foreign aid and agricultural development and then inject those senses into the budget debate back home. He believed the rich world, and the United States in particular, could do much to end the paradox.

Hall journeyed to northeastern Kenya to inspect the feeding efforts and was relieved to find that no one was being left to die. He would be happy to report to Congress that U.S. aid—both from the government and individual citizens—was leading the way, that "money that is being donated is getting through, people are being helped. That's a great lesson; these (aid) programs are working. And they work well."

He had just returned to Nairobi from one trip to the hunger relief efforts and would be heading out the next the morning to Dadaab, the sprawling refugee camp in the scrubland of eastern Kenya that was being overrun by tens of thousands of Somalis fleeing hunger and conflict. He was gathering plenty of ammunition to blast away at the budget cutters back home who would slash this aid. He was tired, horribly jet-lagged, but still, he told Alliance to End Hunger colleagues traveling with him, he was eager "to go to Congress and speak to the members that aren't aware of some of the good things that we do, that really speak well of the United States. It's some of the best stuff that we do overseas. A lot of our members are not educated to this, and they need to be."

In fact, before Hall had left the United States, the House of Representatives had passed proposed legislation that would cut 75 percent of the funds going to food security and the kind of emergency hunger relief efforts that he had just witnessed. "This (cutting of foreign aid) is not the United States, this isn't the kind of country that we are," Hall said, his voice coming alive with anger and impatience. "I think righteousness exalts a nation, and this is what we're good at," he said, referring to the relief efforts.

He and his Circle of Protection colleagues had spoken to members of Congress who had no idea of the impact of foreign aid, particularly agricultural development and hunger relief. One congressman acknowledged his ignorance—and his budget-cutting zeal to eliminate foreign aid—this way: "I didn't know what it did; it just had money in it, and I just wanted to eliminate the money."

Hall paused after relaying this story. He winced. "This kind of thinking has got to stop," he said. "I think that there are some people who don't care, but for the most part, they don't know. It's a mystery to me. I don't know if it comes under the heading of stupidity or. . . . It doesn't make sense to me. It's just so frustrating to see this. It comes under the heading of uneducated."

Another pause, another wince. "We have some members of Congress that used to brag that they didn't own passports."

Hall offered a macabre chuckle. "They've never seen a famine, never seen malnutrition. The best way to get anybody's attention, especially a legislator, is to bring them and show them and let them walk around and see it and smell it. When they see it they'll have a change of heart. And if the heart isn't changed, we should get rid of them. God help them."

Rather than getting Congress to come to the Horn—particularly those members who view foreign travel as unpatriotic—a flotilla of concerned Americans, like Hall, were determined to bring the Horn to them. Kenya became a must destination for officials who had been heavily lobbying to preserve foreign aid spending, such as Rajiv Shah, the administrator of USAID; Jill Biden, wife of the vice president; and Ertharin Cousin, the U.S. ambassador to the United Nations food and agriculture agencies in Rome. While visiting with the refugees, they also spoke with the governments in the region, urging them to step up their agricultural development plans. For the African paradox on display in Kenya and the Horn, the simultaneous feast and famine, laid bare the truth that had so long been ignored by the global community: emergency aid won't prevent the next famine, only agricultural development will. And it would be so much cheaper. Food aid number crunchers had calculated that it cost five or six times more to deliver a ton of maize as American food aid to Africa than it did to provide smallholder farmers in Africa with the seed and fertilizer needed to produce an extra ton of maize themselves.

The Obama administration seized on the Horn's feast-famine paradox to push its Feed the Future initiative. On August 11, as Tony Hall and his delegation waded into the hunger camps in Kenya, Secretary of State Hillary Rodham Clinton walked up to a microphone at the International Food Policy Research Institute in Washington, DC.

"We need to rise to the level of this emergency by acting smarter and faster than we have before to achieve both short-term relief and long-term progress," she said in a speech intended for the ears of Congress as much as for anyone else. By the time she spoke, U.S. humanitarian aid to the Horn was approaching $600 million for the year; that was about the same amount some in Congress were preparing to whack from the president's Feed the Future request. "Think of what it would mean if we do succeed. Millions of people would be saved from the current calamity. Millions more would no longer live tenuous existences, always prepared to pick up and move to find food if drought or conflict or other crises occur. Parents would no longer have to endure the agony of losing their children when the food runs out. And food aid from countries like the United States would be needed much less frequently because we are now supporting agricultural self-sufficiency." Clinton unleashed a flurry of one-two punches: short-term relief, long-term progress; invest money now, save in the future. This aggressive strategy had been effective in Ethiopia, she said. That country was requiring much less food aid in this drought than it did in the drought-fueled famine of 2003. Then, thirteen million people on the doorstep of starvation were fed by the outside world. Since then, the Ethiopian government, supported by the United States and other donors, had established the Productive Safety Net Program, which helped smallholder farmers diversify their crops, created local markets, better managed water resources, and increased the nutritional content of their food. That program had helped nearly eight million people, Secretary Clinton said. In the 2011 drought, fewer than five million were dependent on food aid.

"This is still an unacceptably large number, but it is also an astonishing improvement in a relatively short period of time," she said. "And it is evidence that investments in food security can pay off powerfully."

Replicating such progress elsewhere, she maintained, "would be a transformational shift for the people of our partner countries. It would be a new era of security, health and economic opportunity, peace and stability. And it would signal a new chapter in the world's relationships with the people of these countries. As they become themselves able to care for their families, they will become real models and examples of prosperity and stability and they will become partners to do even more to help people live up to their own God-given potential."

People like Sanet and Zipporah Biketi, who had just brought in their harvest—perhaps fifteen times more bountiful than their previous one—while fellow Kenyans were saved from starvation by food brought in from abroad. They so wanted to become the models of the prosperity and stability that Clinton and Obama envisioned.

ONE ACRE'S ANDREW YOUN was one of the few NGO leaders who wasn't rushing to the drought-stricken areas of Kenya and Somalia or visiting the hunger refugee camps and the food aid distribution sites. Instead, he was attending harvest-training sessions for One Acre farmers and helping to clear cobs from stalks.

"The harvest is very rewarding, especially coming right after the hunger season, going from not having enough food for your families to having more than enough to eat," Andrew told a group of farmers near Kabuchai as he joined them in their work. He yanked off the cobs and tossed them into a pile that grew rapidly as other farmers pitched in. "No family can eat all of this, so for the first time they have maize to sell. You can see right here the transition from subsistence farming to farming where they can make a profit."

He estimated that One Acre's fifty-thousand-plus farmer customers would bring in a harvest capable of not only feeding their own families but also, in aggregate, of producing a surplus to feed an additional three hundred thousand people. "Famine is a horrible tragedy, but it should send the signal that more food needs to be produced," Andrew said. "Famine is a wake-up call to the world. As human beings, we respond to emergency needs. But we can't Band-Aid this problem forever. We need relief aid, but the only permanent solution to famine is permanent and sustained increases in food production. We have to invest in long-term agricultural development."

It was far better, Andrew believed, for the world to hear the *whack, whack, thump* of the maize harvest than the cries of the hungry. And far better to accommodate dreams than assuage nightmares.

"Harvest time is a time to dream," he said as he continued husking. "To dream of improving lives, feeding families, sending children to school, investing in livestock. To dream about how to chart their path out of poverty. It's important for the farmers to be able to achieve those dreams. It's important to know that climbing out of poverty is a multiyear process. It takes several years of good harvest after good harvest."

WITH THE HARVEST DREAMS came a new burst of energy on the *shambas*. Like the first rains brought an invigorating freshness after the extended dry season, the harvest introduced a new optimism after the long *wanjala*. Cyrus and his three boys scrambled to put a new, conical thatched roof on their round storage bin. Francis sharpened his machetes and cleared out his storage huts. And Zipporah and Sanet hustled to find plastic mesh storage bags to hold all their maize once it dried. They would need ten times as many bags as last year when they used only two, and they couldn't buy enough through the One Acre package. So the Biketis scoured three different markets before they accumulated twenty bags, paying prices ranging from fifty to seventy shillings per bag.

By the third week of August, the farmers of Kabuchai had completed their harvests. In Lutacho, Leonida had been planning to pick her maize in September, but now she was working double time to bring in the harvest before there would be any more weather damage. Heavy rain had continued to fall on her side of the Lugulu Hills. The rain should have tapered off by mid-July, but a month later it was still coming down. The stalks, heavy with cobs, bent easily with the added moisture. Worried that the next big rain or wind would knock them over into the dirt and mud, where rotting would quickly begin, Leonida decided to move up her harvest by several weeks. So on August 20, a cool, overcast morning, the *Amua* members gathered on her *shamba* and began to pick clean the field like a swarm of locusts. *Whack, whack, thump*, the stalks were cut and stacked. Twist, poke, strip, toss, the husks were removed and piled.

Leonida, wearing a red sweater, long brown skirt, and a yellow-and-brown bandana, orchestrated the action. As the *Amua* team methodically moved across the field, Leonida's three youngest daughters and her two nephews joined them to haul the cobs into storage. They formed a kind of bucket brigade: Jackline and Dorcas stuffed the cobs into bags, the boys lugged them to the yard in front of the house, and Sarah dumped the cobs into a pile. From there the cobs were carried to the round storage bin or to the storeroom where Gideon normally slept.

After several hours, the work was finished. A rare sound of celebration on Leonida's *shamba*—music—was heard. Three musicians, friends of Peter, arrived and spread out on a bench under a row of trees bordering the field. Two men strummed homemade guitars; the third set the rhythm by beating on the bottom of a plastic bucket with his hands. One of the guitar players was dressed in a funky, blue-striped suit that looked like pajamas. The other guitarist had an ear of corn sticking out of his shirt pocket. As they played a jaunty tune, the members of *Amua* began to dance.

It was a festive pause on their exodus from misery to the land of milk and honey. The harvest was in. The *wanjala* was over. Leonida, dancing with her friends, smiled broadly and shouted above the music, "We're changing our lives."

CHAPTER 6

SIRUMBI

(Second Planting)

With the maize harvest in and her family's food supply seemingly secured, Leonida focused on harvesting her other top dream. Along with the daily task of drying the maize cobs—moving them out of the storage bins and into the sun during the day and then moving them back into storage at night—she worked to secure Gideon's place in school for the crucial final term when he would be taking the advancement tests.

Earlier in the year she had applied for financial assistance from her local government councilors under the Constituency Development Fund, which the national budget provided to parliamentary districts for community improvements and education scholarships, called bursaries. But she heard nothing from them. So in August, with the high school principal's "NO PROMISES" payment deadline looming, she more aggressively pressed her case with the officials in Webuye who also covered the area where Milo High was located. Since Leonida was a village elder, she knew the mayor and other councilors from various meetings over the years. And Peter's brother, who lived in Webuye, also knew them. After six trips and much cajoling of secretaries, Leonida finally secured a meeting with the mayor.

She succinctly outlined her financial difficulties, saying Gideon, a top student, would likely have to drop out of school. She showed the mayor her balance of nearly twenty thousand shillings with Milo High. The mayor considered the figures and agreed that it was too much for Leonida to afford. Your Gideon must stay in school, he told her.

The mayor's office gave her the scholarship application. She immediately arranged a bike ride down the dirt road to Milo High, where Principal Mutambo signed the form. Leonida then returned to city hall and handed the application to the Constituency Development Fund office.

Then she waited. Would this be another false promise from a government official? Or would this one actually come through? Those questions were still hanging in the air when Gideon returned to school on September 7. The principal accepted the application as a start; it was a more solid prospect than a promise of payment from a parent. Then, on September 13, Leonida received the words she had been so hoping to read. It was a copy of the letter to the principal of Milo High from Lincoln Barasa, the constituency office manager, referencing the case of Gideon Wanyama.

"We write to kindly ask you to allow the student in class, for his bursary form is being processed and the check for the same will be forwarded to you as soon as it is ready. Thank you in advance."

Leonida closed her eyes and said a little prayer. "God is good," she whispered. A huge burden had been lifted from her shoulders.

It revitalized her dream of her children getting high school educations. Next up would be Jackline, who was now beginning intensive study with her one hundred eighth-grade classmates for the tests that would qualify them for high school next year. Every morning at 5, Jackline left the house to be at school by 5:30 when the studying began. It was still dark, so Leonida walked with her. At lunchtime, Jackline trudged home and then headed back for afternoon classes. She was home again at 5 p.m. for dinner and chores, and then once more returned to school at 6 for evening studies. With nightfall, Leonida walked back to school to meet Jackline at 9, then they strolled home together.

"Work hard," Leonida would tell her daughter. "You don't want to do all this work and end up with nothing."

Jackline's ambition was to become a nurse, and she knew she needed to be good in science and math. Her mother beamed when she returned one day with a graded math test. Leonida read through the word problems:

- Three girls eat meat. One eats one-half kilogram, one eats one-fifth kilogram, and one eats one-eighth kilogram. How much did they eat?
- A mother has 540 shillings to share among three sons. How much does each son receive?
- Lutacho Farm has 96 rows of vegetable stems. There are 96 vegetables stems in each row. How many stems are there?

There were ten questions. Jackline scored 100 percent. Leonida laughed in delight. "I can't do this math, anymore," she told her daughter. "In school, I found it easy, but not today."

Leonida was confident Jackline would do well and qualify for a good high school. With Gideon in his final year, that would mean two tuitions next year. She hoped Gideon's scholarship would continue, and she would try to get one for Jackline, too. But she was also making other plans, counting on the increased diversity of her farm.

The maize harvest had Leonida and the other One Acre farmers looking at their land in a new way; seeing the potential of surplus production spurred them into greater activity in the second planting season, the *sirumbi*, which usually began with the onset of the so-called short rains in September. This year, though, the long rains never seemed to end, so the farmers got busy planting a variety of vegetables once the maize was cleared. In the past, the *sirumbi* had been considered as the lesser growing season because the lighter, shorter rain wasn't particularly suited to maize. One Acre field officers encouraged farmers to plant another set of crops beside maize to diversify their diet and income. Beans were perhaps the most popular second season choice, even though the yields were spotty; they provided an important source of protein and they also nourished the soil, adding nitrogen that would later be needed by the maize. One Acre offered a package of bean seeds and fertilizer for seventeen hundred shillings. But until the organization could obtain a better bean variety that would be resistant to disease that hampered yields, many farmers preferred to plant bean seeds they had saved from the previous harvest.

During the *wanjala*, Leonida had thought hard about her second-season strategy, how she could manage her *shamba* to provide food and income throughout the year. Sweet potatoes would be her main *sirumbi* crop; she would use cuttings from a plot of starter potato plants she had grown by her banana trees. Some of the sweet potatoes were planted between the maize stalks in June and the rest after the maize was harvested. By early September, low, leafy green plants dotted the field where the maize once stood. The first sweet potatoes would be ready to eat in December. Leonida would finish the harvest by February so she could begin preparing the field for planting maize with the advent of the long rains. She was counting on the sweet potatoes to diversify her family's diet, but she was also planning to sell a good portion of the crop to pay school fees.

After the maize harvest, Leonida had also planted cassava and *sukuma wiki* to be ready to eat in May, June, and July, to help hold back the *wanjala*. And she planted a small trial plot of an early maturing variety of maize to see how well it would perform in her soil. That maize, she estimated, would be ready to eat in April.

In addition, twenty-one chicks were scampering around her *shamba*, along with her five hens and one rooster. The chicks had hatched on September 17, and Leonida was quick to get them vaccinated with medicine administered in eye drops. With that protection against rampant disease, she hoped the chicks would survive and grow to be hens and then would be ready for sale in April.

This agriculture strategy to line up food to eat throughout the year also would allow Leonida to spend less on maize. Surplus crops, along with the milk sales, would generate additional income. The chickens would provide a more comfortable emergency cushion for health issues or unexpected school fees. Her remaining quarter-acre of sugarcane would be ready to harvest around June, delivering a mid-year burst of income.

In addition, Leonida had joined an informal savings club with her neighbors, which they called a merry-go-round. The eighteen members each contributed one hundred shillings every Tuesday; each week, one member would get a payout of eighteen hundred shillings. Leonida was planning for her windfall to come in November or December, and she would use the money to pay down her One Acre Fund credit.

She was also pondering the possibility of entering the formal finance sector. After suffering through the punishing maize price fluctuations during the year, Leonida considered a way to harness that roller coaster for her benefit. This was her plan: She would get a loan from the Kenyan Women's Finance Trust—a microfinancing facility for women entrepreneurs—and then go into business as a maize trader. She would buy maize at the mill in Webuye at the bottom of the hill, where the price was usually a little lower, and then bring it back up the hill to sell at a kiosk she would set up at the end of her property right beside the well-trod pathway to church. She would add five shillings per *goro-goro* for her profit. Her customers would be her neighbors, who would pay for the convenience of buying maize within a short walk of their *shambas*. The income would be set aside to pay high school fees, if the scholarships didn't come through.

It was an ambitious strategy, but Leonida had learned so much during the year after her early maize sale and the subsequent struggles to raise money. In the markets, she discovered, timing was everything.

THE FARMERS IN KABUCHAI had also been busy in the *sirumbi*. Francis planted patches of maize and beans with seed that he had saved from the year before, and he also planted onions and *sukuma wiki*. Mainly, though, he concentrated on his true agriculture love: tomatoes. He planted more than two thousand stems, transferring them from seedbeds and carefully tucking them into the soil. According to his plans, this greater diversity would help him turn the market to his advantage. If he needed cash, he could sell vegetables while holding on to his surplus maize until the price increased.

"One Acre has given me the spirit to find money in the soil," he told his wife, Mary, as they nurtured the tomatoes.

Francis had already sold one bag of the early maturing non–One Acre maize he had planted between the rocks, and he bought a solar lamp offered by One Acre for seventeen hundred shillings. It provided better light for his children to complete their homework, and it would also relieve the constant need to buy kerosene. But the lamp also got Francis thinking. He examined the little solar mechanism and wondered, "If I get a bigger solar panel, as big as my table, maybe I could finally watch television." His black FM/shortwave radio was his only connection to news of the world. He had long hoped to buy a television so he could see how other people lived and how farmers in other countries worked.

For instance, he was curious if he could grow tomatoes without chemical spraying. The chemicals were expensive, and he feared they were dangerous. One spray carried a warning about needing to wait two weeks after application before eating the crops. Francis worried that his children would see a ripe tomato and pick it for a snack, unaware of the time frame. Also, he couldn't afford to buy the protective spraying gear. He wore boots and some old clothes when he sprayed, but he didn't have gloves, hats, or a mask.

"If we can escape these chemicals, every person will be free of worrying about what they are eating," Francis explained to his son Geoffrey, who would be buying most of the tomatoes for his restaurant stew. A new shop that offered Internet connections had just opened in the Kabuchai market several doors down from the restaurant. Geoffrey had signed up for an e-mail address and was learning how to navigate the World Wide Web. He told his father he would search "organic" and see what he could learn.

For the moment, Francis was maintaining his old-fashioned vigil, keeping an eye on the weather. The rain needed to stop. A burst of hail a few days earlier had left black spots on some of his tomatoes. Now thunder again rumbled in the distance. "More rain is coming," Francis told Mary. "We really need to build a greenhouse."

ZIPPORAH AND SANET were also keeping their eyes on the sky. Every morning they searched for clouds. If it looked like a sunny day, Zipporah would haul out a few bags of cobs and spread them over the flat rocks behind the house to dry in the sun. If rain threatened, she kept the maize inside. When the maize was on the rocks, Zipporah needed to remain close to home, in case rain appeared; if it did, she would hurriedly sweep the maize into bags. Any cobs left out in the rain would spoil quickly with mold.

A hard surface like the rocks provided an ideal platform for drying. Not only would the sun bear down on the maize from above, but heat would rise up from the rock below. A grassy surface would be moist with the morning dew. In the post-harvest weeks, the paved roads were lined with farmers drying their maize in the sun.

After arranging the maize in the morning, Zipporah headed to the field, where her *sirumbi* crops were flourishing. Instead of a thicket of maize, the one-acre rectangular field was now a lush vegetable garden. Following the maize harvest, Zipporah and Sanet planted peanuts, beans, *sukuma*, sweet potatoes, peas, and a small patch of maize seed the farmers had received from Western Seed in a trial of a new variety. In the middle of the field, a flame tree showed off its flamboyant red flowers.

The diversity reflected the hard lessons they had learned during the brutal *wanjala*: keep the family healthy with a balanced diet, keep the income flowing with an assortment of crops that ripen at various times.

Each crop had been planted with a specific purpose. Sweet potatoes would be good for lunch as a substitute for maize. Beans provided a protein-rich complement with maize in *githeri*. Peanuts would be ideal for breakfast with tea. The *sukuma* and peas would nutritionally bolster the *ugali* at dinner.

The vegetables also served a common agricultural purpose. They were part of a crop rotation strategy, renewing and softening the soil, giving it a break from the harsh demands of the maize. By working the soil in this second season, the Biketis hoped they would need to do less plowing in advance of the maize planting.

Like Leonida, Zipporah and Sanet also were counting on the crop diversity to provide a fairly steady stream of income; the beans would be ready at the end of October, the peanuts in November, the sweet potatoes in December, the *sukuma* would produce throughout the year. Zipporah hoped to be able to sell some produce every week so she could buy other household items like kerosene, salt, and sugar—the sugar price in particular had remained shockingly and stubbornly high at two hundred shillings per kilogram.

Sanet was planning to use some of the vegetable cash for his animal-trading business, which had dried up earlier in the year for lack of capital. He was also counting on the maize harvest being able to feed his family through the year, allowing them to save money by not having to purchase maize at the high market prices. Those savings, he calculated, would also leave more cash available for his trading. And it would open the possibility of beginning a poultry business; their three hens had hatched twenty-one chicks shortly after the maize harvest. Sanet was hoping to build a chicken coop with a metal roof—the second metal roof on the *shamba* after the maize storeroom.

Zipporah chuckled at Sanet's vast ambitions for the maize. She teased her husband, noting that men had rarely helped with growing maize when it was only a subsistence crop with meager harvests; they left the work to the women, who toiled alone in the fields. But once the maize yields multiplied, producing a surplus that could be turned into income, then the men suddenly roused an interest in the crop.

"When a couple worked that way, with the men not being involved in the farming, they would fail. It's the way most families around here worked," Zipporah told Sanet. "But when we sit together and decide what to do, it's better. There's more harmony in the house."

The household health was certainly improving. After the maize harvest, the Biketis began eating *ugali* twice a day, for lunch and dinner. It seemed like gluttony compared to the missed meals during the *wanjala*. But right now maize was all they had. As soon as the vegetables were ready, Zipporah would be changing the daily menu. *Ugali* would be served once a day, at dinner. Though David was still haunted by his cough, his body tone and skin color were improving, and the stomach swelling seemed to be receding.

The main goals of stretching the maize were to vary the diet and throw off the shackles of the market. Zipporah felt liberated not having to purchase maize for the month after the harvest. She and Sanet hoped to be food self-sufficient in 2012, eating their own reserves until the next harvest; any market purchases of food would be by choice, not by necessity.

And any sales, too. The maize price in the market was now back down to sixty shillings for a *goro-goro*. "Even if the price goes to one hundred shillings, we won't sell," Zipporah told Sanet. They must be patient and wait until June, she said, so they could turn the tables on the *wanjala*, transforming the Biketi family from victim to victor. "Next year," she vowed, "we will sell when we can get the highest price during the *wanjala*."

AFTER HARVESTING her maize, Rasoa turned to beans. She had signed up for One Acre's bean offer and on a cool, moist morning she planted on a plateau between the rocks behind her house. It was land that belonged to her husband's family, and she was joined by her three boys and several sisters-in-law and their children. Rasoa unfurled the One Acre planting string and the adults began the precise work, digging holes along the string with their *jembes*. For beans, the fertilizer use was even more judicious than with maize. Rasoa had fashioned her own scoop, attaching a cap from a Fanta orange soda bottle to the end of a stick; in each hole she now dropped only one-third of a cap. Row after row they planted with painstaking, back-bending labor for the better part of the day. Later, Rasoa planted other *sirumbi* crops, particularly tomatoes and cabbage, on the half-acre of land beside her house where her One Acre maize had grown.

One day in early September, the Wasike *shamba* was shaken with the tragic news that Rasoa's little nephew, the son of her older brother, had died. It was a sober reminder of the fragility of life in the African countryside, and how quickly fortunes could change: from the joy over a bountiful harvest to the sorrow over a child's death. As the young bean sprouts worked their way out of the soil, a young life was gone.

The five-year-old boy had complained of a stomachache. His mother walked with him two kilometers to the hospital. There, they encountered a shortage of medicine. With little treatment, the boy declined quickly and died. The family wasn't certain of the cause of death, but they suspected a severe case of malaria. And surely, they believed, the rugged *wanjala* had also taken a toll.

In the grandfather's house, the body of the boy was laid on a bed in the living room and covered with a green-and-blue blanket. "It is a common thing in this area. We bury a lot," said the grandfather, who was sitting in a chair beside the bed. He frequently pulled back the blanket and tenderly touched the boy, feeling his face and chest.

"Yes, a lot of people die from malaria," said another elderly man who was among the mourners in the room. "We are a poor people. Because of it, we have lost very many people."

"They bring the nets to protect us, but still we have malaria," Rasoa said. "Also, too many people drink bad water; they get typhoid. They get treated in the hospital, but then they go home and drink more bad water." Many of the residents of Kabuchai, Rasoa included, drew their water from wells on their *shambas*, but it still needed to be purified in some manner.

Rasoa also suspected her nephew didn't receive the proper medicine. "When someone is at a hospital, they need to pay money before they get treated," Rasoa explained. "Doctors and nurses want to get paid before they treat. Without money, there is no proper treatment. I think that is the case here."

The bed was in a corner of the living room. The walls behind the bed were covered with precise chalk drawings of animals: a lion, rabbit, chicken, antelope, kangaroo. There was also, incongruously, a drawing of a man who looked like a bearded Paul Kruger, the South African leader from the nineteenth century who had established Kruger National Park, one of Africa's famous wildlife refuges.

Written above the bed on one of the walls was a reference to a Bible verse: Isaiah 60:1–2. It was the same that was on the pulpit banner in Leonida's church. "Arise, shine."

The grandfather read from Romans 14:7–8. "No one of us lives for himself only. None of us dies for himself only. If we live, it is for the Lord." And, "If someone has done wrong to you, don't seek revenge. It is better for you to forgive."

Also, Luke 6:27. "Love your enemies."

For the burial, relatives dressed the boy in a white shirt and then laid him in a casket. He was buried on a family plot, which had become a cemetery.

Amid the crying and lamentations, Rasoa remained stoic. "We must accept it," she told her family. "It is God's will. Life goes on."

And it did, at a slower pace after the second season plantings. At the end of September, Rasoa was back working with LifeStraw, checking up on how the water filters were working. One discovery was that rats seemed to like the rubber tubes and the balloon pump, so a number of the contraptions, gnawed to pieces, had to be replaced. With her new LifeStraw earnings, Rasoa also replaced the calf that had died. This time, she and Cyrus went big and sturdy. Cyrus searched the cattle markets and bought a mature bull for twenty-four thousand shillings. They planned to get into the plowing business. Not only would they save several thousand shillings by plowing their own field, but they would also make money plowing for their neighbors. Cyrus calculated he could make back the investment in one season.

He and Rasoa also decided to regularly deposit money in their *Haba na Haba* account for future school fees. They wanted Tim to join his younger brothers at the Baptist School; one year's tuition for all three would total nearly twenty thousand shillings. Their goal was to keep seven bags of maize this year to feed the family until the next maize harvest. Their main mistake last year, they knew now, was that they had sold low and then had to buy high. Like the other farmers, they were determined to reverse their fortunes. "It was painful, but we learned what we need to do," Rasoa told Cyrus. "We need to manage our maize."

AS SEPTEMBER TURNED to October, the greatest activity on the *shambas* was the shelling of the maize cobs, which were now sufficiently dry. It was a family affair. Living rooms became the arena of action; furniture was pushed along the walls or taken out into the yard. The cobs were dumped on the dung floors and everyone pitched in with their hands. Each family had one or two of the gray, conical, metal shellers. Those without the mechanical aids used their thumbs. The shellers worked especially well on dry cobs; if the kernels were still a little moist, the thumbs were most proficient. The parents did some shelling during the day while the children were in school, then at night, after dinner, with the light of the kerosene lamps, they all gathered on the floor for a couple of hours of family shelling.

The children often turned it into a competition. Who was the fastest sheller? Who could clear the most cobs in a certain time? Wrists flipped furiously. Thumbs worked in a blur. In the Biketi house, oldest daughter, Cynthia, was often the champion. Middle son, Arnest, usually won in the Wasike family, with the oldest, Tim, in hot pursuit. Francis, the wily veteran still nimble in his fifth decade, set the pace in the Mamati clan. Among the Wanyamas, the middle girls, Jackline and Sarah, were often in the lead.

The white kernels flew off the cobs, scattering across the living room floor. At the end of each shelling session, the kernels were swept into the large mesh-plastic storage bags. In the morning, the kernels would be spread over the flat rocks or the yards, as the cobs had been, and another drying phase would begin. If the sky was clear and the sun intense, the kernels would need two or three days before being dry enough for final storage. It was an imprecise science, calculating the proper dryness. None of the farmers had moisture meters, so they put a kernel between their teeth and gingerly bit down. If there was a crisp cracking sound, the kernels were ready for long-term storing.

Both Rasoa and Zipporah had to move up the start of shelling to prevent spoilage on the cobs. The rain had continued to fall after the harvest, and the thatched roof over Rasoa's storage bin leaked. Zipporah had the opposite problem. While the metal roof of her storeroom kept the rainwater out, the tightly constructed walls and floor kept the moisture of the cobs in; there wasn't enough air circulation for evaporation.

About three weeks after the harvest, Zipporah and Sanet noticed dark mold forming on some cobs. Alarm gripped the *shamba* with the fear that everything in the storeroom was rotting and all their hard work would be lost. Zipporah climbed into the bin and hurriedly tossed out all the cobs that were spoiling. The bad cobs filled one bag, which Sanet sold to people who make maize alcohol, a blindingly potent concoction. He then ordered that shelling of the rest of the cobs should begin immediately, as the individual kernels would dry easier than the cobs.

The shelling—hours of wrist-turning, thumb-flicking repetitive action—provided an opportunity for grand contemplation, particularly of future plans. One morning, Rasoa and Cyrus sat together in their living room surrounded by kernels and white dust. It looked like it had snowed overnight. Cyrus had the idea that he could speed up the shelling by beating the cobs with a stick. He had stacked all the furniture against the far wall of the living room and dumped a bag of maize in the corner by the door. Then he flailed away. The kernels flew all over the room, as did little pieces of the cobs. What they were left with was a bigger cleanup task and even more bits of cobs that still had to be shelled. He discovered why One Acre didn't recommend the stick-flailing method of shelling.

Cyrus would open the M-Pesa shop later in the morning so he and Rasoa could make a dent on the mess that remained. Rasoa tuned the radio to lively Gospel music. Cyrus sat beneath the message "I love my God" written on the wall. Rasoa sat with her back to the reference to Ruth 1:16–17. As they shelled, they talked about their plans to buy more cattle to grow their plowing business. They discussed how the boys were doing in school. And, they determined, the best way to afford better education and more cattle was to expand their One Acre land. Rasoa, like Leonida and Zipporah, had ambitions to become a "super farmer," which, in One Acre parlance, was a farmer working two acres or more. She hoped to rent an extra plot next year and to perhaps plant on some of her mother-in-law's land. Cyrus, too, wanted to become a One Acre member and plant maize on the half-acre of the *shamba* beside the pathway to the market where sugarcane had been growing.

If they were both One Acre members, Cyrus said, they could have a competition to see who would produce the most maize and who, by extension, was the better farmer. "It will be me," Cyrus boasted.

Rasoa rolled her eyes and flashed a broad smile. "No," she said, "I will win. You will need my help."

At 10 a.m., Cyrus received a call on his cellphone. People were lining up outside the M-Pesa. He needed to open the shop. Rasoa carried on the shelling by herself and was soon joined by a neighbor and one of Cyrus's sisters. The talk turned to community health problems.

"You know, I wanted to be a nurse," Rasoa said. That dream was dashed when she had to leave high school in her second year for lack of money to pay the fees. Instead, she trained to be a community health worker. This morning, Rasoa was wearing a T-shirt from a past stop-malaria campaign of the federal Ministry of Public Health and Sanitation that distributed bed nets. The T-shirt proclaimed: *MBU NJE! SISI NDANI!* Mosquito Out! People In!

Rasoa had twenty households under her care; she would regularly check in with them and discuss any health concerns. Were they using their nets? Did they treat their well water? Were they eating a balanced diet?

"Right now, we're looking for another thing. A hand-wash machine," Rasoa told the women shelling in her living room. She described it as a type of jerry can with a tap, sitting up on a stand, with a bar of soap, just near the outhouse. "So you could wash your hands after visiting the toilet."

"We also want every household to have a washing rack," she continued. "It would be a place where you can dry the utensils and pots and pans after washing them. It's important that they dry. You don't want to use them when they are still wet because the water isn't good."

Rasoa led the shelling through the morning, until the boys came home from school for lunch. Then she disappeared to the cooking hut to serve up the *githeri*.

On the other side of Kabuchai market, Zipporah and Sanet sat down to shell after lunch and after their children had returned to school. Little David joined them on the floor. Chickens wandered in and out, pecking at the cobs that Zipporah dumped on the floor.

As the shelling commenced, the conversation focused on future construction plans. Sanet explained how he would rebuild the store-room before the next maize harvest. "It's not allowing enough air to pass through to dry the cobs," Sanet said. "I'll take down the maize stalks from the walls and use branches from eucalyptus trees. They'll provide better ventilation. And I'll raise up the floor. The air is also supposed to come up from the bottom."

Then Zipporah turned to their boldest ambition: building a new house. "We shall build a brick house, with iron sheets for the roof," she said, smiling broadly.

It would be a bigger house, with five rooms instead of the current three. Zipporah and Sanet had already sketched out a floor plan: there would be a living room, bedroom, storeroom, a study room, and a bathroom that would feature a shower connected by hose to a tank of water outside the walls. The house would measure 28 feet by 19 feet, for 532 square feet, nearly double the present 300 square feet. The new kitchen would be in a separate building, also made of brick and an iron roof. They had learned from the present house, where the kitchen was right beside the bedroom, that it was better for the family's health to keep the smoke out of the main living quarters. The storeroom would house the bags of food and tools such as the *jembes*. "The maize will have its own room," Zipporah marveled. For now, the maize would be stored in the bedroom, along the wall farthest from the roof leak.

"I have been thinking of this house for a long time," Sanet said.

"Yes, we've had these plans for two years now," Zipporah added. "We didn't have any means to get started on the building."

Now, as the shelling continued and the kernels accumulated, Zipporah and Sanet began to believe they finally might be able to finance their dream house. They had already begun to price the cost of construction. They would make their own bricks, and they could round up enough family members and friends to help with the labor. The main cost would be the metal roof. Each three-meter iron sheet cost 850 shillings, and they would need about thirty-six sheets. If they got the twenty bags of maize they were hoping for, they might be able to swing it. And maybe even splurge on a concrete floor.

The first priority, though, would be setting aside enough maize to feed the family through the year. "We might be safe," said the ever-cautious Sanet. "It will depend on how wise we shall be."

AS LEONIDA SAT on the floor of her living room one late September afternoon, she seemed to be a woman at peace. Her younger children were all in school, and she was beginning her shelling. Piles of maize cobs surrounded her; she was anxious to measure the size of her harvest.

Melsa, Leonida's second-oldest daughter, sat beside her on the floor. Melsa was nine months pregnant, due any day. Her first child, twenty-one-month-old Gertrude Nafula (born during the long rains of 2010), crawled among the cobs. Melsa had come home from her work on the tea plantation to give birth.

"I'm about to be a grandmother again," Leonida sighed as she watched Gertrude. "And Melsa, this is your second child and you aren't yet twenty-two."

This gathering of three generations over the maize harvest prompted Leonida to reflect on family size in rural Kenya. "We used to think that the more children you had, the richer you were," she told Melsa. Children provided labor, and social security in their parents' old age. "But," Leonida added, "we can't think that way anymore."

It had long been customary for development experts to look at Africa and point to population growth as exacerbating, if not directly causing, many of its problems—particularly hunger. Even casual observers of the continent would ask, Why do poor farmers have such big families when they struggle to feed all those children? The same could once have been asked of developed countries when they were largely agrarian; in the United States, at the beginning of the twentieth century and through the Great Depression years, large farming families were common, often with four or more children who pitched in with the labor. That's largely the case today in rural Africa, which, in terms of its agriculture, is stuck in the 1930s.

But with development, with better education opportunities, particularly for girls, family sizes in the United States shrunk. And Leonida believed the same thing would happen in Africa—"It *must* happen," she said. Leonida paused in her shelling to fish out her cellphone from the mound of kernels. She placed it on top of the pile and continued shelling.

"Today, if you don't educate your children, you're not really a person at all," Leonida told Melsa. "And if you have so many children, how can you educate them all as a farmer?"

She considered herself Exhibit A. This year of mighty struggle to keep her children fed and in school during the harsh *wanjala* provided plenty of evidence. It was clear to her that One Acre farmers with the larger families, and with children in high school, were lagging behind the other families in the exodus to Canaan.

Among her friends and neighbors, it was no longer the number of children that defined a person's wealth, but the education standards the children had achieved or would be able to achieve. Leonida said family size is a frequent topic in community meetings. "People ask me, 'How many children do you have?' Seven, I say. Then they ask, 'How many doctors or secretaries do you have?'"

None, she would answer. None had even completed high school. In Kenya today, Leonida conceded, "A person with one child who is a doctor or a lawyer is above a person with seven children who haven't been educated."

Family planning and contraception were widely available in the rural areas of Western Kenya. The clinic in Kabuchai and the hospital in Webuye provided birth control in the form of IUDs (known as "coils" locally) and pills, patches, and injections. It was even possible for women to have a tubal ligation and for men to have a vasectomy, though they were rare.

"It is better to have a small family; it is easier to manage," Leonida said. With seven children, she conceded she came to this realization too late. Francis, after nine children with Mary, had come to the same conclusion. Zipporah and Rasoa had decided to keep their families relatively small, aiming to stay with four and three children, respectively. Rasoa believed family planning was important as farmers began thinking of farming as a business rather than subsistence.

"We see how much we have to plan and save if our three boys are all to go to high school," Rasoa said to Cyrus as they discussed the issue. "And we also want to improve our living standards, have a better house."

Zipporah learned from experience. She grew up with eight siblings. Sanet's family had nine boys and ten girls. She marveled at her own sister with eight children. How will you educate them all? she often asks her. Didn't you see how we couldn't finish high school because we were too many children in the family?

"We must learn as we go through life," Zipporah has told her. "We must learn from our struggles."

BY MID-OCTOBER, when the shelling was finished and the kernels dried and stored in ninety-kilogram bags, the harvest results from the farmers' One Acre fields were clear.

Zipporah and Sanet reaped twenty bags from their one acre. It was the miracle of their prayers.

Rasoa and Cyrus had thirteen bags from a half-acre. It was better than they had hoped. "In all the years I've been planting maize, I never had a harvest this good," Rasoa told Cyrus.

Francis and Mary harvested twelve bags from their half-acre and son Geoffrey reaped eight bags from his plot, even though they each lost a couple of bags when heavy rains knocked over some stalks. In the end, it was a harvest so bountiful that Francis climbed the rocks behind his house and offered a prayer of thanksgiving.

Leonida ended up with seven bags from her half-acre. It was below her initial hopes but in line with her lowered expectations once she realized her soil had been depleted by the years of sugar-cane growing. Also, the extended rains on her side of the Lugulu Hills had exacted a significant price.

Leonida surveyed her *Amua* colleagues, and they all harvested a couple of bags less than expected. Agnes Wekhwela shelled fourteen bags from her one acre; she estimated that mold from the heavy moisture claimed another four bags. Margaret Lumunyasi and Elizabeth Namasaka each reaped eight bags from their half-acres. Alice Barasa and Beatrice Arinyula joined Leonida with seven bags.

"The rain was too much and leached away the fertilizer," Agnes concluded. "At the end, the stalks were yellow, which was an indication of too little nutrients, too little fertilizer."

Their field officer, Kennedy, confirmed that the rains had lowered yields throughout the Lutacho area. But neither the rains, nor the losses, were heavy enough for the One Acre insurance to pay out; the harvests were still two or three times greater than non–One Acre members were reaping. The rains, Kennedy told the *Amua* group, normally tapered off by the time the farmers would be applying their top-dressing fertilizer, which added nitrogen to the soil. Nitrogen was crucial to high maize yields, but it was also particularly soluble. The prolonged rains muted the impact of the top dressing.

The farmers all believed that the fertilizer they applied when they planted, even though it was in tiny amounts, was the difference-maker in their harvests, along with the better seeds. Margaret Inyuma, who had just signed up to be an *Amua* member, offered further proof. Farming on her own this year, she harvested only two bags of maize on her half-acre. The main difference was that she didn't apply much fertilizer. She used some cow dung, but she didn't have nearly enough for the entire plot.

Rasoa's experience also convinced her of the advantages of fertilizer use. She had planted an additional half-acre of maize beyond her One Acre plot. There she used the same variety of seed, which she had purchased in a shop, but she didn't use fertilizer. She harvested only three bags, which was less than a quarter of her One Acre yield. She would prefer to farm without adding the fertilizer, since it was the most expensive part of farming. But her three cows didn't produce enough manure to cover her land. And her family couldn't survive on the lower yields.

"The best thing about One Acre is that it provides all the fertilizer we need," Rasoa told her husband, who was about to sign up to be a member himself. "I couldn't afford to buy fertilizer on my own, and you can see what happened. The yield was less than a quarter."

One Acre was conducting composting trials, where farmers built organic mounds layered with manure, dirt, grasses, and maize stalks. And it was also looking into conservation agriculture methods, where the stalks and husks remaining from the harvest would be left on the field or mixed in with the dirt to preserve moisture, prevent topsoil erosion, and return nutrients to the soil. But they were difficult practices for the smallholder farmers to adopt, since they needed the stalks and husks as fodder to feed their cows, particularly during the *simiyu*, the dry season that could stretch for several months. Few farmers had enough grazing space, and any land set aside to grow Napier grass for the cows meant less land to grow food for the family. The farmers also knew that if they left the stalks and husks covering the field, other farmers would think it was going to waste, and they would take it away for their cows.

One Acre's Andrew Youn, who had posted fertilizer price charts on his bedroom wall, believed fertilizer in modest amounts was vital for smallholder farmers to conquer hunger. "One sack of fertilizer can mean the difference between feeding your family or not," he often said. The farmers' soils had been heavily depleted over time. And smallholder farmers didn't have enough land to take a portion out of production to let the soil recover, nor did they have enough livestock to go totally organic.

"To increase production, you can either clear more land to grow more crops, or you can improve productivity on the land you have," Andrew said. Clearing forests to create arable land, he maintained, contributed more to greenhouse gas emissions and global warming than fertilizer production. "We can see the impact on families of unreliable rain. So I want to limit climate change," he said. "If the world needs more food, and clearly it does, we need to be improving yields rather than clearing more land."

The Kenyan government also recommended modest fertilizer amounts, the standard measure being the one soda bottle cap per plant of maize and one-third of a cap per bean plant. "Best of all would be to mix the chemical fertilizer with manure, but most farmers don't have enough manure," said Charles Mutinda, the Kenyan maize breeder who was leading the nitrogen-efficient maize trials at the foot of Mount Kenya in the central region. "Can we do without fertilizer in Kenya? I don't know. I doubt it."

He noted that soil fertility was emerging as a major challenge throughout Kenya as family *shambas* had been subdivided over the generations to accommodate the families of grown-up sons. That required more intensive agriculture. "Years ago, if you needed to grow more food, you planted more land," Mutinda said. "Now, you need to grow more on smaller plots. And the soils have been so depleted. That's why we are trying to come up with something new."

SOMETHING NEW WAS also needed on the storage front. Preserving the maize for many months—warding off weevils and combating mold—until the price rose to an attractive level for sale or it was consumed by the family was one of the biggest challenges of smallholder farmers. The One Acre members sprinkled little packets of actellic dust—a chemical powder that repelled pests but was judged safe for humans—over the kernels as they stored them in the bags. In the past, many farmers spread ash from the cooking fires over the dried maize as protection from weevils. But that typically lasted only for two months. The actellic dust, which was part of the credit package, could extend the protection for several more months, perhaps up to a year.

The farmers then piled up the bags in their bedrooms, elevated a bit off the ground. The bedroom was usually tucked behind the living room, far from the door, so there was little light; if there were windows, they were smaller and usually shuttered. It was in most cases the coolest, darkest, driest area of the house, so the best place to store food. And it was the safest place, with the farmers sleeping beside their most precious asset. House break-ins and maize theft were the most common criminal acts in the rural areas.

The farmers also wanted to keep the maize hidden from the prying eyes of relatives and neighbors and even strangers who stopped by the *shamba* for a visit. As harvests increased, so did covetousness, which could be more damaging than the weevils. A dark corner of the bedroom was like a secret bank account in Switzerland: no one could know how much you have.

"I don't want anyone to see our food, how much we have," Francis told Mary as he lugged the bags from their storeroom just off the sitting room to the bedroom. The gregarious Francis would go out of his way to help his neighbors, but the maize of his hard labor was another thing. "This food is for our family," he said. "We're not going hungry!"

Rasoa displayed the same protective instincts, which she tried to balance with the communal responsibility to share. "It's good to share; you can share for one or two days. But then they come back and ask for more if they know you have it, if they can see how much you have. If the maize is out in the sitting room, it's too big a temptation. If people see the maize, there's no way you can refuse to assist," Rasoa explained to her One Acre group. "In the bedroom, the maize is private and safe. I can share with someone for one day and when they come back I can say I don't have enough for my family."

She spoke the words without meanness but with a logic sharpened during the difficult *wanjala* and an ambition to get ahead. There was also a nagging distrust of the storage methods, that an attack of the Osamas could quickly shred the security of a maize surplus. It had happened to Rasoa and Cyrus two years ago, when weevils infested two bags of maize, wiping out most of their harvest. It was before Rasoa joined One Acre. Then one year ago, they had avoided the weevil problem—and the prospect of sharing—when they sold their maize in January and bought the calf. Now, Cyrus was again pushing to hedge their bet on storage. Rasoa didn't want to sell any of the maize just for the sake of selling, just to keep it from the weevils or to remove the responsibility of sharing. But Cyrus had a plan. He argued they should buy another bull, to build up the plowing business—after all, they needed at least two bulls—and to earn more money to save for the boys' education. Rasoa agreed; she liked the idea of turning her maize into an investment rather than cash to be stashed in the bank account. So they made a bold move: they sold eight bags of maize—half of their combined harvest—for about twenty-four hundred shillings a bag. That was double what they received when they sold in January to buy the calf. A few days later, Cyrus returned from the livestock market with a husky bull. They named it "Buffalo."

They now had eight bags of maize remaining. Rasoa calculated that would be enough to feed the family until the next harvest, if the storage succeeded.

DEVISING A BETTER storage system that would eliminate the tremendous post-harvest losses and allow farmers to hold on to their maize as long as they wanted was one of the holy grails of agricultural development.

The Kenyan government and some NGOs were promoting a warehouse receipts system, where farmers would take their maize and other grains to big concrete warehouses. They received a receipt for their deposit and could decide to sell at any time. For smallholder farmers, though, that was a bit cumbersome, Andrew Youn thought. It involved a transport cost, taking the maize to the warehouses in the bigger cities, and a quality standard that would be difficult for the smallholders to measure. And it required a level of trust, leaving your maize in strange hands. Even government officials promoting the system admitted it would be inefficient for farmers with less than twenty bags of maize.

One Acre staffers were instead focusing on a better home storage system. For one year they had been conducting a trial program that offered training in maize handling, storage, and education about the value of holding on to maize deeper into the year. In the first round, farmers in the training program who stored their maize longer and sold it later for higher prices increased their income on average by about four thousand shillings.

In addition, One Acre was following emerging innovations by others on the storage front. Various agricultural research institutes and universities were working on new bags that might be able to preserve grains, such as maize, for a year or longer without needing chemical protection. And a growing number of private companies were tinkering with designs for silos and other storage containers that could be used by individual households.

"It's the next big thing," said Chandu Shah of Kentainers, a Nairobi-based company that designed products like water containers, well liners, and latrines. Their black polyethylene cylindrical water tanks were ubiquitous in Kenya and east Africa. Now Kentainers was working on grain storage.

The Kentainer factory was in an industrial park near the Nairobi international airport. It was reachable via a wretched dirt road under constant construction that snarled impossibly during evening rush hour. Big trucks, little trucks, pickup trucks, *matatus*, and cars of all nature maneuvered in competing directions. A two-lane road grew to three, then four, then five, then six lanes of traffic. The vehicles shoved their way forward, inching past a riot of small businesses: hair salons, butcher shops, vegetable stands, shoe stores, and a place called the Rocky Driving School. The Holiness Church and the Christ Embassy ("giving your life meaning") competed for business beside the Temptations pub and grill.

The small shops gave way to a busy row of factories. The Kentainer yard provided an oasis of order in the chaos. Just beyond the gate were rows of enormous water tanks. Behind them were a couple of prototypes of grain storage containers made of the same material but much smaller. The thick plastic would keep out the weevils, even the Osamas, and the containers would be small enough, holding from four to ten bags of maize, that they could be kept inside a house.

Kalpesh Patel and Paul Madoc were working on a ventilation system and an airtight sealing method, the thorniest problems. One objective was to create the possibility of drying the maize kernels inside the container. It would relieve the farmers of hauling their maize out of storage to dry in the sun and spare them having to look out for approaching rain or thieves. These containers would also promote an air of secrecy. No one could tell how full they would be or if they contained maize or water.

Kentainers was working with the U.S.-based Meridian Institute, which specialized in bringing together diverse partners to tackle complex problems, including agriculture and food security issues. They were keen to reduce post-harvest losses with innovations that would be particularly attractive and affordable for smallholder farmers. "We can make the product and provide the sales network," said Patel, "but the questions are how to make it self-sustaining, so the farmers don't need any skills to maintain it, and how to make it for the range of forty to fifty dollars."

The market, Patel noted, was potentially huge. "Seventy to eighty percent of Kenyans are farmers," he said. "And they lose so much of their harvest. If we can reduce the loss, and if farmers can store their maize and wait for a better price before selling, with one harvest they can recoup the cost. We're all looking for new solutions."

Madoc had his mother in mind while he worked on the design. She farmed an acre of maize and resolutely battled weevils and grain borers. "With this container, she wouldn't have to worry about them anymore," he said, thumping the thick, plastic shell. "I want these for our farm." Then he expanded his ambitions. "Imagine if we increased national production by 20 percent just by saving the maize from being spoiled. How important is that for the country?"

In another part of Nairobi, a company called GrainPro Inc. was also plunging deeper into the quest for a better storage method. It was developing what it called safes and cocoons—PVC plastic coverings for grain bags that could be hermetically sealed with a zipper to kill insects and stop the growth of aflatoxins. It also offered airtight bag liners and a collapsible dryer case, which provided a canvas like surface for drying kernels that could then be rolled up, kernels and all, like a tarp covering a baseball field at the first sight of rain. GrainPro's grandest project was a GrainKeep Center, a small conglomeration of the cocoons and tents where smallholder farmers could bring their maize to be dried, weighed, and stored. They were portable and could be located close to a cluster of villages to provide easier access to farmers in remote areas. But without microfinance lending, few smallholder farmers in east Africa could afford any of these products, which were largely made in the Philippines.

North of Nairobi, at the foot of Mount Kenya, three silver metal peaks rose on the farm of Marie Njoki Nderi. They were silos, just like those that dotted rural America but were a rare sight in Africa. For years, Marie had been on the frontline of fighting off the Osamas. And for most of the years, it was a losing battle. She was a science and physical education teacher and her husband was an engineer in the ministry of water. Together they operated a larger commercial farm, planting twenty-five acres in maize and beans. They would harvest about 150 bags of maize each year and store them in a shed. It wouldn't be long before weevils attacked, tearing into the bags, even those with the actellic dust. Marie would scramble to salvage what she could, selling the maize as fast as possible, but still she would lose up to half her harvest. Some bags would be lost outright to the weevils; others had to be sold prematurely at a lower price. Her annual losses amounted to tens of thousands of shillings, sometimes up to one hundred thousand shillings.

In 2010, Marie heard about a new innovation being developed by the local Catholic diocese and CIMMYT, the international maize and wheat improvement center. The diocese was interested in new storage solutions to stop the wastage at its schools, which purchased tons of maize to feed the students. CIMMYT was hoping to provide farmers with an incentive to grow more maize; if they could store it while waiting for a better price, they would grow it. Officials from the diocese promoting the silos came to Marie's school, and the principal suggested to Marie that she might be interested in the presentation. She immediately saw the possibilities and bought three silos, each standing about six feet tall, with storage capacity of twenty bags of maize. She paid 20,000 shillings for each silo; the price was set at 1,000 shillings per bag of storage capacity.

After her first harvest, when the kernels were dry, she filled the silos with sixty bags. Following the instructions, she lit a candle and set it on top of the maize in each silo and then she sealed the top

with a rubber liner. The candles burned for about ten minutes, con-
suming the oxygen. When the flames went out, the silos would be
airtight, and any weevils inside would die. At least that was the
idea. Marie was told not to open the silos for at least one-and-a-half
months. When she had a buyer, she asked others to open the silo.
She was too nervous to watch, fearing that weevils would come
pouring out with the maize.

"I don't want to be there," she told them. "I'm afraid what you
might find."

The silos were opened, and the maize was in fine shape. Marie
breathed a huge sigh of relief and pocketed a nice profit. The ninety
bags of maize she didn't put in the silo had been sold for 2,500
shillings a bag. The sixty bags of silo-stored maize she sold two
months later went for 3,700 shillings a bag. The price difference of
1,200 shillings per bag meant she recouped the cost of the silos, plus
some, in one harvest.

CIMMYT meanwhile was trying to work out the logistics bugs
of the silos. The price would have to come down to be affordable for
smallholder farmers. And smaller silos, with a capacity of five or ten
bags that could fit inside houses, would be more desirable to them.
Scaling up sales would be a challenge, since so far metal artisans
had individually made all the silos. They were also a bit fragile; any
dents or rust could ruin the airtight nature.

As she brought in the 2011 harvest, Marie was looking to buy
three more silos. Curious visitors came to see her new storage innovation and do the savings calculations. "We must conquer the pests
before they conquer us," she would tell them, gently patting the
silos. "We all want to make as much from our maize as possible."

IT WAS THIS GOAL—maximizing the value of maize—that was
driving up membership in One Acre. "The innate desire of the farmers to improve," Andrew Youn said on a hot October afternoon. He

was sitting on a couch outside his room in Bungoma, slowly eating a bowl of vegetable soup that he hoped would chase away a mild case of the flu. "The human component is so important in what we do."

Andrew had estimated that One Acre would be serving fifty thousand farmers by the end of the year, but now he was revising that to seventy-five thousand. And he expected that number to double by the end of 2012. "We've figured out the marketing, how people pass on knowledge," he said. "In Asia, the Green Revolution seemed to spread organically; it spread like a virus. Africa is different; people live in different geographic proximity. People want to act in a group."

To channel the existing social network, One Acre identified member farmers dubbed "replication agents." They were particularly enthusiastic and community oriented, and One Acre encouraged them to form their own groups. While farmers could see how a neighbor who was a One Acre member improved her yields, they often needed someone to actively recruit them to join. "Instead of a stranger telling farmers that this is a good idea," Andrew said, "they need to hear it from someone they trust."

Someone like thirty-six-year-old Gladys Wafula, who was selected to be a replication agent by Kennedy as he sought to expand his roster of farmers in the Lutacho area from 158 to about 300. Gladys herself was in her first year as a One Acre member, but she had quickly spread the word with an evangelical zeal. "I want my whole area to be educated in the new methods of farming, to learn new skills," she told Kennedy as she assembled her new group under a row of shade trees on a day for registering new members. "Education is powerful. That's what reduces poverty." There was also a more practical reason why she wanted all her neighbors to increase their harvests. "If everyone in an area joins One Acre and produces more, it reduces the jealousy of some people. It reduces the temptation to steal."

She had recruited seventeen new members and named their group *Baraka*. Blessings. They were gathering now, in early October, with some forty other One Acre recruits in a more remote area of Lutacho, far from any church or school where they could meet. To expand, Kennedy was traveling farther and farther from the main market area. As Gospel music blared from a radio, he set up a table at the edge of a field. The farmers sauntered over one by one to sign a membership contract and pay the one-hundred-shilling registration fee.

Gladys beamed as she watched the procession. The *Baraka* members were her neighbors. Early in the year, they had noticed how she had enough seeds to plant and they didn't. They watched her maize grow and saw her yield triple. They asked what she had done to her land. She told them she had joined One Acre, and she invited them to become members as well.

"It was easy, really," she told Kennedy.

Particularly after the *wanjala*. It had been the worst Gladys had ever experienced, numerous were the days she had nothing but a cup of tea. All her neighbors were suffering, too; nobody wanted to ever see such a hunger season again.

"It was so bitter this year," a neighbor, Emily Nanjala, told Gladys. "Many days I didn't have food for lunch or dinner. Please, can I join One Acre?"

Eliud Juma battled hunger and high school fees for two children and an underperforming maize crop. "What is your secret?" he asked Gladys when he saw her maize. "I must know."

Enrollment was rising, even as the credit amounts for the One Acre products were increasing in the new year to 5,600 shillings for a half-acre and 10,500 shillings for one acre. Fertilizer prices were

up, and One Acre was adding a few more items to the bundle it provided: four storage bags, ten doses of deworming treatment for children, and a one-year supply of water treatment per member. It was
an important part of One Acre's financing, but Andrew was wary of
hitting the point where farmers would resist joining—or even drop
out—because of the cost. Field officers were hearing some com-
plaints about the credit increase from veteran members who suggested that beyond the basic package of seeds and fertilizer and
training they should have the option of accepting the other items,
like the health and water treatments. But when they did the calculations, the farmers saw that the cost for the total package was still far
below what they would be paying if they had to buy the seed and
fertilizer on their own in the shops, if indeed the shops would even
have them in stock.

Andrew's budget strategy was that One Acre's field operation
would support itself in several years. One Acre had an $8.3 million
budget, $5.5 million for its fieldwork with the farmers and $2.8 million for its research and development and infrastructure. Its field
revenues, collected from farmer payments, were $4.5 million. Donor
funding covered the rest of the organization's expenses. Andrew's
goal was for the field operations to break even.

While the new member registration continued in the field
through the post-harvest period, the research and development of
new products continued in Bungoma. One that was about to enter
the trial phase was a program called School Fee Loans for Maize
Storage. The One Acre staff was learning from the experiences of
Leonida and other farmers: one of their great needs was cash at the
beginning of the year to pay high school fees, which forced them to
take some maize out of storage and sell at lower-than-desired
prices. This trial program was an attempt to help on both fronts, to
promote longer-term storage and relieve the cash pressure for

school fees. Farmers participating in the program would be required to store at least six bags until January. In return, One Acre would provide a loan of 6,000 shillings to make an initial school fee payment. Four of the bags would need to remain in storage until May, when they would be sold to repay the loan plus 1,100 shillings in interest (which matched the lowest rate charged by Kenya's commercial banks). Based on historic maize price averages, the four bags would have a total worth between 5,000 and 6,000 shillings in January and at least 12,000 to 14,000 shillings in May—and much more if the price soared like it had this year. So, after selling, the farmers would have enough to pay off the loan plus something left over to buy a goat or pay additional school fees.

It would be an attempt to slow the spinning poverty cycle that consigned the farmers to selling low and buying high if they wanted to keep their children in school. And, if successful—if farmers, with this incentive, could store their maize until May, if the smallholders' maize could be seen as collateral—the program could convince microfinance organizations to step up their rural lending for education. And it might even draw Africa's commercial banks to see smallholder farmers as viable clients; as it was, less than 3 percent of the banks' lending went to the rural areas, even though that was where the vast majority of the population lived.

In addition to connecting to rural Kenya's social network to boost enrollment, One Acre was also extending into the growing global network of agricultural development to better serve its farmers. Andrew dispatched one staff member to Nairobi to coordinate with other NGOs and government agencies; he knew that for smallholder agriculture to really take off, farmers needed technology innovations, policy changes, and access to financing that One Acre itself couldn't provide. Some One Acre farmers were already benefitting from products developed by organizations such as KickStart

International, which made simple irrigation systems, and Village Enterprise Fund, which provided start-up capital for small business ventures, including vegetable growing. There was increasing two-way traffic of shared interest. Earlier in the year, Village Enterprise's Kenya director had himself become a One Acre member to increase his own maize production.

AN IMPORTANT PART of the agricultural development network was the African governments. Rwanda's agriculture minister Agnes Kalibata had welcomed One Acre's work in her country, and now Kenya's agriculture ministry was doing the same. Wilson Songa, the agriculture secretary, had met with Andrew and his colleagues and then invited One Acre to be on one of the ministry's "think-tank" committees—the Agribusiness and Financial Services Thematic Working Group.

A plant pathologist, Songa was the top agriculture professional in the ministry, which was based in Nairobi's Kilimo House (Agriculture House). A flashing neon sign at the entrance proclaimed, "Kilimo House is a corruption-free zone." Scrolling underneath were phone numbers where anyone could report cases of corruption.

Songa, a welcoming and expansive man, held court in his office overlooking the capital city. One Acre, he said, was doing "very good work." Work, in fact, he wished the government was able to do more of—like providing access to farming inputs and extension advice. One Acre, in turn, knew that its work was influenced by government policy, which set the framework for agricultural development, be it improving access to markets, supporting prices, or expeditiously releasing new seed varieties.

"Smallholder farmers are our main focus," Songa insisted. "They are responsible for more than 60 percent, 70 percent of food production." Then he proceeded to bemoan the government's inability to better aid the smallholders. Storage facilities, extension services, transport, and irrigation were all lacking. The government, he said, didn't have money to support prices during times of wild fluctuation, which, he acknowledged, sapped the farmers' incentive to produce as much as they could. He lamented that Kenya had become the latest poster child for Africa's feast-famine paradox, acknowledging with great frustration that potatoes were rotting and aflatoxins were attacking maize in some parts of the country, while people were starving in others.

He conceded that new seed varieties were often slow in getting to the seed companies and to the farmers. And he pointed out that a lack of coordination between the ministries often hit the smallholder farmers hardest—for example, the state treasury dispersing money for fertilizer imports only after the rains came and the farmers had planted, or the inability of the education department to speed up its support to schools in order to relieve the pressure on farmers to pay school fees when the maize price was lowest.

All this took its toll on the national agriculture output. The maize harvest was expected to yield thirty-two million bags, which was well below the production of thirty-eight million bags in a "good year." In a report on the harvest, the agriculture ministry blamed the decline in maize yields, in part, on fertilizer and seed shortages during the planting season, like those that had bedeviled the farmers in western Kenya who weren't One Acre members.

But Songa was optimistic that Kenya's agriculture was turning around. The ministry, he said, was streamlining to bring all the functions together under one chain of command; all those involved in seed research and development, for instance, would soon be grouped in one unit, instead of competing offices, offering the promise of a speedier release of new seed varieties. The agriculture budget had swelled to 11 percent of government spending, finally meeting the 10 percent level that African governments had committed to back in 2003. Songa predicted annual 10 percent growth in agriculture through the year 2030.

He also said Kenya's agriculture was benefitting from greater outside investment. China, India, and Brazil were showing keen interest in investing in agricultural development, he said, more than the United States, even with the Feed the Future activities. In fact, he noted, the next day he would be flying to China. "They are very keen to talk; they offered to fly us first class," he said. China, he surmised from the summit agenda, was keen on infrastructure projects—roads and irrigation and providing agriculture machinery, like tractors. The Chinese, he said, "seem to have no time to waste" when it came to agricultural development.

Africa, Songa said, should share that sense of urgency. "Why are we still having hunger problems in Africa," he asked, "when we know the way forward?"

ANOTHER CRUCIAL COMPONENT of Africa's agricultural development would be the growth of local seed companies. That was certainly important for One Acre, because it could grow only as far as the availability of seeds would allow.

Take, for example, the better bean seed that Seth Silverman had been tracking. He shared in the farmers' disappointment over the poor performance of the existing bean seeds. Now, at long last, in early October, his confidence grew that the better beans were within reach.

"Here you see that the KK8 beans are in the ground and flowering," said Janey Leakey, as she opened up a slide show presentation on her laptop. Seth and One Acre colleague Kalie Gold crowded around the computer, which hummed on a picnic table at the One Acre compound in Bungoma. Kalie had been out in the field with

Leakey, showing her several of One Acre's seed trials. Now they all examined a photo of beans flourishing in a plot on Leakey's Leldet Ltd. seeds company farm in Nakuru.

"This is exciting," Seth said.

"I planted seventy kilograms of the KK8," Leakey said. Those were the disease-resistant beans developed by breeder Reuben Otsyula at the Kenya Agricultural Research Institute in Kakamega. Leakey had been trying to get her hands on the seeds for a couple of years, but they had been awarded exclusively to a Kenyan NGO that never developed them. She planted the seeds in August shortly after receiving them and was well into the first round of seed multiplication. Seth was hoping to buy at least several tons to offer to One Acre farmers.

"We've got the demand signal, we want to get the beans out to the farmers," Seth said. "But we're totally stuck at the breeder seed level."

"The farmers are at the end of the process, and nobody thinks about them," Leakey said.

"Ideally, we'd like to offer farmers beans for the short rains so they could alternate their crops: maize in the long rains, beans in the short rains. But we don't have a good bean."

"Yet!" said Leakey. "You don't have a good bean yet."

"Yet!" Seth said, laughing. The good bean, he and Leakey hoped, was there on the screen in front of them.

Janey Leakey grew up on farms and tea plantations across eastern Africa. She married Nigel Leakey, a member of Kenya's famous clan of paleoanthropologists and conservationists, and together they founded Leldet and began to focus on supplying seed to the utterly neglected smallholder farmers. Leldet became the first seed company in Kenya to offer seeds in small packages, and to stress diversification with what are known as "orphan" crops, those that had been ignored in the push to established cash crops like maize and wheat. They included cowpeas, pigeon peas, millet, sorghum, and various beans. The seeds were bundled into packets of 60 or 80 or 400 grams and sold for ten or fifteen shillings. Smallholder farmers who couldn't afford the two- or five-kilogram packs of seeds snapped them up.

"Risk mitigation is the big thing for farmers. Small seed bags at low prices reduce the risk," Leakey said. "The women farmers have change in their pockets, so you can sell a lot of small packages."

Leldet and One Acre, along with Joe DeVries at the Alliance for a Green Revolution in Africa, had become allies in the battle to pry new seed varieties from the research institutes and the government control boards and get them growing in the fields. Seth told Leakey that access to improved seeds, particularly beans, "is important to our long-term value proposition to our farmers."

Long term. Leakey smiled at that phrase. "How long will you be here?" she asked Seth.

"We're here for good," he replied, meeting her smile with one of his own.

In that case, Leakey said, it was important for One Acre to consolidate its gains, to sharpen and intensify its extension work, and to advise farmers on crops they may be planting beyond the One Acre package. And she suggested that One Acre's growth ambitions incorporate the growth of the seed companies. Above all, she said, farmers were wary of unreliable seed supplies. "That's why farmers keep seed from their harvests, in case there are shortages the next year," she said.

For months, One Acre had been stockpiling seeds in its Bungoma warehouse for the next maize planting season. It didn't want to get caught in the shortages that had haunted so many other farmers. With enrollment of new members soaring, the demand for seed and fertilizer had more than doubled; One Acre estimated that in 2012 it would be distributing about 500 metric tons of seed and 5,000 tons of fertilizer.

"You have to be able to keep up with the demand," Leakey counseled. "Because once the farmers see the result of these seeds, the demand goes up." She laughed. She was looking forward to delivering Reuben's high-potential beans next year and then sitting back and watching the orders for the following season roll in.

THE BETTER BEAN SEEDS couldn't arrive soon enough, for the bean harvest that began in October had disappointed many farmers. Germination was inconsistent. The rains were too steady and heavy. Hail pounded the plants. Root rot rampaged.

Rasoa had been expecting to harvest more than sixty *goro-goros* from the quarter-acre of beans she had so meticulously planted. She harvested only twelve. The year before she had harvested fifty-two *goro-goros* of beans and sold thirty-five for more than seventy-five hundred shillings. She would keep this year's measly harvest for her family's consumption and forego the extra income.

The second planting season had been one of mixed results for Rasoa. Her quarter-acre of cabbage flourished in the rain, and she reaped five thousand shillings from selling a portion of that harvest. The pumpkins also did well, adding a new item to her menu. But their cows had destroyed the quarter-acre of maize during the days when Rasoa was out doing her LifeStraw work. Cyrus was busy at the M-Pesa, and the boys were in school. Nobody was home to keep the cows out of the field. Other animals, neighborhood dogs, snatched a half-dozen of her chicks. It all gave more urgency to Rasoa's plan to open a little shop for daily necessities at the edge of their property, near the busy pathway that led to the school. She could work there and keep an eye on the crops.

The shop, though, would have to be made of bricks, as would their new house. For in early November, one particularly heavy rain washed away Rasoa's cooking hut, which was made of mud and sticks. Fortunately, no was in there when it collapsed. And the pots and pans had been removed for washing. Undaunted, Rasoa built a new fire pit in the storeroom attached to the house. She remained philosophical, and smiling.

"With farming, you need to accept that you can lose or gain," Rasoa told her children. If nothing else, the disappointing *sirumbi*, following the euphoric One Acre maize harvest, provided a good lesson in the ups-and-downs of agriculture. "You can't give up," she reminded the boys. "You need to encourage yourself and put in a good effort the next year."

At the Biketi *shamba*, the beans also didn't do well. Zipporah had lowered her expectations from the start when the germination was poor. But her other crops, the peanuts, sweet potatoes, peas, and *sukuma*, had come in strong. As planned, the vegetables and nuts were allowing Zipporah to scale back the use of their maize, increasing both the diversity of their meals and the longevity of their One Acre harvest.

The Biketis, too, suffered a structural loss. One night, a downpour dissolved much of their mud outhouse. Fortunately, no one had been in there at the time, either. The next day, Sanet tried to patch up the walls, and he draped a piece of plastic for the roof. Reconstruction would need to wait until the dry season finally arrived.

Up in the rocks overlooking Kabuchai, Francis had also been battling the unseasonable weather. He didn't know what was happening; the hot dry season should have arrived weeks earlier. But as October gave way to November, a damp cold persisted. His half-acre of beans performed poorly; he reaped fewer than twenty *goro-*

goros. All-day rains confined him to his house. He missed working with his tomatoes. And he feared for them. A late blight had mounted an attack. The tomatoes had already matured and were on the verge of harvest. Then several days of particularly heavy rain, and some hail, finished them off. Francis lost nearly the entire crop, the red tomatoes lay rotting in the field. He had hoped to make fifteen thousand shillings in tomato sales; he ended up with only five thousand.

His dream of creating a tomato empire wouldn't die, though. When the rains diminished and the sun returned, he was back in the field with Geoffrey, who had been counting on featuring the tomatoes in his restaurant. They planted another five hundred stems. Francis shared Rasoa's stubborn resolve. "I'm not giving up," he promised his son.

THE RAINS HAD BEEN less punishing on the other side of the Lugulu Hills, so Leonida's second-season crops were doing well, compensating in some measure for the rain-impacted One Acre maize harvest. She was especially proud of her half-acre of sweet potatoes. While awaiting the birth of her grandchild, Leonida eagerly worked the field with her *jembe*, clearing the weeds and aerating the soil. On October 11, Melsa went into labor. Leonida had prepared the storage hut where Gideon slept when he was home to be the delivery room. She expected Melsa's second child to be a smooth birth. But as the day wore on and the labor intensified, Melsa grew ever more uncomfortable. Leonida sensed something was wrong. She kept a vigil through the night and the next morning, with no sign of imminent birth, she knew Melsa needed better care at the hospital in Webuye.

A bicycle or *piki-piki*, a motorcycle, obviously wouldn't do; too many people had died while bouncing over the bad roads on the way to the hospital. So Leonida urgently arranged for vehicle trans-port. There were very few cars in the area, and the only driver avail-able demanded four thousand shillings. The only asset Leonida had on hand that she could quickly turn into such a sum of cash was, praise God, her One Acre maize. She sold one-and-a-half bags at nearly 3,000 shillings per bag for the transport, and then a bit more for cash to show the hospital that she could pay for whatever treat-ment was needed. That evening, they sped over the washboard dirt road and down the hill to the hospital.

The doctors and nurses saw that Melsa was in great distress and feared that mother and baby might die. Leonida, terrified, stood aside as Melsa was rushed into the operating room. The C-section delivery was a success—another girl!—but Melsa was very weak. She would need to remain in the hospital for two weeks. And Leonida often stayed there, too, working with the nurses to restore Melsa's strength. Leonida thought she herself might faint when the hospital presented her with the bill: thirty-eight hundred shillings. She considered selling a cow, but resisted. The cow was vital for the family milk business, and it would soon be delivering a calf. And her chicken brood was severely depleted by a mongoose-like animal that lived in the sugarcane and devoured half the chicks. So Leonida sold another one-and-a-half bags of maize.

Melsa was still in the hospital the weekend of October 22 when Leonida, back in Lutacho for church meetings, got a call from Gideon's school. He had been taken to the Milo hospital. She spoke with a doctor there. The information was sketchy, but Leonida sur-mised that Gideon was suffering from both malaria and pneumonia. A second phone call from the hospital brought the news that Gideon was fainting.

Consumed with worry, exhausted from her time in the hospital with Melsa, Leonida hurried over to Janet's pharmacy and described Gideon's symptoms. Joint pain, fever, chills, headache, general body malaise, loss of appetite, chest pain, and congestion. Janet rounded up the treatment—painkillers, quinine tablets, antibiotics. She put it all on Leonida's tab.

Next, Leonida scrambled for money. She knew that without an advance payment, there would be little care in the hospital. She sold more maize. After a sleepless night, Leonida stirred before the sun came up, preparing for the journey to Milo. Melsa and the baby still needed her attention, but Gideon's condition was grave. She hopped on a *piki-piki* and headed back down the hill to Webuye and then further on to the Milo hospital.

Leonida was shocked when she saw her son. Gideon, hooked up to an IV drip, was lying motionless. He wasn't talking or eating. His eyes were closed. Teachers from the school were gathered around the bed. Leonida cried. She thought Gideon was dying.

She never left his side. The hospital was overcrowded with patients, so Leonida slept on the floor next to her son's bed. Medicine was chronically short, but thankfully Leonida was able to give Gideon what she had brought from Janet. For four days, there was no response, and Gideon didn't seem to be improving. Then on the fifth day, he asked for water. A nurse brought a Fanta orange soda. He drank half the bottle. He began to eat little amounts of food, mainly rice. Slowly, Gideon began to recover. For two weeks, he remained in the hospital. Again, Leonida stayed with her child.

During that time, Gideon's classmates were beginning to take their series of final exams, the ones that would determine if they advanced to the final year of high school. Gideon feared that all his work had been for nothing. Leonida worried that her investment had been wasted. For if Gideon missed the tests, or failed them because he lacked the weeks of preparation, he would have to repeat the third year.

Gideon left the hospital in early November and returned to school. Principal Mutambo, who had seen about 10 percent of the student body drop out during the year for lack of fees, now had some two dozen students laid up sick with the same nasty concoction that struck Gideon. Mutambo wanted Gideon, one of his prized students, to take the tests. For one week, as his smile and good nature returned, Gideon worked with a teacher to prepare. He crammed day and night. When the exam results were posted, Gideon was elated. He had passed. And not only that, he ranked fifteenth in his class of forty-five students.

When Leonida returned home, tired to the core, she found Melsa and the baby were doing well. The Milo hospital bill came to fifty-nine hundred shillings. Leonida sold two and a half bags of maize to cover it. The dual ordeals had cost five and a half bags in total. Now only one bag was left from the One Acre harvest. It sat on the chair in the corner of the living room.

But Leonida felt rich beyond measure. Everyone had survived. Her new granddaughter, fittingly, had been named Lauren Nekesa. Lauren Harvest.

Leonida gathered the family and thanked God for their One Acre harvest which had given them the ability to conquer the health challenges. She knew what likely would have happened if, like her friend Margaret, she had planted on her own and reaped only two bags of maize.

"Without the One Acre maize," Leonida told her husband, "we would have lost our children."

CHAPTER 7

SIKUKU

(Festival Days)

As Christmas neared, Leonida's *shamba* was wrapped in a festive mood of lightness and laughter that exceeded even the celebrations on planting and harvesting days.

Leonida and the children had decorated the living room walls with pages from old Kenyan newspapers, some as far back as 2008. Those pages carried colorful photos of birds and animals and fashion models and soccer players and shoes—BATA OCTOBER SALE 30% OFF, screamed a footwear advertisement. The headlines were particularly bold and large, no matter the incongruous topics: "Sex Claims Haunt Top School," "Corruption in Grand Coalition," "The Drab Side of Modeling," "Kenya-US Differ Over New Libya," "Woman Accuses Husband of Defiling a Minor." A paper chain was draped above the window opposite the door. Colorful strips of cloth, torn from rags, dangled from the ceiling beam under the

metal roof in the living room. Other cloth strips were tied like rib-
bons to the two clotheslines in the yard.

Gideon and some friends applied a fresh layer of mud to the
outer side of the house walls. It was a common holiday task to spiff
up the homestead, but also a necessity after the ravages of the rainy
season. Gideon was very happy to be home, and alive. With a broad
smile, he repeated a passage from the New Testament, Philippians
4:4, as he worked: "Rejoice in the Lord always; and again I say,
Rejoice."

Two weeks before he would begin his final year of high school,
he now told his mother he was becoming more interested in his
agriculture studies. "You see, I want to make sure no one suffers
from hunger and poverty. I will make known to them the goodness
of agriculture," he told her. "I can teach them how to work the land
properly, how to diversify their crops, how they must eat smart."

Leonida beamed and laughed, delighted at her son's enthusiasm. Materially, she may have been back where she was at the start
of the year: her maize was nearly gone, and she was staring at a new
mountain of school fees. But mentally she was in an entirely different place: the gloom and worry and doubt that restricted the last
Christmas meal to boiled bananas was replaced by an optimism and
determination that she could splurge a little now and plan a feast of
chicken and beef and other treats rare during the year. She had
weathered a brutal *wanjala*, and what seemed like constant sickness
in the household, and had emerged with a clearer map for the journey from misery to Canaan. The fact that it would be a long and
arduous trek hadn't changed, but now she was confident that they
would make it.

Leonida's desire to become a One Acre super farmer, planting
two acres of maize or more, was keener than ever. She and Rasoa,
Zipporah, and Francis realized that they would need to expand

their harvests in order to comfortably feed the family, cover emergency health expenses, and fulfill their dreams of high school educations for all their children. A quantum leap in production on a half-acre wasn't enough to produce a quantum leap in quality of life. They also saw the necessity to create farm-based businesses in order to get a measure of independence from the price swings of their main asset and main source of food, be it Leonida with maize trading, Rasoa with a general store, Francis with tomatoes and greenhouse vegetables, or Zipporah with chickens and bricks. They ended the year wiser on the importance of storage, managing credit, establishing income streams, and diversifying their farms and diets.

And so, as Christmas neared, they had all already gotten a head start in paying off their One Acre loans for the next year. Leonida had sold some sweet potatoes and used her merry-go-round payout to retire half her credit. She had also given one bag of her One Acre maize to the Lutacho primary school to cover the school fees and lunchtime meals for Dorcas for the entire year. It was a huge relief; Leonida wouldn't have to worry about her youngest and most vulnerable next year. "You will be safe from *wanjala*," she told her daughter.

BY THE END OF THE YEAR, all the farmers referred to *wanjala* as if it were a person, or a monster. And they all believed they had him on the run.

On December 22, Francis attended the launch meeting of Africa Potential Growth, a new community improvement group. About thirty community workers in Kabuchai had gathered in the assembly hall of the local technical training school. The treasurer suggested they start small, focusing on achievable goals. He reminded them of the philosophy of Mother Teresa: If you can't feed one hundred, then feed one.

After the *wanjala*, relieving hunger was a consensus top priority. Benedetta Mabele, a home economics extension advisor with the ministry of agriculture, said that half of the families in their area didn't eat three meals a day. Their diets were heavy on carbohydrates and thin on protein. They ate meat maybe once a month; they overcooked vegetables, boiling away the nutrients. The mothers rarely came to health centers for information. So, she suggested, this new organization needed to go to the homes with information on nutrition. She said the community needed to take control of its own health, as the agriculture ministry had little money to support her supposed extension activities.

"We have no motorbikes to reach the families, no teaching materials, no pots and pans for cooking demonstrations," she said. "We're supposed to show how to properly prepare food to maximize nutrients, but how can we do that without even pots and pans?"

Francis vigorously nodded his head as he listened. Then he rose from his bench and told the group about One Acre Fund and the efforts to reduce hunger through better agriculture practices. He said he had harvested twelve bags of maize on a half-acre. This news was greeted with a flurry of questions about how to join.

After the meeting, Francis returned to his *shamba*. The rains were finally tapering off, so his new tomato stems were looking better. He and Mary were anticipating a big Christmas family gathering. John Willy, their second-oldest son, would be coming from Nairobi. Francis wanted to speak to him about becoming a One Acre member as well, so together, including Geoffrey, they would have three plots of maize.

In his dreams, Francis saw a harvest of forty bags on his *shamba*. There would be no hunger in his house for as long as he lived. His

Christmas present to his family would be this prediction: "We will see *wanjala* no more."

RASOA, TOO, BELIEVED they had seen the last of *wanjala*. From her harvest, she had eight bags of maize stored in their bedroom and a bull purchased with maize sales that was grazing just outside the door. Her dairy cow had a male calf on December 14, so the future of their plowing business was looking good. Cyrus and the boys were putting a fresh layer of mud on the house for Christmas. Inside, new colors decorated the walls: a red-and-yellow plastic strip from a Coca-Cola promotional campaign, "Refresh yourself this Christmas"; and a green poster with a homespun poem. "My house, my house is small. There's no mansion for a millionaire, but there is room for love and friends. That's all I care about."

Rasoa was feeling comfortable about the future. She and Cyrus would be planting an entire acre of maize with One Acre Fund, and their bulls had already plowed the field once. A couple more sessions with the plow, and the soil would be ready. She had learned the importance of storing to take advantage of price fluctuations and believed the eight bags of maize would be enough to get them through until the next harvest. "For now," she told Cyrus, "I won't cry again that my children are lacking food."

But tears from another tragedy came soon enough. Several days before Christmas, they heard that Cyrus's younger brother was in the hospital battling for his life. His health was declining rapidly; the hospital staff feared it was HIV/AIDS and were conducting a battery of tests. Rasoa and Cyrus sold two bags of their maize at eighty shillings per *goro-goro* to help the family pay for the treatment. They knew the hospital wouldn't do much without an advance payment.

That left six bags in the bedroom. Still, Rasoa figured she could stretch them through next August; each bag should last for a one and a half months. There just wasn't much of a cushion.

ZIPPORAH LOOKED at the bags of maize stacked to the top of the walls in their bedroom and ran through her calculations. Sixteen bags remained from their harvest of twenty. They had eaten four since August, but the pace of maize consumption was slowing as the vegetables from the second planting were harvested. She, too, would keep six bags to feed the family until next August. That would leave ten bags to finance the construction of their new house—the house that maize would build.

The work had already begun. In late November, Sanet made the first bricks. On a barren corner of land at the edge of his field, he cleared away the topsoil and attacked the next layer of reddish clay. He mixed a shovelful of clay with water and put the muddy mixture into a brick-shaped wooden frame. Once the mud hardened in the sun, he flipped over the frame, and the brick popped out. Now, two days before Christmas, he was up to twelve hundred bricks. Sanet was storing them in the same shed where he had kept his maize cobs.

As he made the bricks, Sanet pondered his house. He retrieved his old blueprint and drew it afresh, with bold, thick lines and precise measurements. The living room would be 187.5 square feet, the bedroom 117, the study 90, the storeroom 71.5, and the bathroom 28. He confirmed his earlier calculations: Thirty-six iron sheets would do it for the roof, plus another four if there would be a veranda beyond the door. Construction would begin when he had made six thousand bricks, and when the maize price was high enough that they could sell ten bags to buy the metal roofing. Sanet figured that would be May or June. It would be the height of the *wanjala*, but not on his *shamba*.

"I'm expecting *wanjala* won't be seen here again," he said to Zipporah as she served a lunch of boiled sweet potatoes and beans. David filled up a bowl. He had stopped coughing. He was wearing a colorful Houston Astros Roger Clemens shirt. It hung flat over his belly.

THE BIKETIS BEGAN the year as the poorest of the four families, and now, at Christmastime, they were rich with food and ambition. The house blueprint, the sixteen bags of maize, and the silenced cough were all evidence that hunger and poverty could be conquered through agricultural development. The experiences of Leonida and Rasoa and Francis, as well, demonstrated that access to seed and advice and financing and small amounts of fertilizer did indeed work toward multiplying yields and increasing incomes.

A week before Christmas, they and the smallholder farmers of Africa received a present from the United States Congress. The year of budgetary warfare ended with the survival of vital agricultural development programs that directly impacted them. The House and Senate, approving the fiscal year 2012 appropriations omnibus bill, allocated $1.17 billion to global agricultural development and food security (which included Feed the Future), up slightly from fiscal year 2011. And they put $135 million into the Global Agriculture and Food Security Program (GAFSP), the World Bank multilateral trust fund, also an increase from 2011. But the allocations still fell short of fulfilling American promises. In 2009, President Obama had pledged $3.5 billion to the G-8 L'Aquila three-year food security commitment; the fiscal year 2012 appropriation brought the U.S. total to $3.26 billion. And the GASFP funding left the United States more than $100 million below its pledge.

The bellicose baying of some Republican legislators out to defund USAID subsided. And USAID continued to make Feed the

Future and agricultural development its cornerstone activity. Some of the new congressional allocations would soon be trickling down to the farmers in western Kenya. For shortly before Christmas, One Acre learned it would be receiving funding from two USAID programs: a three-year, $2 million grant under a project established to encourage collaboration between USAID and smaller NGOs; and $1 million from a public-private partnership program in which USAID matched funds provided by a private-sector entity—in One Acre's case the Pershing Square Foundation. One Acre planned to use this funding to support its operations in Kenya, particularly to expand to new areas in Western and Nyanza Provinces.

AT 5:30 P.M. on Christmas Eve, Leonida lit a pile of sticks in her cooking hut. The preparation of the Christmas feast had begun. First up was the *mandazi*, a square doughnut without the hole. Leonida filled a silver cauldron with water; the pot's outside was charred black. She set the pot in the fire between three stones. Sitting on a low stool, just a foot off the ground, right beside the fire, she mixed flour and sugar and water in a second pot. She added special *mandazi* yeast and a bar of yellow fat. She kneaded the mixture with her hands, and then rolled it out with a Fanta orange soda bottle. Smoke filled the hut, and the temperature rose. As the dough took shape, Leonida said a little prayer, asking God that the hunger from the past *wanjala* would never return to her house. "Never again, never again," she said.

Leonida cut the pastry into squares and dropped them into a pot of boiling cooking oil. The dough sizzled, puffed and turned a golden brown. Leonida fished them out with a spoon and set them aside to dry.

Dorcas, wearing a pink dress, entered the hut carrying a bundle of sticks, which she fed to the fire. It was her fifth birthday and she delighted in the excitement; she had never seen a feast like this. Dorcas was followed by Sarah, who appeared balancing a plastic bag of *sukuma* leaves on her head. Jackline grabbed a small knife and sliced the *sukuma*. Leonida began making the *chapati*, rolling out the wheat flour for the round, tortilla-like bread.

Outside, under the avocado tree, Gideon read the Bible, preparing for the Christmas church service. Two members from *Amua* stopped by. Agnes talked about her hopes that the weather would "behave" better next year; she was sure it would. Alice braided the hair of the girls. Over by the house, Peter had turned his bike upside down and was working on the chains. He tuned the radio to a music station. The two orphan boys tended the four cows in the field. A parade of neighbors wandered through the *shamba* with Christmas greetings.

Shortly before seven, with night descending rapidly, Leonida emerged from the cooking hut with a big butcher knife. She sharpened it on a rock and went off to find the hen she had chosen for the feast. Jackline started a fire outside the hut and filled another pot with water. Leonida carried the chicken to the edge of the field beside the pumpkin patch. She plucked a few feathers from the neck and then sliced with the knife. There was a flutter of the wings and then quiet. Leonida wiped the knife in the grass. She couldn't remember the last time she had done this; it had been so long since she had prepared a chicken.

Leonida laid the chicken in a pot and carried it to the fire. Jackline poured in some steaming water and, when it cooled a bit, began to pluck. The feathers pulled off easier when wet. Sarah dumped some beans into the water boiling on the fire and Leonida prepared a few chunks of beef. The little marmalade kitten darted in and out of the action, skirting the fire, hoping to catch a scrap of meat.

The *shamba* was dark, except for the fire. Thunder rolled in the distance. A few streaks of lightning flashed. A light sprinkle fell.

Leonida and Peter smiled; rain on Christmas, they said, was good luck. A drunken neighbor stumbled past the house, singing his holiday greetings. The girls doused the fire and moved the food into the cooking hut. The preparation was finished for the evening.

CHRISTMAS DAY DAWNED bright and hot. Leonida's family stirred early and washed up quickly. For breakfast, there was *mandazi* and juice, a combination they hadn't known during the year. Peter put on a gray-green suit. Gideon wore a white shirt and tie; the two younger boys skipped the ties. Dorcas and Sarah wore identical white dresses with purple sashes around the shoulders and waist. Jackline was all purple. Leonida stepped out of the house in a white-and-blue dress. They all inspected themselves in the cracked rearview mirror.

A photographer from Lutacho came by on his bike. Leonida had hired him for some family portraits. She lined everyone up in the yard between the huts, and they smiled broadly for the camera. Leonida ran into the house and came back with a trophy. It had been awarded to her two years earlier for coaching the Lukusi market women's soccer team. Now, finally, she would have her picture with it.

At 9:30, Leonida and the girls began the thirty-minute walk to the big Kenya Assemblies of God church in Lukusi. Peter and the boys had left earlier. They were among the first to arrive. By 10:30, the pews were filling up and the singing and preaching had commenced. Pastor Fukwo, wearing an olive-green suit with bright white shoes, led the celebration of the birth of Christ. Congregation members jumped up to thank God that they had survived the *wanjala*. They sang Christmas songs such as "Joy to the World" in English and Swahili. Gideon and another boy banged on cowhide drums. A greater racket arose outside when the band from the neighboring Salvation Army Church marched by with horns and drums and flags.

By noon, Leonida's family was back at the *shamba*. Two tables were arranged under the big shade tree, chairs and couches were carried out from the house. Any worries had been put in abeyance for the day. Yes, Gideon's school fees for his final year of high school would be more than thirty thousand shillings, and they couldn't be sure of his scholarship being renewed. And Jackline tried not to think of her high school qualifying test scores. (She would hear three days later that she received passing marks, but just barely; rather than go to a low-quality high school as her scores would dictate, she decided to repeat eighth grade and try for better results.)

Leonida and the girls served the food, forming a procession from the cooking hut to the tables. Beans and tomatoes, *ugali*, chicken, beef, *chapati*, and *sukuma*. And for dessert, bananas. There was so much food and very little conversation; this was a time to eat, not talk. It was such a grand feast that even Peter, in his sixth decade, rubbed his eyes in disbelief. He told his family he had never eaten so well. Surely, he thought, they had already arrived in the land of milk and honey.

IN KABUCHAI, Zipporah returned from Christmas church and cooked up an afternoon meal of chicken in tomato sauce, boiled bananas, and *chapati*. David had seen the chicken being slaughtered. Now he told his mother he couldn't eat it. Zipporah laughed and gave him extra *chapati*. There was no maize on the menu because Zipporah was determined to make her reserves stretch. And Sanet, whose second name was Sikuku for his birth on Christmas Eve in 1976, wasn't big on celebrations. Far better, he thought, to have a feast when they could eat it in their new house.

Francis was surrounded by his children and grandchildren, as he sat in the shade of the avocado tree. When Mary served dinner, just after nightfall, the adults moved into the living room. She had set the table with her nicest dishes and silverware, and they gleefully dug into a feast of meaty chicken with tomato and pepper stew, rice and a traditional *ugali* made from sorghum and millet. Francis beamed. He was proud to see his clan gathered together, eating so well.

It was well into the night before Rasoa had the opportunity to serve Christmas dinner. It was a somber meal—just *ugali* and *sukuma*—for the day before they had learned that Cyrus's brother had died. Several family members were staying in their house. Cyrus and Rasoa would contribute a bag of maize for the funeral. Just five bags would remain in the bedroom.

THE DAY AFTER Christmas, Leonida was in her field, bending deeply over her *jembe*, digging up sweet potatoes. There were still plenty to be harvested, and there would be plenty to eat for the next two months. Then she would begin the plowing for the One Acre maize planting in March. Leonida stood up, slowly straightening her back. It was a clear, blue day, hot, with a persistent breeze. There were no clouds in the direction of Mount Elgon.

Leonida surveyed her *shamba*, and she saw the future. Once the the last of the sugarcane was cut, the field would be a vast, green sea of maize in the long rains season, and assorted vegetables in the short rains. She imagined the bags of food filling her bedroom and storage sheds. But there was still work to do. Leonida bent deeply again and hacked at the soil with her *jembe*. Here is where she would bury the *wanjala*.

ACKNOWLEDGMENTS

To Leonida Wanyama, Rasoa Wasike, Zipporah Biketi, and Francis
Mamati and their families, I am grateful beyond measure. These
farmers, humble and kind to the core, graciously welcomed me,
time and time again, to their *shambas*, invited me into their homes,
and shared with me their joys and sorrows, triumphs and failures
throughout a remarkable year. From the very beginning, they
embraced a common desire: they dearly wanted their stories as
African smallholder farmers to be told and, through their stories, to
instruct and inspire. They understood they would have nothing to
gain personally by answering my incessant questions but believed
they would enrich many others by drawing attention to the every-
day struggles, and the eternal potential, of rural Africans. The
scenes in this book come from our time together or from their

recounting experiences that I missed. I pray that I have faithfully presented their stories.

I am also thankful for all the other farmers and residents of western Kenya who gave me their time and their thoughts. Whether they appear in these pages or not, they have all added to this mosaic. Special thanks go to the dedicated workers of One Acre Fund, be they in the field or in the Bungoma office. Andrew Youn and Stephanie Hanson opened the doors and kept them open, and, along with Tony Kalm, embraced the storytelling and facilitated my reporting. Particularly indispensable was Ebrahim Kigame, who was my guide to the geography, language, culture, and spirituality of western Kenya, and, on top of all that, he kept me safe and in good spirits through all our travels together.

Whether in Bungoma or Nairobi or points in between, many people aided my reporting along the way: the drivers and innkeepers, who kept me going; the scientists, entrepreneurs, government officials, and aid workers, who kept me informed; and the assorted agricultural experts, who kept me headed in the right direction. And lending their camaraderie, common sense, and cinematic perspective—and a seat in their van, the *Hakuna Matatu*—were the filmmakers Joshua Courter and Giulia Longo Courter, who also repeatedly demonstrated the power in the one-two punch of words and images.

Providing support from the home base were many colleagues at the Chicago Council on Global Affairs, in particular Marshall Bouton, Elisa Miller, Lisa Eakman, Sung Lee, Maggie Klousia, Robyn Jacobs, and Diane Gilbert. I'm also grateful in numerous ways for the support of many organizations on the frontlines of the fight against hunger through agricultural development, particularly the Bill & Melinda Gates Foundation, the Skoll Foundation, and the Alliance for a Green Revolution in Africa, as well as the International Maize and Wheat Improvement Center, the Alliance to End Hunger, Bread for the World, ONE, Concern Worldwide, and the United Nations' World Food Program and Food and Agriculture Organization.

I also owe much gratitude and admiration to PublicAffairs for an uncommon commitment to stories about hunger and poverty, and, specifically, for embracing this narrative of smallholder farmers in Africa. Many thanks to founder Peter Osnos, publisher Susan Weinberg, managing editor Melissa Raymond, senior editor and marketing director Lisa Kaufman, and production editor Lori Hobkirk. Lisa provided unwavering encouragement, a driving curiosity, and an insistence that the farmers' voices be heard loud and clear. Laurie Liss, my agent, recognized that *Enough* wasn't enough for me and knew there were more stories to be told.

Finally, everlasting gratitude to my wife, Anne, who shaped this book in many ways, not least by her ardent and vigilant reading of draft after draft. And to our children, Brian and Aishling, who understand and believe.

INDEX

Roger Thurow is a senior fellow for Global Agriculture and Food Policy at the Chicago Council on Global Affairs. He was, for thirty years, a reporter at the *Wall Street Journal*. He is, with Scott Kilman, the author of *Enough: Why the World's Poorest Starve in an Age of Plenty*, which won the Harry Chapin Why Hunger book award and was a finalist for the Dayton Literary Peace Prize and for the New York Public Library Helen Bernstein Book Award. He is a 2009 recipient of the Action Against Hunger Humanitarian Award. He lives near Chicago.